THE VIRTUE OF UNCERTAINTY

LOOKING FOR EVIDENCE IN RELIGION

THE VIRTUE OF UNCERTAINTY

LOOKING FOR EVIDENCE IN RELIGION

EUGENE R. MOUTOUX

BUTLER BOOKS

Published by Butler Books
www.butlerbooks.com

ISBN: 978-1-941953-62-4

This book is dedicated to

Phyllis Taylor,

my friend and companion of the last ten years,

who has made my "golden years" golden.

I am grateful to Kim Vivian, who proofread the first version of this book, *It Ain't Necessarily So: A Liberal Looks at Religion,* and to Larry Barnett, who proofread *The Virtue of Uncertainty: Looking for Evidence in Religion.* Kim, an old friend from graduate school at UC Santa Barbara, is a retired German professor and author of scholarly books as well as novels and poems. Larry, who lives in Southfield, Michigan, has become my friend as, over the course of many years, we have discussed one of his favorite pastimes and mine, sentence diagramming. Both Kim and Larry offered many helpful stylistic and content-related suggestions. I am similarly indebted to my significant other, Phyllis Taylor, a retired intensive-care nurse, who read and commented compellingly on many sections of the manuscripts of both books; and to her sister, Gayle Hanratty, author of a recently published book of short stories, whose professional comments on the first thirty pages of the first book got me started in the right creative direction. I also wish to thank members of a breakfast club to which I belong for their contributions. I have always valued the artistic talent of my son Tom Moutoux, who has contributed drawings for several of my books and, for this book, the painting on the cover and the figure on the title page.

Contents

Part V: Popular Delusions

Part VI: Questioning Faith

* * * * *

Biblical quotations used in this book are from the New American Catholic Edition, 1952 (Douay version of the Old Testament and Confraternity Edition of the New Testament). In referring to the books of the Bible that have one name in the New American Catholic Edition and another in most other bibles, I have used the names of the latter. Thus, for example, instead of 1 Kings, 2 Kings, 3 Kings, and 4 Kings, I have used 1 Samuel, 2 Samuel, 1 Kings, and 2 Kings; and instead of 1 and 2 Paralipomenon, 1 and 2 Chronicles. Likewise, I have used the more modern numbering of Psalms, according to which, for example, "The Lord is My Shepherd" is Psalm 23, not Psalm 22. For the sake of consistency, I have changed some names from the New American Catholic Edition to the corresponding names used more commonly today; for example, Noah is used for Noe, Joshua for Josue, Isaiah for Isaias, Elijah for Elias, and Messiah for Messias.

"The problem with writing about religion is that you run the risk of offending sincerely religious people, and then they come after you with machetes."

- Dave Berry, "Berry's first commandment: Machete attacks are not allowed"

"The things that you're liable to read in the Bible, it ain't necessarily so."

– from George Gershwin's musical *Porgy and Bess*

Introduction

"I can live with doubt, and uncertainty, and not knowing. I think it's much more interesting to live not knowing than to have answers which might be wrong. I have approximate answers, and possible beliefs, and different degrees of certainty about different things, but I'm not absolutely sure of anything, and there are many things I don't know anything about, such as whether it means anything to ask why we're here. . . ." - quantum physicist Richard P. Feynman, *The Pleasure of Finding Things Out: The Best Short Works of Richard P. Feynman*

* * * * *

On a warm, sunny morning in the spring of 1959, I was walking slowly back and forth on a large second-floor balcony above the dining hall of the Canisianum, a Catholic seminary in Innsbruck, Austria. From the balcony or from the garden below, one had a grand view of the snow-capped Nordkette (the Alpine mountain range on the north side of the city), which begins its ascent no more than half a mile from the seminary, just on the other side of the gray-green waters of the Inn River. My bishop, Henry Grimmelsman of the Diocese of Evansville, Indiana, had sent me to Innsbruck to study theology for four years and then, near the end of my course of study, to be ordained a priest. I was in my first year of graduate studies, a year sometimes called First Theology. If one had to study theology (yes, I thought I had to), the Canisianum was the place to be because of the natural beauty of the area. On this day, I was reading a typed text that accompanied a course entitled "De Ecclesia Christi" ("About the Church of Christ"), which included passages from the Bible in support of the Catholic Church's claim to be the one, true church: "And I say to thee, thou art Peter, and upon this rock I will build my Church, and the gates of hell shall not prevail against it" (Matthew 16:18, 19) and "Go, therefore, and make disciples of all nations, baptizing them in the name of the Father, and of the Son, and of the Holy Spirit, teaching them to observe all that I have commanded you; and behold, I am with you all days, even unto the consummation of the world" (Matthew 28:19, 20). As I read, I was troubled, for I knew that these biblical passages could not function as valid evidence until their reliability had been established. And the text did not address that issue. How does one know that what the Bible says is true? It was not a doubt exactly, at least not a doubt that I was ready to acknowledge. But it was an important question--a question that I could not answer. I figured the answer would come with further study. It did not, however, and my journey toward religious uncertainty was underway.

After graduating from high school in 1953, I spent nine years as a Catholic seminarian: the first five years at St. Meinrad Seminary in southern Indiana and the final four years in the Canisianum in Innsbruck. Two months before scheduled ordination to the priesthood, and two days after ordination to subdeaconate with its vow of celibacy, I made one of the most important (albeit much belated) decisions of my life: not to become a priest. I was troubled by doubts about Jesus' divinity, which made the idea of becoming a priest intolerable. How could I teach and preach what I myself found unconvincing? A door opened for me, and I was finally able to admit that I wanted to get married. I left the seminary as a subdeacon. By the time I succeeded in obtaining from Rome a dispensation from my vow, I was 28 years old. I had not even kissed a girl since high school. Two months later I met my future wife; ten months after that, we were married.

In the early years of marriage, I began to distance myself intellectually and emotionally from my religion but continued with an external, and somewhat hypocritical, attachment to the Catholic Church because of my employment in a Catholic high school, my residence in a small rural town, and my concern for my very religious mother. When my family and I moved from Indiana to California in 1975, I was released from these pressures. My wife, who had never been enamored of Catholicism, and I severed all ties with the Catholic Church. In time, mostly through reading, I settled comfortably into agnosticism. In a way, it is tempting to think of my seminary years as, by and large, a waste of time, but, of course, they were not. My wife and three children would never have been a part of my life if I had chosen a different path after high school. Also, without the seminary, I would not have learned German and Latin, subjects which I ended up teaching for some forty years. Finally, *sans* seminary, this book would not have happened. The seminary-to-book line may be a tortuous one, but I do see *The Virtue of Uncertainty* as an ironic result of my principal seminary studies: philosophy and theology.

I hope in this book to acquaint the reader with a multitude of reasons why the supernatural claims of Christianity in general, and of the Catholic Church in particular, are without merit. With this in mind, I expect that most readers of this book will come from the ranks of those who either have begun to question Christian dogma or have already distanced themselves from it. I do not expect many Christian fundamentalists, who are absolutely certain of their religious beliefs, to read this book. And that is too bad. Surely some of the impetus behind the intolerance (even hatred) that we observe in our polarized world is rampant religious certitude. I intend to make the case that Christians are never justified in ascribing certainty to any of the tenets of their faith. It is simply not certain that the Bible is the infallible word of God, that Jesus is divine, or that any Christian church is the true church. Indeed, the preponderance of evidence points in the opposite direction. My hope is that some of the evidence I provide will filter out to fundamentalists. My message to them, and really to everyone, is this: Let us, religious and non-religious alike, climb down from our certainty horses and walk and talk with open minds. To believers I say: Make a leap of faith if you must, but having made that leap, do not say that you have arrived at certitude. Truckloads of maybes cannot deliver certainties. The reasons people give for their religious beliefs do not rise above the level of the possible.

It is not my intention--in this book or elsewhere--to condemn religion or to demean those who believe in it. Indeed, throughout the world millions of people find in religion both a comfort and a reason to act morally. Still, I know from personal experience and from conversations with others that it is possible to arrive at these things without religion, through an approach to life that focuses not on a divine overseer, whom we do not know, but on our fellow human beings, whom we do. This approach, called humanism, stresses acts of kindness performed solely because they make life better for everyone. And while I believe that the world would be a better place if all humans were humanists, I do not want to pull the carpet of religion out from beneath the feet of believers and leave them desperate for a replacement. In this book, I am not selling humanism; I am selling uncertainty. I intend to show that religious certainty flies in the face of evidence and rational thought, and ought to be forgone.

The Virtue of Uncertainty examines Christianity's origin, its purported revelations, its sacred book, its moral principles, its doctrines, its theology, its history, and its effects on society. My modus operandi is somewhat desultory; thus, you will not find a straight line leading from the beginning of the book to the end. But every chapter does, I hope, contribute evidence toward the confirmation of my thesis: that doubt ought to be a *sine qua non* for Christians. Most chapters begin with salient, sometimes humorous, quotations. Each chapter consists of either research-based material or my personal insights, or both. In the course of reading the book, you will, for better or for worse, get to know me as I relate relevant personal experiences. Scattered throughout the book, at the ends of most chapters, you will find the answers of friends and relatives of mine to questions I asked them about religion. Several of the respondents are former Catholics, three are secular Jews, and two are Unitarians; most self-identify as atheistic or (like me) agnostic. None of them consider themselves experts in the area of religion, which is why I hope you will find their answers refreshing. This book is meant to be an adventure. I hope you will enjoy it.

Part I: God

Chapter I
Does God Exist?

"To be certain of the existence of God and to be certain of the nonexistence of God seem to me to be the confident extremes in a subject so riddled with doubt and uncertainty as to inspire very little confidence indeed." - Carl Sagan, *Broca's Brain*

"Tonight, instead of discussing the existence or non-existence of God, they have decided to fight for it." - Monte Python, "The Wrestling Epilogue"

Attempts to Prove God's Existence

St. Anselm (c. 1033-1109), Archbishop of Canterbury, defined God as "that than which no greater can be conceived" (a literal translation of Anselm's original Latin "id quo maius cogitari nequit"), and he used this definition as the basis of his famous proof for the existence of God, the ontological proof. The proof goes like this: If God were not real but imaginary, then God would not be that than which nothing greater (i.e., more perfect) is able to be conceived, for existence is greater than non-existence; therefore, God exists. What could be simpler? But not so fast, say the opponents of this proof. You cannot simply define God into existence. Who says that existence is greater than non-existence? And what is meant by "great" in the realm of the metaphysical? Does human greatness, or perfection, really have anything at all to do with a metaphysical being? How would we know? Can we know anything at all about a divine being or beings? Might he, she, it, or they be in a realm entirely unknown and unknowable by humans? But, beyond that, some opine that one can define a perfect anything into existence. I can define Island X as an island so perfect that no more perfect island is able to be imagined. Does Island X necessarily exist? Have I proved the existence of the absolutely perfect island? Even if I could state precisely the qualities of such an island, its real (as opposed to imaginary) existence would be altogether uncertain.

St. Thomas Aquinas proposed five proofs for God's existence. In a Thomistic philosophy course at St. Meinrad Seminary in 1956-57, my classmates and I were introduced to all five. Perhaps you are familiar with the fifth proof, which has become rather famous, the proof from design, or the "God as watchmaker" proof. Aquinas did not actually use the watchmaker reference; there were no watches in his 14th-century world. In any case, as the modern equivalent of the proof goes, imagine you are walking along a beach and find a pocket watch. Would you wonder for a second if someone made the watch or not? Everything about the instrument cries out that someone made it. So it is with the world, the proponents of this proof say. They point to the "intelligent design" in the universe. Look at the order in the universe: the moon goes around the earth, the earth with its moon goes around the sun, as do the other planets. They stay in their orbits; they do not collide. And these same kinds of orbits by similar planets, we now know, happen elsewhere in our galaxy and in galaxies beyond ours.

There are two principal objections to this proof, it seems to me. Collisions happen all over the place in the universe, in our galaxy, even in our solar system. Meteors, some of them larger than houses, crash into planets, causing immense damage. Signs of such collisions dot the moon and the planet Mars and can be seen in abundance on our earth as well. A black hole in our galaxy gobbles up stars, some of them many times the size of our sun. And even galaxies collide. Scientists know that our sun will die in several billion years. In the subatomic realm, randomness is the order of the day. So much for an orderly universe. Even if one were to concede the claim of a well-ordered universe, how would we know that the universe had a maker? Everything we are familiar with in the universe, with the possible exception of matter itself, has been caused by something else in the universe, that is true. And even if our universe is, let us say, a universe within a universe within a universe, it seems logical to assume that causality as we know it functions within that physical system. But when we get beyond everything in the universe and ask about the ultimate cause, we must confess ignorance. We have no evidence that the causality we are familiar with applies beyond the realm of the physical. Maybe the physical building blocks of our universe have always existed. Or maybe the universe was created by a god altogether unlike anything or anyone we can imagine. Maybe a creator god does not have a mind; maybe god is an almighty force or potency. Maybe the universe (all that exists) is god. The maybes go on and on in a realm in which we know nothing. We have to admit, it seems to me, that the perceived design in the universe may be simply the result of eons of randomness and natural selection.

René Descartes, a brilliant philosopher and mathematician of the 18th century, added a second ontological proof to Anselm's proof for the existence of God. Anselm held, and Descartes agreed, that God, the supremely perfect being, must exist because, existence being greater than non-existence, if God were only imaginary, he would not be supremely perfect. To this, Descartes added the idea that man's idea of God as a perfect being must have as its cause a perfect being, because the effect cannot be greater than the cause. This perfect being is God. In my opinion, this argument would be weightier if one could show that man has a perfect idea of God as a perfect being. But for all we know, man's concept of God is utterly imperfect. What would be the characteristics of a perfect God? How could we, finite creatures, have any idea? Take omnibenevolence, for example. While it is customary among believers to think of God as the omnibenevolent creator of the world, this idea is not borne out in our observations of the world. All kinds of bad things happen to humans and to other sentient beings. For all we know, omnibenevolence has nothing to do with God.

The atheist scholar Walter Kaufmann suggests (but does not ascribe to) a proof for the existence of God that I had never thought of as a proof: "If Jesus was trustworthy, God exists; Jesus was trustworthy; therefore God exists."[1] The proof is valid if its minor premise (Jesus was trustworthy) is true. Millions of people believe that Jesus was just that and feel confident that their belief in God is on a solid foundation. Others would insert "the Bible" in place of "Jesus" in the proof, like this: If the Bible is trustworthy, God exists; the Bible is trustworthy; therefore God exists. Once again, if the minor premise (the Bible is trustworthy) is true, the proof is valid. I suspect that more Christians base their belief in God on one of these two syllogisms (albeit informal) than on the proofs offered by Thomas Aquinas and Anselm; if so, they have built their castles on sand, because the minor premises are highly questionable. Any astute, open-minded reader of the Bible discovers that Jesus' trustworthiness is quite questionable and that errors of all kinds abound in the Bible: factual errors, contradictions, inconsistencies, and absurdities.

Immanuel Kant, who thought that all theoretical proofs for the existence of God were invalid, presented a morality-based argument that, according to him, leads to belief in God as a "postulate of practical reason." Kant held that every rational, moral person necessarily desires that moral virtue be a condition for happiness; but such a desire would be nonsensical without a belief that moral actions can achieve such an end. Since one cannot achieve this end in this life (so goes the argument), it is necessary that every rational, moral person believe in an afterlife, and thus in God, who makes the afterlife possible. Kant's moral argument follows C. Stephen Evans' general scheme of moral arguments: "1. There are objective moral facts. 2. God provides the best explanation of the existence of objective moral facts. 3. Therefore, (probably) God exists."[2] Of course, the argument requires, for its validity, a particular God: the theistic God of Christianity, who, because he is all-good, would not create man with a desire for an afterlife that does not exist. But what if God and nature are the same thing (pantheism)? Can the same assumption be made of such a God? Or what if God is totally transcendent, which would mean that man has no idea of God's attributes? What if God is pure energy and has no mind at all? How can such a God be thought to guarantee that human desire for an afterlife not be nonsensical? I for one find the moral argument unconvincing; indeed it has been widely criticized. One should keep in mind that, while Kant considered himself a Christian, he did not attend church; in fact, he considered prayer a superstition.[3]

Pascal's Wager

"There might be many gods, including one who favors people like Pascal; but the other gods might overpower or outvote him, à la Homer. Nietzsche might well have applied to Pascal his cutting remark about Kant: when he wagered on God, the great mathematician 'became an idiot .'" - Walter Kaufmann, *Critique of Religion and Philosophy*

* * * * *

"Let us then examine this point, and say, 'God is or He is not.' [...] Let us weigh the gain and the loss in wagering that God is. Let us estimate these two chances. If you gain, you gain all; if you lose, you lose nothing. Wager, then, without hesitation that He is."[4] This is the famous "Pascal's Wager" in a nutshell. This strange bet was proposed by none other than the eminent mathematician Blaise Pascal. Here is his rationale for wagering: There is no way of proving that God exists or does not exist. Still, one has to take a position with respect to God: one has to believe in him or not. One has to wager finite pleasure against eternal loss. If one wagers that God exists, and God really does exist, then one wins an eternal reward. If one wagers that God exists, and God does not exist, then one loses only something finite. If one wagers that God does not exist, and God does not exist, then one loses nothing. If one wagers that God does not exist, and God does exist, then one loses everything: heaven (and, Pascal might have added, one goes to hell). Pascal's God, we must keep in mind, is the omnipotent being who, according to Christianity, rewards good people with heaven and punishes bad people with hell. In a wager, if the stakes are an eternal good (or the avoidance of an eternal evil) on the one hand and a finite good on the other, one must always bet on the side of the eternal good, says Pascal. On its face, this assertion is true; however, it assumes that we humans know that God, if he exists, grants to those who believe in him an eternal reward or punishes those who do not believe in him with an eternal torment. But we do not know this at all. It is possible that God dislikes people who try to wager their way into eternal happiness, and rewards those who refuse any part in such a wager. Perhaps God is more pleased with people who, seeing no reason to believe in him, do not believe, but instead enjoy the innocuous pleasures of this earth that believers eschew. Pascal recommends that unbelievers begin to act as believers do, thereby making eventual belief possible. If you act like a believer, you might become a believer. But is that not disingenuous?

The philosopher William James, who wrote at length about the reasonableness of faith, found nothing reasonable about Pascal's Wager, calling it a "mechanical calculation" and opining that if he were God, he would probably enjoy excluding Pascal's gamblers from their eternal reward. If you are a Christian or are open to the Christian message, James asks you to imagine what you would think of a Pascal-like offer from a prophet of another religion: "I am the Expected One whom God has created in his effulgence. You shall be infinitely happy if you confess me; otherwise you shall be cut off from the light of the sun. Weigh, then, your infinite gain if I am genuine against your finite sacrifice if I am not!" You would reject the offer because the prophet offers you a dead hypothesis; you have little or no tendency to act on it.[5] Okay, so Pascal's Wager does not persuade James, but why would anyone find it persuasive? James explains: "[O]ur non-intellectual nature does influence our convictions, that is, "pure insight and logic, whatever they might do ideally, are not the only things that really do produce our creeds."[6] According to James, who is ever the pragmatist, Pascal's Wager, nonsense though it is, works for some people because it makes them feel good. I say nonsense is nonsense. As an unreliable anchor for faith, it should never be used to persuade others.

In my opinion, Pascal went overboard with religion. Although rational as a mathematician and as a physicist, he lived in the realm of the irrational in his thoughts about religion. Read his famous work of 1670, *Pensées*, which helped to establish him as a philosopher. Here are three of many puzzling statements by Pascal:

 - "Do you think that the prophecies cited in the Gospel are related [i.e., told] to make you believe? No, it is to keep you from believing."[7] Does this not paint an ugly picture of God?

 - "There is sufficient obscurity [in Scripture] to blind the reprobate, and sufficient clearness to condemn them and make them inexcusable. [...] If

God had permitted only one religion, it has been [sic] too easily known; but when we look at it closely, we clearly discern the truth amidst this confusion."[8] When I look at Pascal's words closely, I discern nonsense.

- "And thus, instead of concluding that there are no true miracles, since there are so many false, it must be said, on the contrary, that there are true miracles, since there are so many false; and that there are false ones only because there are true; and that in the same way there are false religions because there is one true."[9] By this logic, there must be a true Santa Claus because there are so many false Santas.

One would think that statements like these would shake most people's faith in Pascal's philosophical acumen.

Theodicy: Why Is There Suffering in the World?

"Is God willing to prevent evil, but not able? Then he is not omnipotent. Is he able but not willing? Then he is malevolent. Is he both able and willing? Then whence cometh evil? Is he neither able nor willing? Then why call him God?" - attributed to Epicurus

"It is worth remembering that if God created the world and all things in it, he created smallpox, plague, and filariasis [infection caused by roundworms]. Any person who intentionally loosed such horrors upon the earth would be ground to dust for his crimes." - Sam Harris, *The End of Faith: Religion, Terror, and the Future of Reason*

* * * * *

I belong to a discussion group that meets biweekly for breakfast. Over coffee, oatmeal, and bagels, we talk about whatever is on our minds; often the topic is religion. One of the members, a retired lawyer who is using some of his retirement time to work on a Ph.D. in physics, calls himself an atheist. He does not believe that God exists; however, he is not certain that God does not exist. Not believing in God's existence is not the same as denying the existence of God. Anthony Flew, a prominent atheist, prefers that the word "atheist" be used to describe someone who does not believe in God's existence, that is, someone who is simply not a theist.[10] Such a person can be called either an atheist or an agnostic. He or she finds no evidence that a creator God who takes a personal interest in the world exists but also finds no evidence that such a God does not exist. I am such a person.

While I disagree with those atheists who deny outright the existence of

God, I do know what leads many of them to do this if the deity whose existence they deny is defined as an all-good, all-knowing, all-powerful being--a perfect being. They ask, as I do, how such a being could permit suffering to exist in the world. If God is all-knowing, he knows about our suffering (why God should be masculine is a mystery to me, but I will follow tradition for now); if he is benevolent, he wants to get rid of it; and if he is almighty, he can. So why doesn't he? The adamant atheist's answer is this: God does not get rid of suffering because God does not exist, period. Except for the word "period," which for me bespeaks certainty, I tend to agree, but I remain uncertain because I do not know if words like "perfection" and "goodness" have any meaning at all when said of a supernatural being (more about that later). This much I can say confidently: A being who is omniscient, omnipotent, and omnibenevolent (in the sense in which we humans understand these adjectives) and who is oblivious to human suffering does not exist.

Some medieval philosophers sought to solve the problem of evil by arguing as follows: Suffering is a physical evil. Evil is the privation of, or the absence of, good; as such, it cannot have been created by God. Therefore, God is not the cause of suffering. The German philosopher Gottfried Wilhelm Leibniz rejected this line of argumentation, insisting that God was the author of everything in the universe, including suffering and even sin. According to Leibniz, although God does not decree suffering, he does permit it, and this permission is morally justifiable. Leibniz's argument seems to be that God permits physical evil, i.e., suffering, so that greater spiritual good, i.e., virtue, may come from it. What he seems to have disregarded is that spiritual evil (e.g., despair) can also come from suffering. In any case, he ends up saying that this world is the best of all possible worlds, a conclusion which many think laughable, and which the French philosopher Voltaire satirized in his short novel *Candide*.

Most often, attempts to reconcile a perfect God with the existence of suffering come down to this: human suffering results from man's sinfulness. In the Old Testament, we are told that people (and entire ethnic groups, like Israel) pay for their sins by suffering in this life. God rewards and punishes people in this world, not in the next. Until late in the Old-Testament chronology, there is no mention of an afterlife. And what is wrong, philosophically, with the idea of a perfect God punishing sin with suffering? Perhaps this: A benevolent God would forgive men's sins, realizing (after all, he is also omniscient) that humans, all humans, are weak. Why not give people more strength so that they not succumb to the temptations that God's world offers? In the New Testament, God's punishment for sins, as well as reward for virtue, is deferred until after death. In this life, good things can happen to bad people, and bad things can happen to good people. You may suffer now, but God will make it up to you in heaven. You may sin freely now, but you risk being punished in the eternal fires of hell. In the New Testament, suffering in this world is not seen as a punishment for sin. So, who can complain about suffering if we are repaid for it infinitely in eternity? Well, what about the people who suffer *and* sin and end up in hell? Where is their reward for suffering? Why did God (who is after all omnipotent, which means he could have created humans in any number of ways) create people who would suffer at all, anywhere. He could have created humans and placed them directly in heaven. So why did he not? Would not a benevolent God have done so?

Bertrand Russell agrees but uses a somewhat different approach. He writes: "The usual Christian argument is that suffering in the world is purification for sin and is therefore a good thing. [...] I would invite any Christian to accompany me to the children's ward of a hospital, to watch the suffering that is there being endured, and then to persist in the assertion that those children are so morally abandoned as to deserve what they are suffering. In order to bring himself to say this, a man must destroy in himself all feelings of mercy and compassion. He must, in short, make himself as cruel as the God in whom he believes. No man who believes that all is for the best in this suffering world can keep his ethical values unimpaired, since he is always having to find excuses for pain and misery."[11] I wonder if Russell has Leibniz in mind. Would that a debate between Leibniz and Russell could be arranged! Maybe in another world.

The one book of the Old Testament that receives almost universal praise for literary merit is the Book of Job. And, guess what its central issue is! Yep, the problem of evil. The Book of Job tells a story that goes like this: One day Satan appears before God and receives permission to test the virtue of Job, a man revered by all. Satan proceeds to strip Job of everything he has: he causes Job's servants to be slain, his animals to perish, and his children to die. Job's response is, "The Lord gave, and the Lord hath taken away. [...] Blessed be the name of the Lord" (Job 1:21). Even after Satan strikes Job with ulcers all over his body, Job responds: "If we have received good things at the hand of God, why should we not receive evil?" (Job 2:10) However, he soon adds, "Let the day perish wherein I was born, and the night in which it was said: A man child is conceived" (Job 3:3). Job's friends are no consolation to him, for they try to convince him that his sins are the cause of his suffering. Job points out that the wicked often prosper in this world. None of Job's friends believe in his innocence. One of them even accuses him of blasphemy for saying that God punishes the innocent. Then God speaks directly to Job and shows him that man cannot understand the wisdom of God. Job replies: "What can I answer, who have spoken inconsiderately? I will lay my hand upon my mouth" (Job 39:34). The Lord then bestows on Job more possessions than he had before his troubles began, and he blesses him with many sons and daughters. Job never denies the justice of God, but he is at a loss to explain his suffering. For those who insist on holding onto the traditional theistic view of God, Job's recognition that he, a mere mortal, might not be able to understand the motives of God is as good as any answer I have heard or read. But for many, the case seems strong that at least one of God's traditional attributes must go.

1 Walter Kaufmann, *Critique of Religion and Philosophy*, p. 168.
2. "Moral Arguments for the Existence of God," on the website *Stanford Encyclopedia of Philosophy*.
3. Nick Gier, "Immanuel Kant (1724-1804): The Personhood Puzzle," www.webpages.uidaho.edu.
4. Blaise Pascal, *Pensées*, Section III.
5. William James, "The Will to Believe," II.
6. "The Will to Believe," III.
7. *Pensées*, 568. The entire *Pensées* contains 924 paragraphs. The quotations used here are from W. F. Trotter's translation.
8. *Pensées*, 578.
9. *Pensées*, 818.
10. Terry L. Miethe and Anthony G. N. Flew *Does God Exist? A Believer and an Atheist Debate*, pp. 7-8.
11. Bertrand Russell, *Why I Am Not a Christian*, pp. 29-30.

Do you believe that God exists?

George (retired lawyer, candidate for a Ph.D. in physics, activist in the areas of women's rights and the role of money in politics): *I'm an atheist, I believe in God, and I am certain that God exists. Here's how I explain that: Gods exist. Multitudes of gods have been invented by human beings. Those inventions have a reality in the sense that they affect how human beings act.*

My path away from religion involves making the most honest decisions I can, and this is the most honest decision I can make on the topic. There is never absolute certainty. But, as certain as I can be, as honest as I can be, this is my perspective on religion.

Junior (retired banker, volunteer family and commercial media-tor): *I grew up with blind faith based on examples or parables or miracles. I was a believer for a long time--until I was thirty years of age or so--and then realized that there is no proof that God exists. I wondered about divine omniscience and omnipotence, about divine intervention and such. I wondered why the only good we are able to see in the world is the good that we ourselves produce. The Baltimore Catechism became for me a mythology that I just couldn't believe anymore. I'm still struggling with what it is that a god is.*

Charlie (retired owner of a commercial real estate company, activ-ist for single-payer health care, and volunteer teacher of refugees): *I can tell you that I'm an atheist with respect to the Christian God that I grew up with. What do I believe now? I honestly can't say. I sense a presence, but I can't identify it. It's something bigger. I tend to associate it with the vastness of the universe, the mul-tiverse. A spectacular course I took a couple of years ago was taught by brilliant theologians and atheists, and they came to the conclusion (maybe that's where I'm getting my ideas) that the multiverse is so complex, so beyond our understanding, that it could somehow integrate a presence out there. I just don't have an idea of what it could possibly be.*

Steve (retired professor of psychiatry, volunteer physician in a free clinic): *As a child in Texas, I observed that the most out-spoken bigots and socially prejudiced people in the community were the same ones that most powerfully professed belief in God. The KKK was the prominent Christianity-based example of those overtly espousing such ideas. I did not want to follow that example. These individuals were the ones most likely to be white supremacist and to profess Christianity over Jews and over those of other religions, even over certain Catholics, particularly those Catholics of Mexican heritage. I heard similar stories from my Jewish-refugee parents and other family members who had fled from the predominantly Christian Nazis of Germany in the mid-1930s. Sure, I knew that many people who believed in God did not harbor this sort of hatefulness; still, I never personally ex-perienced anything that showed me that God actually exists--not the benevolent God depicted in the American culture. Nothing has really changed since then. I am not a professed atheist, but I just do not know of evidence that supports belief in God.*

Vince: (secular Jew, active in the Civil Rights Movement in Georgia and Mississippi in the 1960s, and currently involved in the labor, anti-racist, and disability rights movements) *Primitive man, primitive woman saw that it got dark at night. And they got scared. "Please, somebody, bring the sun up." And sure enough, the sun came up in the morning. And they did it again. And sure enough, the sun came up the next morning. And two years later, there was an eclipse. . . ! "O my God!" And they put down a codicil. Thomas Aquinas wrote in the Summa Theologica a proof for the existence of God: Your daddy begat you, his daddy begat him, who begat . . . ? It had to be God.*

* * * * *

I once heard a quaint proof for the existence of God that made an impression on me at the time. The proof went something like this: (major premise) we humans are thankful when unexplainable good things happen to us; (minor premise) thankfulness has no meaning unless there is someone to thank; (conclusion) when we are thankful for unexplainable good things, we thank someone; this someone is God. Leaving aside the weakness of this syllogism, whose conclusion skips without justification from *someone* to *God*, the "proof" bothers me for another reason. Too many of the fortunate people of the earth thank God for their good fortune, forgetting that, if God is really the cause of their health and wealth, he is also the cause of the sickness and destitution of others. How can anyone be thankful to a God who is able to give all people health and wealth and chooses to give these blessings only to some?

Chapter II
Looking for God's Word

"If god doesn't like the way I live, let him tell me, not you." - Unknown

* * * * *

Does God communicate with us humans? How could we ever be certain that a particular idea comes from God and is not just a product of our imagination or a projection of our desire to believe? If God truly wanted to reveal something to mankind, would he/she/ it not do so in an unambiguous manner so that all would accept the revelation unquestioningly? If revelation is questionable, can anyone be blamed for not accepting it? If the guy next door--a nice enough person whom you have known for a long time--announces one day that God has revealed to him that all people return to earth after death as birds, and that it is incumbent upon all living humans to feed the birds generously, are you obligated to hasten to the nearest pet store to buy thistle and sunflower seeds? You laugh, I hope. Okay, what if the lady down the street announces to the neighborhood that an angel appeared to her and told her that she, as a virgin, would conceive a son, whom the whole world should worship, and that this would happen through the agency of the Holy Spirit, without artificial insemination or cloning? Are you obligated to believe her and to worship her son? Is anyone? Surely the claim is so preposterous that not even the woman's nearest relatives and dearest friends are so obligated. All should ask themselves which of two possibilities is more probable: that the woman has been accorded a genuine supernatural revelation or that she is delusional.

According to Richard P. McBrien, Jesus revealed the Kingdom of God "in his word, in his works, in his presence."[1] The implication seems to be that, if you are listening with an open mind, you will accept his "revelations." If an open mind is defined as a mind that silences reason, then I agree: reason silenced, one can hear the things Jesus said and accept them. All it takes is the will to believe. McBrien says that Paul understood revelation to be "the free and gracious action of God by which he offers us salvation through Christ."[2] Of course, if you accept this definition, you have already become a believer. As theologians go, I appreciate McBrien, whose book *Catholicism* was denied an imprimatur. He seems more open-minded (perhaps the word "honest" applies also, but I am not certain) than most. Here is what he says about religious belief: "Belief cannot be demonstrated beyond all reasonable doubt, nor can unbelief be positively disproved. And the same limitations hold true for unbelief."[3] I definitely agree with the first sentence of the quotation, but I have a harder time with the second sentence. I think that unbelief in Christianity can be demonstrated beyond all reasonable doubt; however demonstration beyond reasonable doubt does not yield absolute certainty, which, in my opinion, is beyond our reach as human beings. In other words, I am quite confident that Christianity's claims do not hold up to the scrutiny of reason, but I am not absolutely certain that Christianity is wrong. What I hope is that we--all of us--can disavow certainty with respect to religion. For believers, that would mean not closing the mind to doubts about their religion; for non-believers, it would mean keeping the mind open to the possibility of religious truth. One of the reasons this is important is that there is a two-headed monster tearing at the fabric of American society. This monster's name is intolerance, and its heads are religious certainty and political certainty. My goal in writing this book, in which I will try to show that belief in Christianity is unreasonable, is the wounding of one of the monster's heads: religious certainty. I hope that, as you read this book, you will find the goal attractive, even compelling.

The Bible

"That which is absurd and impossible, that which in any other history would be called falsehood, deception, outrage, and cruelty, cannot be made reasonable, righteous, and true by the added words: Thus saith the Lord."
- Samuel Reimarus, in *Fragments from Reimarus*, by G. E. Lessing

* * * * *

"The things that you're liable to read in the Bible, it ain't necessarily so." These words, from the musical *Porgy and Bess*, are confirmed again and again in the pages of both the Old Testament and the New Testament. The more carefully I peruse the latter--which consists of four gospels, a book called The Acts of the Apostles, twenty-one epistles, and the Book of Revelation--the more clearly I realize that its writers took many liberties with the truth. They invented many "facts" about Jesus and about related topics. In my opinion, the New Testament authors became inexorably convinced that Jesus was, at the very least, a messenger from God and that, to be saved, people needed to believe in him. *What could be more important than that?* might have been their line of thought. If embellishing the truth here and there, indeed, if stretching the truth a mile, might expand the number of believers, then perhaps they would do just that. They might have reasoned that Jesus, had he wanted to, could have done all the marvels they reported, and so it doesn't really matter if he did not actually do them. Fanatics do fanatical things. For them, there's no question that the end justifies the means. And there is probably more going on epistemologically than that. An oral transmission of Jesus' deeds had been happening for about forty years before the first gospel, the Gospel of Mark, was written. Much can be changed as stories pass form one person to another, which everyone knows who has participated in or witnessed the whispered transmission of a story from one party guest to another. The last person in line tells the story that reaches him or her; then the original version is read. The differences can run the gamut from appreciable to astounding to unbelievable. It used to be thought that people in oral (predominantly illiterate) societies, like a large majority of the people in the Greco-Roman world of 2000 years ago, could be relied upon to remember and repeat historical events accurately. However, according to Bart D. Ehrman, recent studies of illiterate societies show that this is not the case. In fact, people in oral societies are less concerned about the accuracy of their traditions than are literate societies.[4]

Informed Christian fundamentalists are quite aware of the errors, the contradictions, and the inconsistencies of the Bible, which they for the most part either attribute to scribal error or label as apparent, doing their darndest to show that the errors are not really errors, the contradictions are not really contradictions, and the inconsistencies are not really inconsistencies. (By the way, if God inspired the authors of the Bible to write without error, would he not also have kept scribes from making mistakes when they copied the Bible?) To its credit, the Catholic Church, which once condemned Galileo for defending a heliocentric view of our solar system (the Bible, after all, talks about the sun rising and setting, even about the sun standing still) has had the good sense of late (let us say since the middle of the twentieth century) to divorce itself from absolute biblical inerrancy. It now maintains that certain biblical errors do not vitiate the essential truths of the Bible, such as the oneness of God, the divinity of Jesus, and the redemption of mankind.

Historically, the Catholic Church has reserved to itself the right to determine which truths of the Bible are essential. This was decreed both by the Council of Trent (1545–63) and by the First Vatican Council (1869-1870), often referred to as Vatican I. The latter council pronounced as follows: "In matters of faith and morals, belonging as they do to the establishing of Christian doctrine, that meaning of Holy Scripture must be held to be the true one, which Holy Mother Church held and holds, since it is her right to judge of the true meaning and interpretation of Holy Scripture. In consequence, it is not permissible for anyone to interpret Holy Scripture in a sense contrary to this, or indeed against the unanimous consent of the Fathers." As far as I know, this council said nothing definitive regarding the extent of biblical inerrancy. Pope Leo III took a hard conservative position in his encyclical *Proventissimus Deus* of 1893: "It will never be lawful . . . to grant that the sacred writer could have made a mistake. Nor may the opinion of those be tolerated, who . . . suppose that divine inspiration extends only to what touches faith and morals." Fortunately for Catholics, these words come from an encyclical, not from a solemn definition of a pope or of a church council. Catholics are not obligated to believe ideas expressed in encyclicals. If they were, they would seem to be stuck in the most ridiculous position that obvious errors were inspired by an all-knowing Holy Spirit. Still, according to Msgr. Joseph Clifford Fenton, Catholics "are bound seriously in conscience to accept the teaching contained in these documents [encyclicals] with a true internal religious assent."[5] What in heaven's name is the difference between "true internal religious assent" and faith? Pity the poor Catholics who have to figure out this stuff.

My own crisis of faith, which occurred in my ninth and final year in the seminary, was occasioned by Jesus' words in the Bible, that his second coming would occur during the lifetime of some of those standing in his presence. Throughout most of my seminary years, I had somehow failed to take notice of this obvious failed prediction And there are other failed predictions of Jesus in the Bible. How I missed them I do not know. In the Gospel of Matthew (17:19), Jesus says, "Amen I say to you, if you have faith like a mustard seed [the mustard seed is tiny], you will say to this mountain, 'Remove from here,' and it will remove." Or, as reported in Matthew 21:21-22: "Amen I say to you, if you have faith and do not waver, not only will you do what I have done to this fig tree [he had cursed the tree, which had then withered], but even if you shall say to this mountain, 'Arise, and hurl thyself into the sea,' it shall be done." There's another example of such nonsense, in the Gospel of John (14:12): "Amen, amen, I say to you, he who believes in me, the works that I do he also shall do, and greater than these he shall do." To the best of my knowledge, no one has ever done works more marvelous than those reportedly done by Jesus. And although the magician Franz Harary was able to make Diamond Head, a mountain in Hawaii, appear to move, he freely admitted that the mountain did not move an inch. No one has ever caused a mountain to rise and hurl itself into the sea.

By all means, read through the Bible, through both the Old and New Testaments, striving to keep an open mind, and ask yourself if an all-good, all-loving, all-powerful God could possibly have inspired the writing of what you are reading. I mean all of it, not just a passage or two here or there ("cherry picking"). Please reach your own conclusions. Do not believe me! At some point in my life, I began to hope that the Bible (and with it the Catholic Church) was wrong. For if the Bible is God's word, then hell (a place of eternal punishment to which, according to the Bible, most people will go) exists. I find that thought disgusting, intolerable. Is it possible that my bias has obscured the facts for me? I don't think so, but if I am wearing blinders, I might be the last person to know. In my opinion, the people wearing blinders are the ultraconservative scholars who, despite the growing opposition of their fellow religionists, continue to maintain that every word in the Bible is true. Well, please read on, and see what you think. In the meantime, keep in mind that the intransigence of fundamentalists may be rooted in the "faulty belief that we can know with certainty when something unproven is correct."[6]

1. Richard P. McBrien, *Catholicism*, p. 207.
2. Ibid, p. 207.
3. Ibid., p. 209.
4. Bart D. Ehrman, *The New Testament: A Historical Introduction to the Early Christian Writings*, p. 48.
5. *American Ecclesiastical Review*, Vol. CXXI, August, 1949, pp. 136-150.
6. Robert A. Burton, M.D., *On Being Certain: Believing You Are Right When You're Not*, p. 160. Dr. Burton's words, which he applies to the malfeasance of certain physicians, apply equally well to the errors of fundamentalists.

Do you trust the Bible? Why (not)?

Kim (retired professor of German, novelist, and poet): *The Bible is an historical document with an agenda, as many are. It certainly is not unbiased. Some/much of the Bible is uncorroborated by another source. Can any such historical document be said to be true? Even if there is some corroboration, how many times is that corroboration unbiased?*

Bruce (retired school counselor, real-estate investor): *I mistrust the Bible for various reasons. Here are a few: 1) The many translations of the Bible produced over a long period of time bring with them a huge possibility of error. 2) I wonder why Jesus didn't write at least part of the Bible himself. 3) Since the authors of the Bible were in part motivated by social control, there would probably have been pressure on them to slant their writing to their beliefs. 4) The words "trespassers" and "debtors," which were used interchangeably in versions of the Lord's Prayer that I heard as a boy, have different meanings. 5) There are too many supernatural events in the Bible for me.*

Chapter III
God in the Old Testament

"But for all their flaws, the Greek and Roman gods, and in fact the gods of all pagan religions, had one universal virtue: They did not require their worshippers to kill anyone who worshipped another god. That distinction belongs to Jahveh." - Craig A. James, *The Religion Virus*

"Believers who try to [read the entire Bible] face a disturbing dilemma: their faith tells them they should read the Bible, but by reading the Bible they endanger their faith." - Steve Wells, *The Skeptic's Annotated Bible*

* * * * *

The God of the Old Testament, Jahveh (aka, Jehovah), threatens no one with eternal punishment; however, his punishments are of the kind imposed by tyrannical rulers of all ages. Jahveh is merciless toward the enemies of the Israelites. Many times he issues commands that all men, women, and children of particular towns be killed. This God is cruel. Richard Dawkins strings together a long list of epithets for the God described in the Old Testament: "a petty, unjust, unforgiving, control-freak; a vindictive, bloodthirsty ethnic cleanser; a misogynistic, homophobic, racist, infanticidal, genocidal, filicidal, pestilential, megalomaniacal, sadomasochistic, capriciously malevolent bully."[1] Steve Allen (1921-2000), comedian and former host of the Tonight Show, had a wealth of biblical knowledge and the ability to express his ideas clearly and engrossingly. He pulls no punches: "It was only when I finally undertook to read the Bible through from beginning to end that I perceived that its depiction of the Lord God--whom I had always viewed as the very embodiment of perfection--was actually that of a monstrous, vengeful tyrant, far exceeding in bloodthirstiness and insane savagery the depredations of Hitler, Stalin, Pol Pot, Attila the Hun and any other mass murderer of ancient or modern history. We cannot have it both ways--either God is such a viciously depraved monster or he is not. But if he is not, then not just a few scriptural passages but a very large portion of the Bible is wrong on a question of the most fundamental importance."[2] There are indeed Old Testament books that deserve respect for one reason or another (the Book of Job and parts of the Book of Psalms come to mind), but some Old Testament books surely deserve ridicule and even condemnation.

The Book of Genesis

Some of the best-known stories of the entire Bible are found in its first book, Genesis: Adam and Eve, Noah and the Ark, Abraham and Isaac, and Sodom and Gomorrah. These stories, although written perhaps to convey moral lessons, nevertheless paint an unflattering picture of God.

Adam and Eve

After Eve and then Adam had eaten of the apple that God had forbidden them to eat, God said to Adam, "In the sweat of thy face shalt thou eat bread till thou return to the earth, out of which thou wast taken: for dust thou art, and unto dust thou shalt return" (Gen. 3:10). And to Eve: "I will multiply thy sorrows, and thy conceptions. In sorrow shalt thou bring forth children, and thou shalt be under thy husband's power, and he shall have dominion over thee" (Gen. 3:16). What becomes abundantly clear is that God's curses apply not only to Adam and Eve but also to their descendents. This is typical of the God of the Old Testament, who time and again threatens to punish--and punishes--not only individual wrongdoers but also their children and their children's children.

Noah and the Ark

"If Noah had been truly wise, he would have swatted those two flies!" - Helen Castle, *The Reader's Digest*, Volume 120

"A Sunday School teacher, having trouble finding subjects to talk about, was discussing with her class how Noah might have spent his time on the Ark. A girl volunteered, 'Maybe he went fishing.' A boy countered, 'With only two worms?'" - *The Rochester Sentinel*, Sept. 16, 2015

* * * * *

The monstrous nature of the God of the Old Testament comes strikingly to the fore in Chapter 6 of the Book of Genesis: "And God seeing that the wickedness of men was great on the earth, and that all the thought of their heart was bent upon evil at all times, it repented him that he had made man on the earth. And being touched inwardly with sorrow of heart, he said: I will destroy man, whom I have created, from the face of the earth" (Gen. 6:5-7). God uses a great flood to destroy all humans and all land animals with the exception of Noah, his family, and enough animals of each species to repopulate the earth. Even if we agree that God has a good reason for destroying the vast majority of humans, what is his excuse for killing the land animals? Has the wickedness of animals also become "great on the earth"? Of course not. To be sure, the great flood, described in Genesis as covering even the highest mountains, is not historical; nevertheless, we can and should wonder about the Old Testament's imputation of cruelty to an ostensibly good and just God. When the flood ends and Noah offers holocausts to the Lord, the latter promises that he will never again destroy every living creature "for the imagination and thought of man's heart are prone to evil from his youth" (Gen. 8:21). It is as if God suddenly realizes something he had not realized before: that humans are the way they are because he, God, made them that way. Like the gods of the ancient Greeks and Romans, the God of the Old Testament is a human invention, with human flaws.[3]

Abraham and Isaac

One fine day God announces to Abraham: "Take thy only begotten son Isaac, whom thou lovest, and go into the land of vision: and there thou shalt offer him for a holocaust upon one of the mountains which I will shew thee" (Gen. 22:2). This cruel command is altogether consistent with other actions of the God of the Old Testament, as you will see shortly. No doubt many conscientious Jewish and Christian parents have asked themselves what they would do if God commanded them to kill their child. It's easy for me. I would say this cannot be the command of a loving God and dismiss it. But Jews and Christians believe in this God. Job said, "The Lord gave, and the Lord hath taken away" (Job 1:21), but Job wasn't asked to wield a knife against his own child. You probably remember the rest of the Abraham-and-Isaac story, so I will be brief. They arrive at the appointed mountain. Abraham has knife in hand, ready to slay Isaac when God's voice stops him. God has conveniently arranged to have a ram stuck in some briers, which becomes Abraham's offering. Horrible though the story is, its presence in the Bible makes it true for some people.

Sodom and Gomorrah

When God informs Abraham that he intends to destroy the sinful towns of Sodom and Gomorrah, Abraham does his best to dissuade the Lord; however, when not even ten good men can be found in those towns, God sends two angels disguised as men to Lot, the only good man there, to tell him to flee with his family. Lot flees with his wife and daughters (his sons-in-law choose to stay), and God rains fire and brimstone on the towns and destroys them and all the men, women, and children. The children too were evil? Lot and family have been warned not to look back as they flee. When his wife nevertheless peeks, she is turned into a pillar of stone. In his *Antiquities of the Jews*, the Jewish historian Flavius Josephus claims that he has seen the pillar of salt that had been Lot's wife. If you are skeptical, you need only travel to Israel, to a place called Mount Sodom near the Dead Sea, where you will be shown a salt formation called "Lot's wife." Anyone looking for an exciting travel destination?

The Books of Exodus and Leviticus

To enable Moses and his brother Aaron to make an impression on the Pharaoh, whom they are to petition for the release of the Israelites from their servitude in Egypt, God transforms Aaron's staff into a magical instrument. In the presence of Pharaoh, Aaron casts down his staff, which turns into a serpent. Alas Pharaoh's magicians also turn their staffs into serpents. Although Aaron's serpent eats the serpents of the magicians, Pharaoh refuses to release the Hebrews. Moses then has Aaron use his staff to turn the rivers of Egypt into blood, but--wouldn't you know it?-- the magicians show that they can change water into blood as well. No dice for Moses and Aaron. Moses and Aaron then cause an army of frogs to descend on Egypt; you guessed it, the magicians can do this as well. In succession, Moses and Aaron conjure up clouds of gnats, produce a swarm of flies, kill the cattle of the Egyptians, inflict boils and swollen brains on humans and beasts, cause hail to fall on the crops of the Egyptians, and bring a plague of locusts, all to no avail. (By the way, the magicians can't get past the gnats.) Finally, Jahveh (who of course is behind all the magic of Moses and Aaron) brings about the death of every firstborn among the Egyptians, and this does the trick. Moses' followers (600,000 men plus children according to Exodus) set out for the promised land. Ah, but wait. God hardens the heart of Pharaoh. He does this repeatedly so that he can work his signs and be glorified (Exodus 10:1-2). Pharaoh, his heart sufficiently hardened, sends his army in pursuit. Everyone knows what happens next: the people of Israel make it through the parted waters of the Red Sea, while the Egyptian pursuers drown when the walls of water collapse. Could God not move Pharaoh to release the Hebrews by means less violent than killing cattle, inflicting boils, causing swollen brains, and bringing about the death of thousands of innocent Egyptian children? Is God so mean-spirited, so egomaniacal, that he needs to show he can manipulate the waters of the Red Sea with dire consequences for Egyptian soldiers? What an abhorrent picture of God the author of Exodus provides. Well, at least it is fantasy.

When the Israelites get to Sinai, Moses announces that anyone who touches Mount Sinai (obviously a sacred mountain) will die, except himself and, later, his brother Aaron. Moses goes up the mountain; when he comes down, although he does not yet have the famous stone tablets, he announces the Ten Commandments to the people . . . and something else: they should make an altar and sacrifice animals to God. But the approach to the altar must not include stairs, lest the people see Moses' private parts (Exodus 20:26). I'm not making this up. Keep in mind that Moses is telling the Israelites what he learned form God himself. And then Moses goes on for three more chapters, reciting law after law that God spoke to him: laws about the treatment of purchased servants (slaves) (e.g., "if the master gave him [i.e., the servant] a wife, and she hath borne sons and daughters, the woman and her children should be her master's"), about how punishments should be meted out (death to a man who strikes or curses his father or mother and to an ox that gores a man or a woman to death). God prescribes death for a man who kills a pregnant woman but a lesser punishment if only the fetus dies (whoops, there goes the literalists' case for the full personhood of fetuses). Witches, bestialists, and those who sacrifice to the gods are also to be put to death--just so you know. And here is one more for good measure: If you work on the Sabbath, you will be executed. It is true; check out Ex. 31:14-15: "he that shall profane it [the Sabbath] shall be put to death. [...] Every one that shall do any work on this day, shall die." I wonder if the millions of Christians working on Sundays at Walmart, Home Depot, Kroger, and thousands of other stores give any thought to this warning. (Yes, I know what Christianity teaches: Jesus abolished the Law of Moses. So, does that mean that God made a mistake in giving it to Moses? And what about the Ten Commandments, which were part of the Law of Moses? Are they no longer binding?) I am skipping tons of prescriptions; as I said, this goes on for three chapters (three pages of small type). The final prescription seems important given the long-standing hostility between Israel and Palestine in our times: "Let them [the inhabitants of the land that God has promised to the Israelites] not dwell in thy land, lest perhaps they make thee sin against me, if thou serve their gods: which undoubtedly will be a scandal to thee" (Ex. 23:33). Does this isolationist precept not have repercussions in modern times?

Then Moses goes up the mountain again. When he comes back this time, he recites six of the most tedious chapters you can imagine about the tabernacle, the Ark of the Covenant, the altar, the vestments, the consecration of Aaron and other priests, monetary contributions, and other related matters. Again Moses goes up the mountain and receives tablets inscribed by the finger of God. In the meantime, the people, disturbed by Moses' delayed return, beseech Aaron to make an idol, a golden calf. Aaron, who even more proximately than the people, has witnessed what Jahveh has done for them, immediately and inexplicably accedes to their request, telling them to bring him golden earrings from their wives and sons and daughters. From this jewelry, Aaron makes them a golden calf, and the people offer holocausts to the idol (Ex. 32:1-6). When Moses returns and sees what Aaron and the people have done, he becomes so angry that he smashes the tablets. Now I ask you: If you were in possession of tablets written by God himself, would you smash them even in your angriest moment? Another mystery. God too is angry, so angry that he threatens to destroy the people. Moses is able to appease God somewhat, but the latter still demands a slaughter. He has Moses tell the sons of Levi that each of them shall "kill his brother, and friend, and neighbor." And they kill about 23,000 men. Nice guy, this Jahveh!

In Chapter 10 of the Book of Leviticus, God kills Aaron's two sons for "offering strange fire." And he promises to kill priests who drink wine when they enter the tabernacle (Lev. 10:9). In Chapter 20, God tells Moses (again) who is to be put to death: anyone who curses his father or his mother, adulterers, active male homosexuals, witches, wizards, people who have sex with animals, people guilty of incest, and men who have sex with women who are menstruating. Finally, in Chapter 21, God tells Moses that people with blemishes (the blind, the lame, in a word the handicapped) may not serve as priests. There are quite a few additional interesting tidbits in Leviticus, but who needs more? Can God be like this?

The Books of Numbers and Deuteronomy

The Book of Numbers offers a smorgasbord of divine atrocities. In Chapter 11, the people complain, and God burns to death those who are at the back of the camp. Again the people complain, and God forces them to eat meat until it becomes repulsive to them and comes out of their nostrils (Num. 11:18-20). Shortly thereafter, God hits the people with a great plague (Num. 11:33). Numbers 14:18 seems self-contradictory: "The Lord is patient and full of mercy, taking away iniquity and wickedness, and leaving no man clear [i.e., leaving no man unpunished]. Who visitest the sins of the fathers upon the children unto the third and fourth generation." That's being patient and merciful? When three Israelites refuse to obey a command of Moses, God causes the earth to open and swallow the men, their families, and 250 of their followers (Num. 16). And it gets worse: On the next day, all of the Israelites complain about the Lord's killing of the previous day, for which God sends a plague that kills 14,700 people. In Chapter 21, the people again complain, this time about the way God treats them in the desert, for which God sends fiery serpents that bite and kill many.

Chapter 22 of the Book of Numbers has a story about a talking animal. It seems that a man named Balaam, ignoring a command of God, is riding his ass to Moab, where he intends to enrich himself by cursing the Israelites. Along the way, the ass thrice sees an angel with drawn sword blocking the way, and avoids the angel each time, twice by veering off the path and once by falling. These maneuvers anger Balaam, who had not seen the angel, and he beats the animal each time, the third time vehemently. Lo and behold, the abused ass speaks and asks Balaam why he beat her. Balaam answers (à la fairy-tale humans, not at all disconcerted by hearing an animal speak), saying that she deserved what she got, that he would have killed her if he had had a sword. The ass reminds Balaam that she has served him well in the past. Now, finally, Balaam sees the angel but does not apologize to the ass.

Moses tells the Israelites that God will deliver to them "seven nations much more numerous than thou art, and stronger than thou" (Deut. 7:1). "Thou shalt utterly destroy them. Thou shalt make no league with them, nor shew mercy to them" (Deut. 7:2). The Israelites are to "destroy their altars, and break their statues" (Deut. 7:5), exactly what ISIS has done with cultural artifacts in territory it has conquered. If a false prophet rises up who tries to induce Israelites to worship other gods, he should be slain (Deut. 13:1-5).

In the Book of Deuteronomy, Moses reminds his people of all that the Lord has done for them, tells them how God will reward them if they are faithful to him, how he will punish them if they are unfaithful, and he lays down a number of rules (some already mentioned in previous books of the Bible). If a family member tempts an Israelite to serve strange gods, that family member should be stoned to death (Deut. 13:6-10). Here are more of God's laws:

- Women should not wear men's clothing. Men should not wear women's clothing. God finds such people abominable (Deut. 22:5).

- If a man finds that his bride is not a virgin and so charges her, she shall, after corroborating examination, be stoned to death (Deut. 22:13-21).

- If a man lies with another man's wife, both the adulterer and the adulteress must die (Deut. 22:22).

- Eunuchs--men whose testicles have been cut off--may not enter the church of the Lord (Deut. 23:1).

- One born of a prostitute shall not enter the church of the Lord (Deut. 23:2).

- If two men are fighting and the wife of one, in order to aid her husband, grabs the testicles of the other man, her hand is to be cut off (Deut. 25:11-12).

Here is what those who don't keep God's commandments can look forward to:

- "The Lord shall send upon thee famine and hunger, and a rebuke upon all the works that thou shalt do. Until he consume and destroy thee quickly, for thy most wicked inventions, by which thou hast forsaken me [sic]" (Deut. 28:20).

- "May the Lord afflict thee with miserable want, with the fever and with cold, with burning and with heat, and with corrupted air and with blasting: and pursue thee till thou perish" (Deut. 28:22).

- "And be thy carcass meat for all the fowls of the air, and the beasts of the earth: and be there none to drive them away" (Deut. 28:26).

- "The Lord strike thee with the ulcer of Egypt, and the part of thy body, by which the dung is cast out, with the scab and with the itch: so that thou canst not be healed" (Deut. 28:27).

- "And thou shalt eat the fruit of thy womb, and the flesh of thy sons and of thy daughters, which the Lord thy God shall give thee, in the distress and extremity wherewith thy enemy shall oppress thee" (Deut. 28:53).

Whoever wrote this litany of laws strained his brain imagining new ways in which the Lord could torture the wicked. Most of Chapter 28 of Deuteronomy--from verse 16 to verse 67--consists of horrible curses that will befall the Israelites if they do not keep the Lord's commandments. Do bear in mind, however, that the ancient Israelites believed that God rewarded and punished people in this life, not in an afterlife. As horrible as the punishments of Deuteronomy are, they are temporal, and do not begin to compare in horror with the punishment promised by Jesus: eternal torture in hell.

The Books of Joshua and Judges

The Book of Joshua also tells of divine atrocities. If you enjoy the old spiritual "Joshua Fit [i.e., fought] the Battle of Jericho," you might enjoy it less in the future. In the Book of Joshua, we read that, when Jericho fell, "they [the Israelites] took the city, and killed all that were in it, man and woman, young and old" (Joshua 6:20-21). Later God commands Joshua as follows: "And thou shalt do to the city of Hai, and to the king thereof, as thou hast done to Jericho, and to the king thereof: but spoils and all cattle thou shalt take for a prey to yourselves" (Joshua 8:2). And Joshua goes on, at Jahveh's bidding, to destroy all the inhabitants of Lebna, Lechis, and Hebron (Joshua 10).

Divine atrocities, so much a part of the books of Deuteronomy and of Joshua, continue unabated in the Book of Judges. The Lord appoints Judah to replace the deceased commander, Joshua, and Judah carries on where Joshua left off: Judah's army slays ten thousand Canaanites and Perizzites in Bezek, puts Jerusalem to the sword and burns it, lays waste the town of Cariath-Sepher, slays the Canaanites of Sephaath, and deals viciously with the city of Luzza. And we're still in Chapter 1. There's much more blood and gore in Judges. It must be edifying reading because it is in the Bible, but I would recommend skipping it anyway. By the way, Jahveh must not have been omnipotent because we read in Judges 1:19 that he "was not able to destroy the inhabitants of the valley, because they had many chariots armed with scythes."

Judges 1:29-40 presents an incident that is even more disturbing than Abraham's attempt to sacrifice his son Isaac. A Hebrew warrior by the name of Jephte made a vow that, if Jahveh delivered the enemy into his hands, he would offer as a holocaust to the Lord "whoever shall first come forth out of the doors of my house, and shall meet me when I return in peace." The Lord did his part: the enemy fell. Sadly, the first person who came from the house to meet Jephte was his daughter. In great distress, her father explained that he had no choice but to sacrifice her. The daughter asked only to be permitted to "go about the mountains for two months" and "bewail my virginity with my companions." Her wish was granted. When she returned, Jephte "did to her as he had vowed, and she knew no man." This time, Jahveh did not intervene as he had with Isaac. Apparently, he was quite satisfied with Jephte's fulfillment of his evil vow.

Archaeologist Israel Finkelstein maintains, with respect to the Bible's claim that the Israelites took the land of Canaan by force, that "there was no violent event, no entry from the outside, not one suggestion of the Exodus. The Hebrews *were* the Canaanites, who had never left."[4] If Finkelstein is right (and his assertion is by no means uncontested), the wholesale slaughter of men, women, and children by the Israelites never happened. Not that that changes the image of God as presented in the Old Testament. This God is ill-tempered, bloodthirsty, monstrous. And the divine atrocities do not stop with the seventh book of the Old Testament.

From 1 Samuel to 2 Chronicles

The Ark of the Covenant was a gilded wooden box about 4'3" in length, 20" in width, and 20" in height. It supposedly housed the two stone tablets on which the Ten Commandments had been inscribed. In 1 Sam. 6:19, God "slew the men of Bethsames, because they had seen [looked into] the ark of the Lord; and he slew of the people seventy men, and fifty thousand of the common people." Yes, looking into the ark was a forbidden act, but did 50,070 people look in? In any case, was slaughtering them the act of a merciful God?

In Chapter 20 of 1 Kings, God kills many thousands of people: "And a man of God coming, said to the king of Israel: Thus saith the Lord: Because the Syrians have said: The Lord is God of the hills, but is not God of the valleys; I will deliver all this great multitude into thy hand; and you shall know that I am the Lord. And both sides set their armies in array one against the other, seven days. And on the seventh day the battle was fought; and the children of Israel slew of the Syrians a hundred thousand footmen in one day" (1 Kings 20:28-29). The Syrians had offended God by saying that God was not Lord of the plains. As a punishment, and to show his power, God killed 100,000 men. Showing off his power seems to be important to the God of the Old Testament. Somehow I doubt that an almighty deity would need that kind of ego boost.

There is a story in 2 Kings 2:23-24 about how Jahveh punished some impudent children. It seems the prophet Elisha (Eliseus) was on his way to Bethel when some little boys mocked him, calling him "bald head." When Elisha "cursed them in the name of the Lord," two bears came out of the woods and "tore of them two and forty boys." While I am not sure exactly what befell the boys, I know I would not want to be "torn" by bears.

The largest God-assisted slaughter of the Bible happens in 2 Chronicles, 14:9-15. With an army of one million men, Zara the Ethiopian came out against the Israelites. Asa, the Israelite leader, called on the Lord for help, and the Ethiopians fled and were destroyed, "for the Lord slew them." The Israelites took the enemy cities and destroyed "an infinite number of cattle, and of camels." If you are interested in violence, 2 Chronicles is the book for you. In fact, if you are interested in violence, you will want to add the Old Testament to your library.

The Book of Psalms

The Book of Psalms has the reputation of being one of the most beautiful parts of the Old Testament. Let us see just how beautiful the psalms are. In Psalm 2, God says: "Ask of me and I will give thee the Gentiles for thine inheritance, and the ends of the earth as thy possession. Thou shalt rule them with a rod of iron, thou shalt break them in pieces like a potter's vessel." That does not sound very beautiful to me. In Psalm 3 the psalmist begs, "Arise, O Lord! Save me, O my God! For thou hast smitten the heel of all who assail me, thou hast broken the teeth of the wicked." In Psalm 9: "Thou hast rebuked the nations, thou hast brought the wicked man to death, thou hast blotted out their name forever. The foes are crushed, cast down into everlasting ruin, and thou hast destroyed cities." And in the next psalm (Psalm 11): "He [the Lord] will rain burning coals and brimstone on sinners." Surely only a sadist would find this beautiful. In Psalm 12: "May the Lord destroy all lips that flatter, the boastful tongue." And in Psalm 21: "May thy hand overtake all thy foes; may thy right hand find all them that hate thee! Put them as in a blazing furnace, when thou appearest. May the Lord destroy them in his anger, and the fire swallow them up! Wipe out their race from the earth, and their seed from among the children of men." And this is only Psalm 21. There are 150 psalms in all. Of course, I have given you a distorted view. Read the psalms for yourself. There are many beautiful passages. But what place is there for the violence?

Steve Allen tells about a central African tribe of savages called Zarubas. These people, Allen tells us, hate other tribes and even glory in their hatred, which is instilled in the minds of infants and children and thus perpetuated from generation to generation He then gives us an excerpt from a Zaruba hymn of praise to their deity: "Oh God, set an evil chief over my enemy and let Kimba (the devil) stand at his right hand. When my enemy be judged, condemn him. Let even his prayer be judged evil. Let his life be shortened and let another man take his village. Let his children have no father and his wife be a widow. Let his children wander in the jungles, begging for their food. O God, let nobody help this man. Do not even let anyone help his father and his children. Let his children in generations to come be cut off. Let their names be blotted out. Let the sins of the fathers and the mothers harass the children down through generations. [...] Happy shall he be who takes and dashes the enemy's little ones against a stone." Then Allen confesses that Zarubas do not exist, that he has changed the name of the tribe of Judah in the Old Testament to Zaruba, paraphrased parts of Psalm 109 and quoted one line of Psalm 137.[5] How can an all-good God be said to have inspired an atrocious prayer? The answer, of course, is that the psalms cannot be attributed to a benevolent God. Like many other parts of the Old Testament that advocate senseless violence, they are an insult to a benevolent God.

The Books of Isaiah, Jeremiah, Ezekiel, Micah, and Zechariah

The salient feature of most of the Old Testament books of prophets (Isaiah, Jeremiah, Ezechiel, and others) is God's threats of punishment, directed sometimes toward the Israelites, sometimes toward the enemies of the Israelites, and sometimes at all people at the end of times. Of the hundreds of examples, I have chosen several to give you an idea of the vindictiveness of the God of the Old Testament:

- Here is what God will do to the Babylonians: "Every one that shall be found shall be slain: and every one that shall come to their aid shall fall by the sword. Their infants shall be dashed in pieces before their eyes, their houses shall be pillaged, and their wives shall be ravished. [...] But with their arrows they shall kill the children, and shall have no pity upon the sucklings of the womb: and their eyes shall not spare their sons" (Isaiah 13:15-18).

- Sometimes it is the Jews with whom God is upset: "And I will defeat the counsel of Judah and of Jerusalem in this place: and I will destroy them with the sword in the sight of their enemies and by the hands of them that seek their lives: and I will give their carcasses to be meat for the fowls of the air and for the beasts of the earth. And I will make this city an astonishment and a hissing: every one that shall pass by it shall be astonished and shall hiss because of all the plagues thereof. And I will feed them with the flesh of their sons and with the flesh of their daughters: and they shall eat every one the flesh of his friend in the siege. . . ." (Jeremiah 19:7-9).

- Once again the Jews are the target of God's wrath: "Because thou [Jerusalem] hast violated my sanctuary with all thy offences and with all thy abominations: I will also break thee in pieces, and my eye shall not spare, and I will not have any pity. A third part of thee shall die with the pestilence and shall be consumed with famine in the midst of thee:

and a third part of thee shall fall by the sword round about thee: and a third part of thee will I scatter into every wind, and I will draw out a sword after them. And I will accomplish my fury and will cause my indignation to rest upon them and I will be comforted" (Ezekiel 5:11-13).

- This is what God will do to the enemies of the one to be born in Bethlehem (Christians understand this chapter to be a prophecy of Jesus): "And I will destroy the cities of thy land and I will throw down all thy strongholds: and I will take away sorceries out of thy hand, and there shall be no divinations in thee. And I will destroy thy graven things and thy statues out of the midst of thee: and thou shalt no more adore the works of thy hands. And I will pluck up thy groves out of the midst of thee and will crush thy cities. And I will execute vengeance in wrath and in indignation among all the nations that have not given ear" (Micah 5:11-14).

- One more, this one aimed at the enemies of the Jews: "And this shall be the plague where with the Lord shall strike all nations that have fought against Jerusalem: the flesh of every one shall consume away while they stand upon their feet, and their eyes shall consume away in their holes, and their tongue shall consume away in their mouth" (Zechariah 14:12).

Yes, the God of the old Testament, Jahveh, is barbaric. Still, not once do the gospels say that Jesus condemned, or even criticized, the Jahveh-condoned violence of the Old Testament. And why would he? After all, God, whose son Jesus claimed to be, had eternal flames waiting for humans whose lives were offensive to him. Jesus' image of God was, therefore, even more monstrous than the image of God in the Old Testament, whose afflictions, horribly cruel and nonsensical, were temporal. And this God, we are told by Christians, loves us.

1. Richard Dawkins, *The God Delusion*, p. 51.
2. *Steve Allen, More Steve Allen on the Bible, Religion, and Morality*, p. xix.
3. Despite the many conflicts between sound science and a literal interpretation of the Bible's creation and flood narratives, the Creation Museum, a 60,000 square-foot facility in Petersburg, Kentucky, attracts 250,000 people a year to its displays, some of which show humans and dinosaurs coexisting in the last 6000 years. In the same state, a Noah's Ark theme park featuring a full-size replica of the famous ark is now open to the public. And the distance between the two monuments to creationist science is only fifty miles. You can take in both in one day.
4. Israel Finkelstein in "Rewriting TelMegiddo's Violent History," *Discover*, November 2015.
5. Steve Allen, "Primitive Religion," in *Steve Allen on the Bible, Religion, & Morality*, pp. 356-357.

Problems with the Old Testament

"Why doesn't the Bible say anything about electricity, or about DNA, or about the actual size of the universe?" - Sam Harris, *Letter to a Christian Nation*

Unfulfilled Prophecies

Some Christian apologists claim to see in the number of fulfilled biblical prophecies a kind of miracle, a proof of the credibility of the Bible. The eminent mathematician Blaise Pascal praised the prophecies as "the very miracles and proofs of our religion" although he stopped short of calling them "absolutely convincing." In Pascal's view, the evidence for the validity of the biblical prophecies is "such that it surpasses, or at least equals, the evidence to the contrary."[1] As I attempted to show in Chapter I, some of the 924 numbered paragraphs of Pascal's magnum opus, *Pensées,* reveal the author to have been an ideologue, a zealot. For reasons that I will elucidate, even though some of the Bible's many prophecies do seem to some Christians to have been fulfilled, they almost certainly were not. Indeed, the many unfulfilled prophecies preclude divine intervention. Let us look at several.

In Chapter 52 of the Old-Testament Book of Isaiah, Isaiah prophesies: "Arise, arise, put on thy strength, O Sion, put on the garment of thy glory, O Jerusalem, the city of the Holy One: for henceforth the uncircumcised and unclean shall no more pass through there" (Is. 52:1). Most assuredly, more than a few uncircumcised people have passed through Jerusalem since those words were written.

Here is a prophecy delivered to David by Nathan regarding the future rule of David and his descendents: "And I will appoint a place for my people Israel; and I will plant them; and they shall dwell therein, and shall be disturbed no more. Neither shall the children of iniquity afflict them as they did before" (2 Samuel 7:10). Who could possibly assert that the Jews have lived undisturbed in the land of Israel since the time of David and Nathan, approximately a thousand years before Jesus? What about the Roman occupation of Israel in the time of Jesus? The prophecy goes on to say that David's son will build a temple. The fact that David's son, Solomon, actually does this is hardly validation of the prophecy. It may have been a reasonable expectation; it may have been a lucky guess; or it may have been an ex post facto prophecy. Important for Christians are the next several verses of the prophecy, which say that David's heirs [of which Jesus is supposedly one] shall rule over Israel forever (2 Sam. 7:11-16). According to the Bible, Jesus admitted to Pilate that he was the King of the Jews. Even if Jesus actually said this, which is by no means certain, it proves nothing. Forever? Israel did not exist for many centuries. Jews were driven from the land of Israel in 135 CE and exercised no control of the land until 1948 CE.

The entirety of Chapter 26 of the Book of Ezechiel tells how the armies of Nebuchadnezzar would utterly destroy the city of Tyre, which would never be rebuilt. Today Tyre is the fourth largest city of Lebanon. Still, many Christians actually point to Tyre as a prophecy fulfilled. According to them, Tyre was destroyed, never mind that its destruction was brought about not by the armies of Nebuchadnezzar, which attacked but never destroyed Tyre, but by the Macedonian armies of Alexander the Great. The island portion of Tyre was in fact never rebuilt. Christians argue that the modern city of Tyre was not built over the ancient city but a short distance away. Thus, according to them, Tyre was never rebuilt, in fulfillment of the prophecy.

Isaiah 17:1 predicts that "Damascus shall cease to be a city, and shall be as a ruinous heap of stones." Believers in biblical prophecy defend these words by saying that the event just has not happened yet. How do you argue against something like that?

The prophet Ezekiel, who wrote around the year 600 BCE, wrote the following: "Therefore, thus saith the Lord God: Behold, I will bring the sword upon thee and cut off man and beast out of thee. And the land of Egypt shall become a desert and a wilderness. And they shall know that I am the Lord. Because thou hast said: The river is mine, and I made it. Therefore, behold I come against thee and thy rivers: and I will make the land of Egypt utterly desolate and wasted by the sword, from the tower of Syene even to the borders of Ethiopia. The foot of man shall not pass through it, neither shall the foot of beasts go through it: nor shall it be inhabited during forty years" (Eze. 29:8-11). This simply never happened. Fundamentalists tried to say that the eruption of a certain volcano could well have caused such desolation, but it turns out that the volcano erupted nearly a thousand years before Ezekiel lived. Nowadays the going answer seems to be that the prophecy hasn't been completely fulfilled.

The prophets of the Old Testament make some pretty wild predictions. Isaiah 30:26 says that when God subdues the enemies of Israel, "the light of the moon shall be as the light of the sun, and the light of the sun shall be sevenfold, as the light of seven days." Isaiah 60:12 offers the Israelites this prophecy: "For the nation that will not serve thee shall perish: and the Gentiles shall be wasted with desolation." How wrong can prophecies be?

And then there is the Book of Daniel, whose author pretended to be writing in the sixth century BCE in order that he might be able accurately, albeit deceptively, to predict happenings in the second century BCE, a time that he knew well because it was, for him, the present. Farrell Till, editor of the *Skeptical Review*, wrote three articles in which he explains how we know that the Book of Daniel is fraudulent: (1) the author did not know several important historical facts that he would have known had he lived in the sixth century BCE; (2) his prophecies for the second century BCE are amazingly accurate; (3) at some point, this accuracy stops.[2] You will probably not be surprised to learn that there are Christian apologists who try desperately to save the Book of Daniel by cleverly manipulating numbers and history in an effort to show that Daniel's prophecy in Dan. 9:24-27 applies to Jesus.[3]

Farrell Till writes that "the men who wrote the Old Testament were just ordinary religious zealots who thought that they and their people had been specifically chosen of God"; their fanaticism "led them to proclaim absurdly ethnocentric prophecies that history has proven wrong, much to the embarrassment of Bible fundamentalists who desperately want to believe that the Bible is the verbally inspired, inerrant word of God."[4] Many biblical prophecies can be shown to be invalid, while none can be shown with certainty to be valid. Just one invalid prophecy ought to preclude divine inspiration of the Bible. It is not hard to find more than one invalid prophecy, as you have now seen, and as you will continue to see in this chapter.

The author of the Gospel of Matthew tries hard to show that various events in the life of Jesus fulfill Old Testament prophecies. He could hardly be less convincing. In Matt. 1:22-23, he says that the virgin birth of Jesus fulfills a prophecy made by Isaiah. If you examine Isaiah 7, you will see that the prophecy has nothing to do with Jesus, and has everything to do with a sign that two kings threatening Jerusalem at the time of Isaiah would be unsuccessful. Furthermore, the Hebrew word translated by Matthew as "virgin" is "alma," which means simply a young woman. The author of the gospel apparently availed himself of a Greek translation of Isaiah, which uses the word "παρθενος" ("parthenos"), which means both young woman and virgin. What Matthew calls the fulfillment of a prophecy is an imaginative invention. In Matt. 2:15, Matthew adduces Jesus' return from Egypt as the fulfillment of the prophecy "Out of Egypt I have called my son." It is not. Even if Jesus as a child did spend time in Egypt (he probably did not), his return from there has nothing to do with the words from Hosea, which refer to the return of the Israelites from their bondage in Egypt: "Because Israel was a child and I loved him; and I called my son out of Egypt" (Hosea 11:1).

Many Christian exegetes do not know what to make of some of Matthew's wild claims of fulfilled prophecy. Take Matt. 2:23, which reads as follows: "And he [Joseph] went and settled in a town called Nazareth; that there might be fulfilled what was spoken through the prophets: He shall be called a Nazarene." The trouble is that neither the word "Nazarene" nor the word "Nazareth" occurs even once in the Old Testament. Another example of a contrived fulfillment of prophecy is Matt. 2:17-18: "Thus was fulfilled what was spoken through Jeremiah the prophet, 'A voice was heard in Rama, weeping and loud lamentation; Rachel weeping for her lost children, and she would not be comforted, because they are no more." Matthew cites these words to show that the (historically doubtful) slaughter of the innocent children of Bethlehem fulfills the words of the prophet Jeremiah about the weeping of a woman named Rachel. To see how disingenuous Matthew's attempted proof is, one need only read a fuller text of Jeremiah in 31:15-17: "Thus saith the Lord: A voice was heard on high of lamentation, of mourning and weeping, of Rachel weeping for her children and refusing to be comforted for them, because they are not. Thus saith the Lord: Let thy voice cease from weeping and thy eyes from tears, for there is a reward for thy work, saith the Lord: *and they shall return out of the land of the enemy*. And there is hope for thy last end, saith the Lord: *and the children shall return to their own borders* [italics mine]." The author of the Gospel of Matthew, who quotes extensively from the Old Testament, must have known that the children in the Jeremiah verses were the children of Israel, who were in captivity.

Isaiah 9:6 gives us another passage that Christians hold up as a fulfilled prophecy: "For a child is born to us, and a son is given to us, and the government is upon his shoulder; and his name shall be called Wonderful, Counselor, God the Mighty, the Father of the World to come, the Prince of Peace." The very next verse excludes Jesus as the fulfillment of this prophecy: "His empire shall be multiplied, and there shall be no end of peace." Well, Jesus has come and gone, and there certainly has been an end of peace. It might be more accurate to say there has been no end of war. By the way, of the almost twenty English-language versions of the Bible, only one, the Douay edition (Catholic Old Testament), has "Father of the World to come"; all of the rest have either "eternal Father" or "everlasting Father" or "Father in eternity." When was/is Jesus ever addressed as "eternal Father," "everlasting Father," or "Father in eternity"? Indeed, to address Jesus in this way would seem to be an assertion of the sameness of God the Father and God the Son, which some Christians consider heretical.

The author of the Gospel of Matthew says, in 8:17, that Jesus cured the many possessed individuals who were brought to him "that what was spoken through Isaiah the prophet might be fulfilled, who said, 'He himself took up our infirmities, and bore the burden of our ill' [Isaiah 53:4]." Isaiah's description of the "suffering servant" in the Book of Isaiah, Chapter 53 bears some similarities to Jesus as we know him from the Bible. Scripture scholars are not in agreement as to whom the words refer, though I suspect that most Christian scholars would apply them to Jesus. Interestingly, most Jewish commentaries and some Christian commentaries hold that the suffering servant of Isaiah is Israel itself. According to this interpretation, the speaker of Chapter 53 is the Gentile kings. I like this interpretation; however, one does wonder about the abrupt change from "we" to "I" between verses 7 and 8. One textual feature arguing in favor of the Jewish interpretation is the use of the past, present, and future tenses to refer to the servant. One of the striking resemblances between the Old-Testament servant and Jesus is that both lay down their lives for our sins. But we must keep in mind that the dogma of Christ's redemptive death probably developed after his death, in which case the prophecy might have been the reason for the invention of its "fulfillment" and thus in no way supernatural. Another reference by Matthew to a "suffering servant" passage seems rather more contrived. The reader is invited to compare Matthew 12:15-21 with Isaiah 42:1-4.

In Matt. 13:13-15, Matthew has Jesus say the following: "This is why I speak to them [the crowd of people who had gathered to hear Jesus] in parables, because seeing they do not see, and hearing they do not hear, neither do they understand. In them is being fulfilled the prophecy of Isaiah, who says, 'Hearing you will hear but not understand; and seeing you will see, but not perceive. For the heart of this people has been hardened, and with their ears they have been hard of hearing, and their eyes have been closed; lest at any time they see with their eyes, and hear with their ears, and understand with their mind, and be converted, and I heal them.'" God's words to Isaiah, clearly echoed by Jesus are harsh and unambiguous: "Go, and thou shalt say to this people: Hearing, hear and understand not: and see the vision and know it not. Blind the heart of this people, and make their ears heavy, and shut their eyes: lest they see with their eyes and hear with their ears and understand with their heart and be converted, and I heal them" (Is. 6:9-10). In my opinion, the most likely scenario is that Matthew, like Mark before him, placed into the mouth of Jesus words that Christians had come to believe Jesus actually spoke, words that had been invented by zealous individuals to match words found in the Old Testament. How can the same Jesus have said the words in Matt. 13:13-15 and also "I have not come to call the just, but sinners, to repentance" (Luke 5:32)?

Psalm 78:2 reads, "I will open my mouth unto parables, I will reveal hidden sayings of old." Although there is no reason to think that these words were intended to be prophetic, Matthew says of Jesus, "All these things Jesus spoke to the crowds in parables, and without parables he did not speak to them; that what was spoken through the prophet might be fulfilled, 'I will open my mouth in parables, I will utter things hidden since the foundation of the world.'" Matthew's lack of concern for details is evidenced by the imprecision of the quotation from the psalm. Also, according to Matthew's own gospel, Jesus spoke to the people often in expository prose, not always in parables. And, in the Gospel of John, Jesus uses no parables at all.

In Matt., 21:2, Jesus instructs two disciples to get an ass and a colt, which he intends to use for his entry into Jerusalem: "Go into the village opposite you, and immediately you will find an ass tied, and a colt with her; loose them and bring them to me." According to Matthew, Jesus did this "that what was spoken through the prophet might be fulfilled, 'Tell the daughter of Sion: Behold the king comes to thee, meek and seated on an ass, and upon a colt, the foal of a beast of burden.'" The relevant passage is Zechariah 9:9: "Rejoice greatly, O daughter of Sion, shout for joy, O daughter of Jerusalem: Behold thy King will come to thee, the just and savior. He is poor and riding upon an ass and upon a colt, the foal of an ass." It is likely that Zechariah used the common Hebraic literary device of parallelism to describe a single animal. After all, why would one man ride on two animals? Does Matthew's misunderstanding of Hebrew parallelism cause him to introduce a second animal (Mark and Luke have Jesus request only one)? At least this time the Old-Testament reference is to a future king and savior; in fact, according to some (or even most) Jewish commentators, the passage refers to the future Messiah. If Jesus really did stage such an entry into Jerusalem, might he not have done so precisely to fulfill a prophecy and thus to point to himself as the longed-for king? (According to Matt. 27:11, Mark 15:2, Luke 23:3, and John 18:33-38, Jesus admitted to Pilate that he was the King of the Jews.) Also, I am not at all sure that "meek" is the right word for Jesus. After all, he excoriated the Pharisees more than once and, shortly after his entry into Jerusalem, cleansed the Temple violently.

Because prophecies are vague, tales can be invented to "fulfill" them. According to Matt. 27:9-10, the purchase of the potter's field with the money (thirty pieces of silver) returned (flung into the Temple) by Judas fulfilled the prophecy of Zechariah 11:12-13: "And I [Zechariah] said to them: If it be good in your eyes, bring hither my wages: and if not, be quiet. And they weighed for my wages thirty pieces of silver. And the Lord said to me: Cast it to the statuary [most translations have "potter" here], a handsome price, that I was prized at by them. And I took the thirty pieces of silver and I cast them into the house of the Lord, to the statuary [potter]." In my opinion, the author of the Gospel of Matthew, who seems to have been intent on unearthing every conceivable allusion to the life of Jesus in the Old Testament, focused on three details in the passage from Zechariah, and then invented a story about Judas returning the money given him to betray Jesus, thirty pieces of silver, by flinging it into the Temple. To draw a connection to the reference in Zechariah to a potter, the evangelist imagined that the returned betrayal money was then used by the chief priests to purchase "the potter's field." It is telling that the other evangelists, two of whom mention the betrayal by Judas for "money," say nothing about thirty pieces of silver, nothing about betrayal money being flung into the Temple, and nothing about the purchase of a potter's field. Matthew seems to have invented the story to fulfill what he considered a prophecy.

Also, we should not be impressed when Matthew tells us that the soldiers' dividing of the garments of the crucified Jesus fulfills a prophecy in Psalm 22. In all likelihood, Matthew invented the scene. There are strong reasons to think that Psalm 22 has nothing to do with Jesus. The person whose garments have been divided up laments that he is being beset by dogs and prays to God to save him from the "lion's mouth" and the "horns of wild oxen." Matthew and the rest of the evangelists seem to have forgotten to mention the dogs, the lion, and the wild oxen on Calvary. Some of the words from this psalm find their way into Jesus' mouth. Are we surprised? Early Christian writers, it seems, saw nothing wrong in inventing stories and data that supported their beliefs. Perhaps the thinking went something like this: I am so certain that it is necessary to follow Jesus to be saved that I will gladly stretch historical truth to bring others to the true faith. After all, the writers might have reasoned that numerous ambiguous Old-Testament passages in some way prophesied events in Jesus life? Walter Kaufmann explains why there were so many of these passages: "Since the Old Testament is a collection of history and poetry, laws and wisdom, folklore and traditions, verses can always be found for every situation."[5]

Robert J. Miller has this to say about Matthew's use of Old-Testament prophecies: "From our perspective it is obvious that Matthew was reading Jesus into the prophecies he quoted. When we examine those prophecies in their own contexts, it is clear, for example, that Zechariah had no foreknowledge of Judas when he spoke about the thirty silver coins, and that Isaiah was not thinking about the birth of Jesus when he challenged King Ahaz with the news that 'the young woman is pregnant and will have a son and will name him Emmanuel' (Isa. 7:14, quoted in Matt. 1:23). [...] Respect for the Bible requires us to understand the prophets as speaking to their own times, with messages that they and their audiences understood in relation to their situations centuries before the time of Jesus."[6]

Samuel Reimarus, an 18th-century groundbreaker in the field of historical criticism of the Bible, wrote: "Among the Evangelists none introduce so many Scripture quotations as Matthew. Yet nothing is more manifest to such as have searched the pages of Scripture, than that they are either not to be found there at all, or not in those books from which they claim to be derived, or else the words are altered. To a rational mind they, one and all, contain nothing in themselves of the matter on account of which Matthew introduces them, and when read with the context, they cannot be drawn over to it otherwise than by a mere quibble in a forced allegory."[7] Following Reimarus's death, an equally bold man, playwright and literary critic Gotthold Ephraim Lessing, published parts of the Reimarus critique as "Fragments of an Anonymous Writer."[8] The cat was out of the bag, and critical biblical research took off from there.

Additional Problems

I do want to give you some examples of the Old Testament's contradictions, inconsistencies, factual errors, and absurdities. In the Second Book of Kings, it is reported that Ahaziah began to rule when he was twenty-two years old (2 Kings 8:26); according to the Second Book of Chronicles, he was forty-two when his reign began (2 Chron. 22:2). One number is right and one is wrong, or else both are wrong; they cannot both be right. Exodus 20:5 has God saying, "I am the Lord thy God, mighty, jealous, visiting the iniquity of the fathers upon the children, unto the third and fourth generation of them that hate me," whereas Ezekiel 18:20 reports the word of God as "The soul that sinneth the same shall die: the son shall not bear the iniquity of the father." Which is it? Along the same line, Deuteronomy 24:16 says this: "The fathers shall not be put to death for the children, nor the children for the fathers: but everyone shall die for his own sin." But Isaiah 14:21 has it this way: "Prepare his [the evil man's] children for slaughter, for the iniquity of their fathers." God often changes his mind in the Old Testament. Here's an example from Exodus 32:14: "And the Lord was appeased from doing the evil which he had spoken against his people." But Numbers 23:19 denies that God ever changes his mind: "God is not a man, that he should lie: nor as the son of man, that he should be changed. Hath he said then, and will he not do? Hath he spoken, and will he not fulfill?"

In addition to the numerous mathematical miscalculations in the Old Testament, one finds an abundance of scientific mistakes. In the Book of Leviticus, we are presented with a list of birds that should not be eaten; among them is the bat. The bat, of course, is a mammal, not a bird; but the author of Leviticus thought it was a bird (Lev. 11:13-19). The text goes on to say that locusts and beetles and grasshoppers may be eaten, "but of flying things whatsoever hath four feet only, shall be an abomination to you" (Lev. 11:23). That should send ornithologists and entomologists scurrying to their reference works. For you amateurs, if you happen upon one of those four-legged flying things, do not pick it up because the very next verse says that you will be defiled, unclean until sunset. Deuteronomy informs us that the camel, the hare, and the coney (probably the hyrax, a small rodent-like mammal) chew the cud (Deut. 14:7). Has anyone heard of a cud-chewing hare? In 1 Sam. 2:8, we read that the earth rests on pillars. Joshua 10:13 says that the sun and moon stood still until the Israelites took revenge on their enemies. There are many such scientific errors in the Old Testament. Here is one more, for you historical linguists: Genesis 11:6-9 tells how the languages of the earth appeared. The transformation from one language to many came about because proud people tried to build a tower (the Tower of Babel) that would reach to heaven. God put an end to the project by causing the workers to speak different languages, so that they could not understand each other. If you thought it took ages for the many languages of the earth to form, go to the back of the class. (Of course, one cannot disregard the possibility that the story of the Tower of Babel is an allegory purely and simply. More about that shortly.)

One finds many additional inconsistencies, contradictions, and even absurdities in the Old Testament. Here are some of them:

- "And the Lord set a mark upon Cain, that whoever found him should not kill him" (Gen. 4:15). Apparently there were only three or four people on earth at the time. What did Cain's mark accomplish?

- "And Cain knew his wife, and she conceived, and brought forth Hennoch: and he built a city, and called the name thereof by the name of his son Hennoch" (Gen. 4:17) The world's smallest city! Good information for a trivia quiz.

- "And the Lord smelled a sweet savour, and said [to Noah]: I will no more curse the earth for the sake of man: for the imagination and thought of man's heart are prone to evil from his youth: therefore I will no more destroy every living soul as I have done" (Gen. 7:21). It took a great loss of life for God to learn that man is weak-willed. Should he not have known this from the start?

- "And Jacob took green rods of poplar, and of almond, and of plane trees, and pilled [seems to mean "peeled"] them in part: so when the bark was taken off, in the parts that were pilled, there appeared whiteness: but the parts that were whole remained green. And by this means the color was diverse. And he put them in the troughs, where the water was poured out: that when the flocks should come to drink, they might have the rods before their eyes, and in the sight of them might conceive. And it came to pass that in the very heat of coition, the sheep beheld the rods, and brought forth spotted, and of diverse colors, and speckled" (Gen. 30:37-39). The Grimm Brothers missed a fairy tale here. Either that or our sheep farmers have a thing or two to learn about breeding sheep.

- "And Israel was initiated to Beelphegor [i.e., gave themselves over to the false god of licentiousness]. Upon which the Lord being angry, said to Moses: Take all the princes of the people, and hang them on giblets against the sun: that my fury may be turned away from Israel. And Moses said to the judges of Israel: Let every man kill his neighbors, that have been initiated to Beelphegor. And, behold, one of the children of Israel went in before his brethren to a harlot of Madian. . . . and when Phinees, the son of Eleazar, the son of Aaron the priest, saw it, he rose up from the midst of the multitude, and taking a dagger, went in after the Israelite into the brothel house, and thrust both of them through together: to wit, the man and the woman in the genital parts. And the scourge ceased from the children of Israel And there were slain four and twenty thousand men" (Num. 25:3-9). It sure is lucky for us that God abandoned his ancient modus operandi.

- "And the Lord our God delivered him [Sihon, the king of Heshbon] to us [the Israelites], and we slew him with his sons and all his people. And we took all his cities at that time, killing the inhabitants of them, men and women and children. We left nothing of them: except the cattle . . . and the spoils of the cities, which we took" (Deut. 2:33-35).

- "Thus saith the Lord: Behold, I will raise up evil against thee out of thy own house; and I will take thy wives before thy eyes and give them to thy neighbor: and he shall lie with thy wives in the sight of this sun"

(2 Sam. 12:11). And did the wives have anything to say about this? You had better believe they did not.

- "Bloody and deceitful men shall not live out half their days" (Psalm 55: 24). Have you not noticed that all the scoundrels die young? And of course the best people all live to a ripe old age.

- "Blessed is he that shall seize and dash thy little ones against the rock!" (Psalm 137)

- "Thou [God] openest thy hand and with benevolence doth satisfy every living thing" (Psalm 145:16). Of course, whoever wrote this had never seen the slums of Mumbai, nor thousands of other slums around the world. If this quotation is factual, every living thing in the ancient world was content.

- "[The Lord] renders justice to the oppressed, gives bread to the hungry. The Lord releases the captives, the Lord opens the eyes of the blind. The Lord raises up them that are bowed down, the Lord loves the just. The Lord watches over strangers, he supports the orphan and the widow, but the way of sinners he confounds" (Psalm 146:7-9). The author of this psalm must not have read earlier sections of the Bible. No divine force renders justice to the oppressed, gives bread to the hungry, releases the captives, etc. Not consistently, that's for sure.

- "And I will feed them [the Israelites] with the flesh of their sons and with the flesh of their daughters" (Jer. 19:9). What a beautiful thought! Just what you might expect a good, all-loving God would say.

- "Therefore the fathers shall eat the sons in the midst of thee [Israel], and the sons shall eat their fathers" (Ez. 5:10). Makes the previous quotation even more edifying!

In defence of some of the Bible's apparent bloopers, one can argue that many biblical absurdities were never intended to be understood literally but allegorically. I am thinking, for example, of the story of Eve and the serpent, the story of Noah and the ark, the story of Jonah and the whale, and, as mentioned already, the story of the Tower of Babel. I have no problem with an allegorical interpretation of these stories. And there is strong historical precedent for allegorical interpretation of the Bible. Origen, Augustine of Hippo, Bernard of Clairvaux, and Gregory the Great were among the important churchmen who found allegorical passages in the Bible. In fact, according to Karen Armstrong, "until the nineteenth century, very few people imagined that the first chapter of Genesis was a factual account of the origins of life."[9] Today, fundamentalists insist that the words of the Bible are literally true; thus, according to them, there really was a talking serpent in Paradise, Noah really did build an ark and load it with pairs of animals from all over the world, Jonah really did survive for three days in the belly of a whale, and all people spoke one language until they tried to reach heaven with a tower. Surely these things are nonsense when understood literally.

What Biblical Archaeology Reveals

"Biblical archaeology has helped to bury the Bible, and archaeologists know it." - Hector Avalos

* * * * *

In an interview with NOVA, William Dever, Professor Emeritus at he University of Arizona, said this: "From the beginning of what we call biblical archaeology, perhaps 150 years ago, scholars, mostly western scholars, have attempted to use archaeology to prove the Bible. And for a long time it was thought to work." However, that time has come and gone, so that today "archaeology raises more questions about the historicity of the Hebrew Bible [Old Testament] and even the New Testament than it provides answers, and that's very disturbing to some people."[10] Dever himself, in 1968, discovered in a cemetery west of Hebron an inscription from the 8th century BCE that says "by Yahweh and his Asherah." Two years later, many such inscriptions were found at a dig in the Sinai. Asherah was the Canaanite mother goddess. This information is disconcerting to some, for it provides evidence that the Hebrew religion was not monotheistic until later--in fact, until after the Babylonian Exile in the 6th century.

Certain biblical characters and events have become historically improbable as a result of the findings, or lack of findings, of modern archaeology. According to Genesis 26:1, "there was a famine in the land, besides the first famine that was in the days of Abraham. Isaac [the son of Abraham] went to Abimelech king of the Philistines, to Gerar." According to Paul Tobin, Isaac's going to Abimelech took place no later than the 15th century, if it happened at all. Unfortunately for biblical literalists, "archaeological finds tell us that there was no city of Gerar and there was no king of the Philistines to meet with Isaac during the historical period in which he would have lived."[11] Tobin mentions four additional anachronisms that disprove the historicity of Abraham.[12] He quotes Thomas Thompson, professor of Old Testament at the University of Copenhagen, who notes that "if the specific references in the patriarchal narratives have been shown to be anachronistic, then they add nothing to the story, but these very references were the historical anchors that supposedly rooted the narratives into history in the first place. Without them how are we to distinguish the narratives from other completely mythical folk tales?"[13]

And then there is Moses. Archaeologists find no evidence for his or the Israelites' presence in Egypt; in fact, there is no archaeological evidence for Moses' very existence. And yet, as you know, it is Moses who is said to have led the Israelites out of Egypt. How many Israelites did he lead? In Ex. 12:37, one reads: "And the children of Israel set forward from Ramesse to Socoth, being about six hundred thousand men, besides children." If you add in women (who, of course, are as important as men, just not in the Bible), that would seem to bring the total number of adult Israelites leaving Egypt to around 1,200,000. The Bible tells us that this immense multitude of people spent forty years in the desert. If so, they must have left behind ample evidence of their wanderings; however, archaeologists combing the desert have not found a trace. The Israelites must have left behind a million or so graves, since the Bible tells us that none of those over twenty years of age when the Israelites left Egypt (except Joshua and Caleb) made it to the promised land (Numbers 14:29-34). Egyptian archaeologist Zahi Hawass says this about the Israelite exodus from Egypt: "Really, it's a myth. . . . This is my career as an archaeologist. I should tell them the truth. If the people are upset, that is not my problem."[14] Archaeologists Israel Finkelstein and Ze'ev Herzog agree that there was no Exodus and no conquest of Canaan.

"If we assume that the story of Exodus is correct," says John W. Loftus, "there should be some archaeological evidence for the exodus, the crossing of the Red Sea, the camping of the Israelites at Mount Sinai, the wilderness wanderings, and their Canaanite conquest. And the archaeological evidence should correspond to the biblical account, but what we find instead is complete lack of it. . . ."[15] The Bible tells us that Joshua and his Israelite army slaughtered all of the men, women, and children in town after town as they took possession of Canaan. The town of Ai was supposedly burned by Joshua and its 12,000 inhabitants killed. This would have happened between 1400 BCE and 1200 BCE. According to Paul Tobin, archaeological excavations there show that Ai was destroyed around 2300 BCE, and there is no evidence at all to show human settlement there after that time. In other words, there was no Ai for Joshua to conquer.[16] John W. Loftus says that Heshbon and Dibon, and Gibeon, cities said by the Bible to have been conquered by the Israelites, did not exist until many years after their "conquest."[17] And remember the walls of Jericho that the Bible tells us tumbled down when Joshua's army marched around the town? It turns out that the walls fell twice, the last time in or before 1500 BCE, at least 100 years before Joshua's arrival. Wikipedia states: "In the face of the archaeological evidence, the biblical story of the fall of Jericho 'cannot have been founded on genuine historical sources' [William Dever]."[18] Oh, and one more thing: the glorious kingdom of David and Solomon was, according to Tel Aviv University archaeologist Ze'ev Herzog, "at most a small tribal kingdom."[19]

Fundamentalists, who take everything in the Bible as literal truth, try hard to dismiss the findings of archaeology. But not the Catholic Church, which, for well over half a century, has officially considered archaeology to be "an indispensable tool of the biblical sciences."[20] In 1943, Pope Pius XII wrote that "the interpreter must, as it were, go back wholly in spirit to those remote centuries of the East and with the aid of history, archaeology, ethnology, and other sciences, accurately determine what modes of writing, so to speak, the authors of that ancient period would be likely to use, and in fact did use."[21] So, if archaeology can show that a particular biblical narrative is not historical, then it is a myth. That is okay with the Catholic Church; after all, the details of fiction do not have to accord with historical facts. It saves the doctrine of the divine inspiration of Scripture. But does it really? Do the contents of a divinely inspired book not have to be edifying? Do they not have to teach us something important about the supernatural and man's relationship with the supernatural? In the Bible, the supreme supernatural being is God. What, pray tell, do the accounts of Joshua's bloody massacres of thousands of innocent people at the command of God tell us about God? Do they not tell us that God is willing to kill anyone and everyone who gets in the way of one group of people whom he has chosen to worship him? Would such a God not be a monster? Not only factual errors can disprove divine inspiration; moral content can do this as well.

1. Blaise Pascal, *Pensées,* 563-565.
2. If you enjoy sniffing out fraud, you will enjoy the complementary articles "Bad History in the Book of Daniel" and "Good History in the Book of Daniel," by Farrell Till, in *The Skeptical Review online,* as well as a section entitled "Daniel: Prophesying the Past" in Paul Tobin's book *The Rejection of Pascal's Wager: A Skeptic's Guide to the Bible and the Historical Jesus,* pp. 114-118.
3. Farrell Till addresses one such attempt in a lengthy article "The Seventieth Week of Daniel" in *The Skeptical Review online.*
4. Farrell Till, "Prophecies: Imaginary and Unfulfilled," on the website *The Secular Web: A Drop of Reason in a Pool of Confusion,* infidels.org.
5. Walter Kaufmann, *The Faith of a Heretic,* p. 224.
6. Robert J. Miller, "Did Jesus Fulfill Prophecy?" from the website of the Westar Institute.
7. Samuel Reimarus, *Fragments from Reimarus Consisting of Brief Critical*

Remarks on the Object of Jesus and His Disciples as Seen in the New Testament, translated from German by Rev. Charles Voysey, p. 45.

8. Into his 18th-century play *Nathan the Wise* Lessing incorporated the parable of the three rings from Giovanni Boccaccio's *The Decameron* (c. 1350). The lesson of the story is that no human can know which religion is the true one; it is even possible that none is.

9. Karen Armstrong, *The Bible: A Biography,* p. 3.

10. William Dever, "Archaeology of the Hebrew Bible," on the official website of NOVA.

11. Paul Tobin, *The Rejection of Pascal's Wager: A Skeptic's Guide to the Bible and the Historical Jesus*, p.89.

12. Ibid, pp. 89-92.

13. Ibid., pp. 92-93.

14. Zahi Hawass, "Biblical Archaeology," Wikipedia.

15. John W. Loftus, *Why I Became an Atheist: A Former Preacher Rejects Christianity*, p. 302.

16. Paul Tobin, *The Rejection of Pascal's Wage: A Skeptic's Guide to the Bible and the Historical Jesus*, p. 102.

17. John W. Loftus, *Why I Became an Atheist*, pp. 305-306.

18. "Battle of Jericho," Wikipedia.

19. Ze'ev Herzog , "Biblical Archaeology," Wikipedia.

20. "Biblical Archaeology," Wikipedia.

21. Pope Pius XII, in the encyclical *Divino Afflante Spiritu*, paragraph 35.

What do you think of the image of God in the Old Testament?

Larry (cultural Zionist Jew, advocate of harmony among all men, gainfully unemployed for forty years): *God is a mythical being depicted to intimidate wild masses of people so that they behave orderly and work toward a common goal. Of course, the barbarous tenor and nature of the stories are absurd, but there are positive messages spread throughout these tales that many religionists crafted into morals, ethics, and human decency. Like all ancient societies, the Israelites celebrated their military victories, exaggerated and perverted by the mythmakers who wrote the Bible. Gods were always interwoven into ancient religious renderings about triumph and subjugation; Gods were used as justification and inspiration for war and mayhem. An element of brutality was (and is) necessary to establish order and to allow human progress.*

Part II:
Jesus and the New Testament

Chapter V
Who Was Jesus?

Jesus in Extrabiblical Sources

"In Jewish and pagan antiquity, in matters of religious persuasion, fabricating stories was the norm, not the exception, even in the introduction of narrative purporting to be true." - Richard Carrier, *On the Historicity of Jesus*

* * * * *

Astonishingly, no information about Jesus is found in non-Jewish and non-Christian writings of the first century, even though, according to Bart D. Ehrman, "we do have a large number of documents from the time."[1] Actually, the first pagan reference to Jesus comes from the year 112 CE in a letter to the emperor Trajan from Pliny the Younger, a Roman governor, who asks for guidelines for dealing punitively with Christians. Pliny wants to know if being a Christian is sufficient grounds for execution (Trajan answers yes, by the way). From Pliny's letter we learn that Christians "were accustomed to meet on a fixed day before dawn and sing responsively a hymn to Christ as to a god"[2]; however, we are given no information whatsoever about the historical Jesus. The Roman historian Tacitus, in his *Annals* from approximately 115 CE, writes as follows regarding the emperor Nero's reaction to the burning of Rome: "Nero fastened the guilt and inflicted the most exquisite tortures on a class hated for their abominations, called Christians by the populace. Christus, from whom the name had its origin, suffered the extreme penalty during the reign of Tiberius at the hands of one of our procurators, Pontius Pilatus, and a most mischievous superstition, thus checked for the moment, again broke out not only in Judæa, the first source of the evil, but even in Rome, where all things hideous and shameful from every part of the world find their center and become popular. Accordingly, an arrest was first made of all who pleaded guilty; then, upon their information, an immense multitude was convicted, not so much of the crime of firing the city, as of hatred against mankind."[3] Other than the fact that Jesus was executed by order of Pontius Pilate, there is nothing in this passage from Tacitus about the historical Jesus.

With the exception of the historian Flavius Josephus, no Jewish writer of the first century mentions Jesus. In his twenty-volume work entitled *The Antiquities of the Jews*, Josephus mentions Jesus in two passages. The surviving text of the first passage is quite controversial. Here it is in its entirety: "At this time there appeared Jesus, a wise man, if indeed it is lawful to call him a man, for he was a doer of wonderful deeds, a teacher of such men as are happy to accept the truth. He won over many of the Jews and many of the Gentiles. He was the Messiah. And when Pilate, at the suggestion of the leading men among us, had condemned him to the cross, those who had loved him previously did not forsake him. For he appeared to them again on the third day, as the prophets of God had foretold these and ten thousand other wonders about him. And the tribe of Christians, so named from him, are not extinct to this day."[4] Many scholars today recognize that this passage has probably been altered, that Josephus, who remained a Jew his entire life, would surely not have written some of the things in the passage. It seems likely that a pious Christian inserted some "improvements." Bart D. Ehrman thinks the original text was probably more like this: "About this time there lived Jesus, a wise man, for he was a doer of wonderful deeds, a teacher of such men as are happy to accept the truth. He won over many of the Jews and many of the Gentiles. When Pilate, at the suggestion of the leading men among us, had condemned him to the cross, those who had loved him previously did not forsake him; and the tribe of Christians, so named from him, are not extinct to this day."[5] I would pare the text additionally by removing the lines that a lifelong Jew cannot be thought to have said, such as "a wise man," "a teacher of such men as are happy to accept the truth," and "those who had loved him previously did not forsake him." My suspicion is that the entire passage is a later insertion. Among other scholars, Paul Hopper, a distinguished linguistics professor at Carnegie Mellon University, rejects the authenticity of the text in its entirety: "The most likely explanation is that the entire passage is interpolated, presumably by Christians embarrassed at Josephus's manifest ignorance of the life and death of Jesus."[6] The context of the passage in question also argues against the authenticity of the passage, as an impressive, balanced article by Peter Kirby points out.[7] The sentence before the passage in question and the sentence after it fit together well. The Jesus passage does not sit comfortably in between. If you are interested in this topic, you can find abundant information on the Internet. Josephus has an additional reference to Jesus in Book 20 of the *The Annals of the Imperial Rome*, where he mentions a man named James, executed illegally by the high priest Ananias in 62 CE. This James, says Josephus, was "the brother of Jesus who is called the Messiah."

One would expect to find words about Jesus and the wondrous events reported in the New Testament among the 850,000 extant words of Philo of Alexandria, a Jewish contemporary of Jesus associated with the house of Herod. Although Philo wrote extensively about the Jewish religion and the politics of the time, one finds not a single word about Jesus. As you see, pagan and Jewish documents of the first century offer very little information about the historical Jesus. This doesn't mean that there are no early extrabiblical Christian sources that purport to give information about Jesus, for there are several. The Infancy Gospel of Thomas was written possibly as early as the second century. It is the account of what Jesus did between the ages of five (made clay sparrows which then came to life and flew off) and twelve (taught in the Temple). Another work that may date to the second century is the Gospel of Peter. It was allegedly written by St. Peter, but we know that many early Christian writers passed themselves off as close associates of Jesus. The fragment of the text that has survived to the present day is the author's first-person narration of the trial, crucifixion, burial, and resurrection of Jesus, and the discovery of the empty tomb by Mary Magdalene and companions. Of special interest are these points: Herod, not Pilate, orders the execution of Jesus; several Roman soldiers pitch a tent in front of Jesus' tomb to guard it; and three huge men and a cross rise from the tomb. Concerning the last point, the heads of two men reach into the heavens, while the head of the one in the middle reaches beyond the heavens. A heavenly voice asks, "Have you preached to those who are sleeping?" Lo and behold, the cross answers, "Yes." Are there any historical facts in this new material? How would anyone know?

The most important early-Christian extrabiblical work is the Coptic Gospel of Thomas, which is called the fifth gospel by a group of mostly liberal scholars called the Jesus Seminar. This unusual gospel, which may have taken preliminary form before the four gospels of the Bible, is a collection of 114 purported sayings of Jesus. Only about half of them resemble sayings from the New Testament. Some have a Gnostic quality (Gnostics stressed salvation by secret knowledge). To give you an idea of the contents of the Coptic Gospel of Thomas, here are several of its unusual sayings:

(1) "And he said: He who shall find the interpretation of the words shall not taste of death."

(7) "Jesus said: Blessed is the lion which the man shall eat, and the lion become man; and cursed is the man whom the lion shall eat, and the lion become man." One would think the final words of this verse

would be "and the man become lion," but I can find no such rendition.

(18) "The disciples said to Jesus: Tell us how our end shall be. Jesus said: Have you then discovered the beginning, that you seek after the end? For where the beginning is, there shall the end be. Blessed is he who shall stand in the beginning, and he shall know the end and shall not taste of death."

(19) "Jesus said: Blessed is he who was before he came into being. If you become my disciples and hear my words, these stones shall minister unto you. For you have five trees in Paradise which do not move in summer or in winter, and their leaves do not fall. He who knows them shall not taste of death."

(37) "His disciples said: On what day wilt thou be revealed [to] us, and on what day shall we see thee? Jesus said: When you unclothe yourselves and are not ashamed, and take your garments and lay them beneath your feet like little children, and tread upon them, then [shall ye see] the Son of the living One, and ye shall not fear."

(114) "Simon Peter said to them: Let Mary go forth from among us, for women are not worthy of the life. Jesus said: Behold, I shall lead her, that I may make her male, in order that she also may become a living spirit like you males. For every woman who makes herself male shall enter into the kingdom of heaven."[8]

Too strange for me! I guess we can congratulate the members of the Synod of Hippo (393 CE) for rejecting the Infancy Gospel of Thomas, the Gospel of Peter, and the Coptic Gospel of Thomas. Of course, the gospels they approved (the gospels of Matthew, Mark, Luke, and John) are far from unobjectionable. Here is how the Jesus Seminar sums up what can be known about the historical Jesus: "We are quite confident that a person Jesus of Nazareth once existed, in spite of a few skeptics who believe that all the stories about Jesus are pure myth. We are confident that he began as a disciple of John the Baptist, that he quit John at some point and returned to Galilee where he launched his own career as an itinerant sage. We believe he spoke about God's domain or God's imperial rule in parables and short, pithy sayings and attracted a substantial following. There is little doubt that he was also a charismatic healer and exorcist and that he was eventually put to death by the Romans around the year 30 CE. Paul of Tarsus, who became a disciple after Jesus' death, claimed that the risen Jesus appeared to him in a vision and that he had also appeared to Simon Peter, one of the original circle of followers. Beyond these meager facts, there is very little hard detailed information."9

Jesus' Birth

Just as two separate creation stories in the Book of Genesis are conflated into a single account for popular appeal, two separate accounts of the birth of Jesus, one in the Gospel of Matthew and one in the Gospel of Luke, become one story in popular literature. Matthew's gospel features three Magi, a slaughter of innocent children, and a flight into Egypt, while Luke's gospel tells of a census of the whole world, of Mary and Joseph's journey to Bethlehem, and of shepherds visiting a child in a manger. Luke makes no mention of Magi, a horrific slaughter, or a flight to Egypt, and Matthew says nothing of a census, a journey to Bethlehem, or shepherds. L. Michael White, the Ronald Nelson Smith Chair in Classics and Religious Studies at the University of Texas, calls the two stories "thoroughly different and mutually contradictory."10

The Magi story has a fantasy element akin to, say, the snake in Genesis: a special star that somehow reveals to the Magi the birth of a new Hebrew king, a star that then stops over the place where the infant Jesus lies in Bethlehem. One wonders how a star can be perceived to stand over a single residence and why God allowed the Magi to be summoned to Jerusalem for their interview with King Herod. If the Magi had not talked with Herod, there would have been no slaughter of the innocents--a moot point, I guess, because such a slaughter almost certainly did not take place. Had the slaughter occurred, the Jewish historian Josephus, who had no love of Herod, would surely have included it in his history of the Jewish people. But Matthew needed the slaughter and the eventual return of Jesus from Egypt to fulfill three prophecies. If you care to check out the Old Testament "prophecies," you will find that the words in the Old Testament do not at all prophesy these New Testament events. In one case, for example, the Old Testament words that Matthew applies to Jesus clearly pertain to the Israelites. You can read more about this topic in Chapter V of this book: "Unfulfilled Biblical Prophecies."

Nowhere in an extrabiblical historical work is there mention of a Roman census of the entire world. The Romans simply never did anything like this. And, practical as they were, they would never have required that each family return to its ancestral home for completion of a census. What an unimaginable interruption of productivity that would have entailed! Furthermore, Luke says that the census took place "while Cyrinus was governor of Syria" (Lk. 2:2). Cyrinus's tenure as governor of Syria began in 6 CE, ten years after the death of King Herod, who, in the Gospel of Matthew, is visited by the Magi and orders the death of innocent children in and around Bethlehem (Matt. Ch. 2). The contradiction seems best resolved by the acknowledgement that one author or both made a mistake. Both Matthew and Luke had to place the birth of Jesus in Bethlehem, because that is where the Jews expected the Messiah to be born. Similarly, both evangelists had to get Jesus to Nazareth, which became known during Jesus' ministry as his native village. In Matthew, Jesus' family, residents of Bethlehem, moves to Nazareth after the return from Egypt, while Luke has the family return to Nazareth, whence they had come.

Is it not strange that Matthew and Luke write such different accounts of the birth of Jesus? And the absence of a birth story in the Gospel of Mark, written some fifteen years before the next gospel (Matthew's), leads one to wonder if no such story had yet been invented and circulated. First-century Gentile converts to Christianity will have been familiar with the stories of the births of gods that included supernatural occurrences. Perhaps they, certain that the birth of their savior had been at least as splendid as the births of pagan gods, imagined and propagated ideas like the virgin birth, the magic star that guided the Magi, and angels who announced the blessed event to shepherds.

Edmond J. Dunn, a Catholic priest, who acknowledges that the biblical stories surrounding the birth of Jesus are not historical, labels them "theologoumenon," a word which Dunn defines as "telling a story that gets across a deep theological truth."[11] What theological truth do the stories of the manger and the angels and the shepherds and the Magi get across? Well, that "Jesus, born of Mary, is special. He is Emmanuel, God with us. He is the Messiah, the Savior."[12] Hmm. If this is what theologoumenon does for the infant Jesus, why can the stories of Jesus' miracles not be examples of theologoumenon, too? Why insist that these stories are historical? After all, they too show that Jesus is special; he is the Messiah, the Savior. And the stories of Jesus' resurrection? No need for them to be historical either. To me, playing the "theologoumenon" card seems like a way for theologians to wiggle out of the embarrassment of the conflicting nativity stories. It is as if they were saying, "Hey, we not only know what is going on with these stories, we even have a sophisticated word for them. Trust us."

The Jesus Seminar published the following conclusions regarding events associated with Jesus' birth:

- "Jesus was probably born in Nazareth, his hometown."

- "Jesus was not born of a virgin."

- "Jesus' father was probably either Joseph or some unknown male who either seduced or raped the young Mary."

- "The world census, the trip to Bethlehem, the star in the East, the astrologers [i.e., the Magi], the flight to Egypt and return, the massacre of the babies, the shepherds in the fields, the kinship to John the Baptist are all Christian fictions."[13]

Truly, the accounts of Jesus' birth are altogether unreliable as history. From them we learn nothing about the life of Jesus.

Jesus' Death

You might be surprised to learn that the gospels do not agree about something as basic as the day of Jesus' death. To understand the discrepancy, one needs to examine the sequence of events at the end of Jesus' life as presented by the gospel writers Mark and John. Jesus was in Jerusalem for the feast of Passover, a celebration to commemorate the passage of the ancient Israelites out of Egypt. In the Old Testament, in the Book of Exodus, one reads that God instructed the Israelites to eat quickly so as to be able to depart quickly. They therefore did not allow the bread to rise but ate unleavened bread. When Jews celebrated this occasion at Passover, their meal consisted of lamb, certain herbs, unleavened bread, and wine. The Passover meal was the first event in a six-day celebration called the Feast of Unleavened Bread. It occurred in the evening because the Jewish day began at sunset. In the Gospel of Mark, Jesus ate the Passover meal with his disciples (Mark 14:12-25). Prior to the meal, the disciples had asked Jesus, "Where doest thou want us to go and prepare for thee to eat the Passover?" Jesus described a location, and the disciples "prepared the Passover." It was at this meal, as described by Mark, that something very important for Christian theology happened: the institution of the Eucharist. Jesus "took bread, and blessing it, he broke and gave it to them, and said, 'Take; this is my body.'" (Mark 14:22). Later that evening, Jesus was arrested and brought before the Sanhedrin, the supreme court and legislative body of the Jews at that time. The Sanhedrin found that Jesus deserved to die. Then, "as soon as it was morning," the chief priests consulted "with the elders and Scribes and the whole Sanhedrin" and "delivered him to Pilate" (Mark 15:1), the Roman procurator, who alone had the authority to order executions. Pilate in turn had Jesus scourged and crucified. The crucifixion occurred, therefore, according to Mark, on the day following the day of preparation for Passover, that is, on the first day of Passover.

Now let us look at the Gospel of John. The author of this gospel does not mention a Passover meal. According to him, those arresting Jesus led him to Annas, whence he was transferred to Caiphas, the high priest, from whom Jesus was led early in the morning to Pilate. The Jews who brought Jesus to Pilate did not enter the praetorium "that they might not be defiled, but might eat the Passover" (John 18:28). We see, therefore, that according to John's gospel, Jesus was arrested before the time at which, in the Gospel of Mark, he ate the Passover meal with his disciples. John writes that "it was the Preparation Day for the Passover, about the sixth hour" (John 19:14), when Pilate had Jesus led away to be crucified. Later that day, according to John, as Jesus hung on the cross, "the Jews, . . . since it was the Preparation Day, in order that the bodies [of Jesus and the two men who were cru-cified with him] might not remain upon the cross on the Sabbath (for the Sabbath was a solemn day), besought Pilate that their legs might be broken, and that they might be taken away" (John 19:31). As best I can understand, John says two contradictory things: Jesus died on a Thursday (the day of preparation for the Passover), and Jesus died on a Friday (the day before the Sabbath, a Saturday). The other three gospels indicate that Jesus died on a Friday. Why the confusion? Bart D. Ehrman suggests that John might have wanted to have Jesus die earlier so that he, as the Lamb of God, might be shown to die on the day of the preparation, the day on which lambs were slaughtered in the Temple in preparation for the Passover meal.[14] For John, symbolic truth might have been more important than historical accuracy, so important indeed that he was willing to omit from his gospel one of the foundation events of Christianity, the Last Supper. But if so, why does he suggest that the day following the crucifixion was the Sabbath? Who knows?

The Internet is teeming with Christian sites that insist that Jesus died on a Wednesday. And they give a reason for this: there were two Sab-baths associated with Passover, one on Thursday and one on Saturday. The argument is that if Jesus died on Wednesday, the day before the Sabbath, he really was entombed long enough to satisfy the biblical prediction that he would be in the grave for three days and three nights. When everyone thought Jesus died on a Friday, Christians struggled to explain the discrepancy between predicted time and actual time. But the problem with this argument, says Tom Brown, is that Jesus also predicted that he would rise on the third day. This prophecy cannot be fulfilled if Wednesday is taken as his day of death. Brown also gives another reason for preferring to stick with Friday: If Jesus had died on Wednesday, the women would have gone to anoint the body on Friday; however, according to Luke 24:1, they did this on "the first day of the week," a Sunday.[15] Some commentators even suggest that Jesus' death occurred on a Thursday; however, this places the Last Supper on a Wednesday, which is not the proper day for a Passover meal. What a mess! If the Scriptures were divinely inspired, as Christians insist, would they be so confusing?

There are several additional inconsistencies in and between the gospel accounts of the crucifixion. Matthew 27:28 says soldiers gave Jesus a crown of thorns and clad him in a scarlet robe; John 19:2 says the robe was purple. According to John, this happens before Pilate gave Jesus over for crucifixion; in Matthew, it occurs after Pilate's pronouncement. Mark 15:25 has Jesus being crucified at the third hour, while Luke 23:44 places the crucifixion at about the sixth hour, and John 19:14-16 implies a time after the sixth hour. Each gospel gives a slightly different wording of the inscription on the cross. Two gospel accounts (Matt. 27:44 and Mark 15:32) say that the two robbers crucified with Jesus reproach him, while Luke 23:39-40 makes a point of saying that only one robber reproaches Jesus; the other rebukes the reproacher. Details differ also regarding the clothing of Jesus for which the soldiers cast lots, regarding just what, if anything, was mixed with the vinegar offered to Jesus, and regarding who mentioned Elijah. I guess the obvious errors do not matter if the gospel writers had no intention of writing a precise historical account, but errors do make it impossible to call the Bible historically inerrant. And some fundamentalists these days still do just that.[16]

Jesus' Resurrection

Paul wrote in his first Epistle to the Corinthians that "if Christ has not risen, vain then is our preaching, vain too is your faith" (1 Cor. 15:14). Paul certainly sounds convinced, but of course zealots always are. Let us see what the gospels have to say about the Resurrection. You might be amazed at how the resurrection stories of the four evangelists differ among themselves. First of all, there's the question of who came to the tomb early on a Sunday morning. According to Matthew, it was Mary Magdalene and "the other Mary"; Mark identifies the women as Mary Magdalene, Mary the mother of James, and Salome; Luke's answer is Mary Magdalene, Joanna, Mary the mother of James, and others (unnamed); John, who gives the most detailed account of post-resurrection happenings, has Mary Magdalene as the sole visitor.

Who's right, if anyone? All tomb visitors find the tomb empty, but they encounter a stranger or strangers: an angel (Matthew), a man in a white robe (Mark), two men in dazzling clothes (Luke), two angels in white (John). In Matthew, the women run to tell the disciples. Jesus meets them on their way back from the tomb, and they embrace his feet. In Mark, the women, having been told that Jesus was risen, say nothing to anyone because they are afraid. Luke has the women returning to tell the Eleven and "the rest" the news. Peter then runs alone to the tomb and finds linen cloths. In John's Gospel, Mary Magdalene, having found an empty tomb, runs and tells Peter that someone has taken Jesus body away. Peter then goes to the tomb with another disciple (thus not alone as in Luke). Mary Magdalene, who apparently returns later to the tomb, looks into it and sees two angels. Then she turns around and sees Jesus but doesn't recognize him. Jesus tells her not to touch him (in Matthew, the women embrace Jesus' feet).

Many years passed between Jesus' death and the writing of the first gospel (Mark's), plenty of time for various stories of his resurrection to have developed. Jesus cannot be dead, his followers and his followers' followers will perhaps have reasoned; therefore, he rose. Steve Allen suggests the possibility of a heightened emotional response to the death of Jesus that might have resulted in imagined sightings such as took place after the deaths of James Dean and Elvis Presley. Stories about such sightings would have been readily believed by ardent followers of Jesus and passed on as unquestionably true.[17] Of course, stories change as they move from one person to another, so that several believed sightings of Jesus could have resulted in many different stories; in fact, we see an indication of this in the various Easter-morning accounts by Matthew, Mark, Luke, and John.

Dan Barker, a former preacher, challenges Christians to tell him what happened on Easter: "The conditions of the challenge are simple and reasonable. In each of the four Gospels, begin at Easter morning and read to the end of the book: Matthew 28, Mark 16, Luke 23, and John 20-21. Also read Acts 1:3-12 and 1 Corinthians 15:3-8. These 165 verses can be read in a few minutes. Then, without omitting a single detail from these separate accounts, write a simple, chronological narrative of the events between the resurrection and the ascension: what happened first, second, and so on; who said what, when; and where these things happened."[18] Barker says he cannot do it and adds that he is still waiting for the Easter narrative a minister once publicly proclaimed that he would send in a few days. One problem is how long Jesus remained on earth after the Resurrection. Mark and Luke indicate that the Ascension happened on the day of Resurrection, whereas Jesus stayed on earth at least eight days according to John's gospel and at least forty days according to the Acts of the Apostles. Jesus ascended from Bethany according to Luke, but from the Mount of Olives according to Acts. Matthew, John, and Paul do not mention an ascension at all.

A website entitled "Atheologica: Subjecting Religion to Critical Thought" makes a good case for asserting that the Canaanite god Baal provided the early Christians a prototype for the resurrection of Jesus. The website maintains that the ancient Israelites were actually "an indigenous tribe of Canaanites," that the Israelites did not conquer the Canaanites but simply broke away from them, and that the Israelites' god Elohim is a variation of the name of the Canaanites' chief god, El Elyon.[19] As you may know, the idea of a resurrected deity was far from unknown in the ancient Middle East. Besides Baal, pagan gods said to be resurrected include the Egyptian god Osiris, the Greek gods Adonis and Dionysus, and the Persian god Mithras, whom Romans made the focal point of a mystery religion. Present-day Christians are, of course, motivated to disprove any pagan influence on the stories of Jesus' resurrection, and so one finds on the Internet seemingly endless Christian attempts to show that no such influence existed.

In an article entitled "The Historicity of the Empty Tomb Evaluated," Peter Kirby quotes Uta Ranke-Heinemann as follows: "The empty tomb on Easter Sunday morning is a legend. This is shown by the simple fact that the apostle Paul, the most crucial preacher of Christ's resurrection, and the earliest New Testament writer besides, says nothing about it. As far as Paul is concerned, it doesn't exist. Thus it means nothing to him, that is, an empty tomb has no significance for the truth of the resurrection, which he so emphatically proclaims. [...] If Paul had ever heard of the empty tomb, he would have never passed over it in silence. Since he gathers together and cites all evidence for Jesus' resurrection that has been handed down to him (1 Corinthians 15), he certainly would have found the empty tomb worth mentioning. That he doesn't proves that it never existed and hence the accounts of it must not have arisen until later."[20] Ranke-Heinemann's reasoning is persuasive; however, I think "proves" is too strong a word here; the author would have done better to say that Paul's failure to mention an empty tomb indicates that such a tomb *probably* did not exist. Skeptics, like believers, must allow strength of evidence to govern strength of conclusions.

Kirby attempts to show that all three later gospels were dependent on Mark for the resurrection story. The changes made by the other evangelists reflect their theological concerns. If this is so, there is really only one early Christian source for the story of the Resurrection. The oldest and most reliable copies of the Gospel of Mark end this way: ". . . and they [the women who had just visited the tomb of Jesus] departed and fled from the tomb, for trembling and fear had seized them; and they said nothing to anyone, for they were afraid" (Mark 16:8). Kirby believes that, if Mark had thought that the women had told the apostles of the empty tomb before the latter went to Galilee, he would not have ended his gospel where he did. Later Christians, for theological reasons, added twelve verses to the Gospel of Mark. The apostles might have begun to believe in Jesus' resurrection during their stay in Galilee and not through visits of their own to an empty tomb. But what if, as Kirby suggests, there was no tomb at all? According to Mark, the women wonder aloud on their Easter morning visit to the tomb who will roll back the stone (Mk. 16:3). Kirby gives a rather compelling reason why the stone could not have been rolled back: it seems that square stones were used by the Jews to close their tombs until around the year 70 CE.[21] Of course, the gospels were written after that year. What we have then, apparently, in the Gospel of Mark is a curious (and suspicious) anachronism.

Mark and Luke have the women coming to the tomb to anoint the dead body of Jesus. Kirby quotes Hans van Campenhausen: "The desire to anoint, 'on the third day,' a dead body already buried and wrapped in linen cloths, is, however it be explained, not in accordance with any custom known to us. . . ."[22] Kirby is not surprised that Matthew and John, who are considered more knowledgeable about Jewish customs, do not mention an intention to anoint. According to Kirby, Pilate should have and would have ordered a dishonorable burial for Jesus, which would have meant that his body was covered with a few inches of sand. Kirby sees the figure of Joseph of Arimathea as a deus ex machina, a contrived person who just happens to be present, who just happens to own a new tomb in which no body had yet been laid, and who just happens to be willing to petition Pilate for an honorable burial for someone whom Pilate considered a common criminal. Bart Ehrman agrees that Jesus would probably not have been given an honorable burial. Ehrman explains as follows: "If [someone] declared 'war' on Rome--which a claim to being the King amounted to [Jesus admitted to Pilate that he was the 'King of the Jews']--the Romans knew how to deal with him. He would be publicly tortured and humiliated, left to rot on a cross so everyone could see what happens to someone who thinks he can cross the power of Rome. And there would have been no decent burial, precisely because there was no mercy or reprieve in cases such as this."[23] Later, says Ehrman, after the body had sufficiently decomposed, it could be dumped into a common grave.

The Mind and Character of Jesus

"If I had the power that the New Testament narrative says that Jesus had, I would not cure one person of blindness. I would make blindness impossible; I would not cure one person of leprosy, I would abolish leprosy." - attributed to Joseph Lewis (1889-1968), publisher, president of Freethinkers of America

* * * * *

If we were to abandon reason and assume that everything reported in the four gospels about Jesus' life between his birth and his death is historically accurate, what kind of picture of Jesus would we get? Would this Jesus not be a perfect human being? In a word, no. The Jesus of the Bible demonstrates many admirable qualities but (heresy of heresies!) quite a few not so admirable qualities as well. One sees indications of the former, i.e., qualities of the gentle Jesus, the idealistic Jesus, in Chapter 6 of the Gospel of Luke, where Jesus says, "Love your enemies. Do good to those who hate you. Bless those who curse you. . . . And to him who strikes thee on the one cheek, offer the other also. . . . Give to everyone who asks of thee" (Luke 6:27-30). And in Matthew's account of the Sermon on the Mount, we find additionally "Blessed are the merciful" and "Blessed are the peacemakers" (Matt. 5:7, 9). Imagine how different the world would be if everyone acted on this advice.

But there is another side to Jesus' character as he is presented in the gospels. First of all, anyone who preaches that God sends certain people to a place of eternal punishment shows, in my opinion, a questionable understanding of God. And Jesus does this over and over. Here is just one example, from Matt. 13:41-42: "The Son of Man [Jesus] will send forth his angels, and they will gather out of his kingdom all scandals and those who work iniquity, and cast them into the furnace of fire, where there will be the weeping, and the gnashing of teeth." Also, Jesus seems to lack compassion when he tells a would-be disciple who has asked to return home to bury his father, to follow him "and leave the dead to bury their own dead" (Matt. 8:22). When another newcomer asks to be allowed to say farewell to his family at home, Jesus' refusal seems to show little regard for love of family: "No one, having put his hand to the plow and looking back, is fit for the kingdom of God" (Luke 9:61-62). These demands seem to be the demands of a zealot. On another occasion, Jesus informs the crowds, "If anyone comes to me and does not hate his father and mother, and wife and children, and brothers and sisters, yes, and even his own life, he cannot be my disciple" (Luke 14:25-26). A thoughtful, compassionate Jesus would have anticipated that the following words of his would cause unspeakable anguish in millions of his followers: "Amen I say to you, that all sins shall be forgiven to the sons of men, and the blasphemies wherewith they may blaspheme; but whoever blasphemes against the Holy Spirit never has forgiveness, but will be guilty of an everlasting sin" (Mark 3:28-29). Surely many Christians have agonized, "What is this sin against the Holy Spirit? Have I committed it? Will I be damned for eternity?"

At times Jesus has an acerbic tongue, as he does in Matt. 23:32, when he calls the Pharisees "serpents, brood of vipers." He even calls them "blind fools" (Matt. 23:17), although in Matt. 5:22 we hear Jesus say that "whoever says 'Thou fool!,' shall be liable to the fire of Gehenna." Would a person of superior morals do something himself that he says will bring damnation to others? One would expect Jesus to be kind to animals; instead one finds him casting some devils into a herd of pigs, which causes them to rush down a cliff into the sea and drown (Matt. 8:30-32). How can one not ask why a humane individual would do something like that? Then, in Matt. 21:18-22, we read about Jesus cursing the barren fig tree, causing it to wither. Mark adds that "it was not the season for figs" (Mark 11:13). Sounds like an anger issue to me. And in Matt. 5:22, Jesus warned, "But I say to you that everyone who is angry with his brother shall be liable to judgment." Mark 3:5 states explicitly that Jesus looked at the Pharisees with anger and was grieved at the blindness of their hearts. Likewise, when Jesus was slapped by an attendant of the high priest, he asked why he had been slapped (John 18:22-23)--instead of turning the other cheek as he had advised others to do. But then, consistency is not one of Jesus' strong suits. Having just upbraided the Pharisees for disregarding one of the laws of Moses, Jesus "declared all foods clean" (Mark 7:19), a departure from the law of Moses, according to which certain foods are unclean. Worse, much worse, Jesus explains to his apostles that he speaks to the multitudes in parables "lest . . . they should be converted, and their sins be forgiven them" (Mark 4:12). This suggestion of divine favoritism, which we find repeated in the New Testament, evokes the ugly thought of predestination. What's more, these words seems to contradict Jesus' words in Matt. 9:13: "For I have come to call sinners, not the just." Jesus seems to say one thing on one occasion and another thing on another occasion.

And the list goes on. One can't help wondering about several of the so-called Beatitudes and Woes as reported in Chapter 6 of the Gospel of Luke. Luke has Jesus say, "Blessed are you poor, for yours is the kingdom of God" (Luke 6:20). Really? Just because you are poor, you get a ticket to heaven? Even if you hate being poor and wish you were rich? Even if you curse God for making you poor? So that his listeners might know what to avoid, Luke mentions four woes. Here is one: "Woe to you who laugh now! for you shall mourn and weep" (Luke 6:25). It sounds like optimists might be headed for hell. Does that make sense? Furthermore, each of the Beatitudes pronounces a condition or an action blessed because there is a reward attached to it. Is it not better to pursue virtue for its own sake, not for the sake of a reward? Should Jesus not have known this and so instructed his followers? An interethnic incident, Jesus' encounter with a Gentile woman who brings her daughter to him to be cured, does not speak well for Jesus' character. He says to her, "Let the children first have their fill, for it is not fair to take the children's bread and to cast it to the dogs" (translation: Why should I help you, who are so much lower than my Jewish supplicants?). When she responds, "Yes, Lord, for even the dogs under the table eat of the children's crumbs," Jesus replies that *because of this answer* [emphasis mine] he will heal the girl (Mark 7:26-29). Sadly, in admonishing the Pharisees, Jesus affirms one of the least appealing laws of Moses: "And he [Jesus] said to them, "Well do you nullify the commandment of God, that you may keep your own tradition! For Moses said, 'Honor thy father and thy mother'; and *'Let him who curses father or mother be put to death'* [emphasis mine]" (Mark 7:9-10; cf. Ex. 21:17). Can one not assume that Jesus also approved of the execution of witches, bestialists, those who sacrifice to the gods, and those who work on the Sabbath, as the Book of Exodus dictates (Ex. 22:18-20, Ex. 31: 14-15)? Indeed, the mind and character of the biblical Jesus do not give us reason to believe that he was the divine Son of God.

What Did Jesus Not Know?

Many years ago, in my final year as a Catholic seminarian, I began to be troubled by a question that had been of great concern to Albert Schweitzer: If Jesus was divine, how could he have erred regarding the time of his second coming? About his "coming upon clouds with great power and majesty," Jesus says in Mark 13:30, "Amen, I say to you, this generation will not pass away until all these things have been accomplished." And virtually the same words are repeated in Matthew 24:34, and in Luke 21:32. According to Matthew, Jesus had also spoken similarly earlier: "For the Son of Man is to come with his angels in the glory of his Father, and then he will render to everyone according to his conduct [at the last judgment]. Amen, I say to you, there are some of those standing here who will not taste death, till they have seen the Son of Man coming in his kingdom" (Matt. 16:27-28). This prediction was not fulfilled. One of the most basic tenets of Christianity is that Jesus was divine. Yet it seems obvious that Jesus made a mistake. What I did not realize at the time is that, if one believes the gospels, one has to admit that Jesus made quite a few mistakes.

In the Gospel of Mark, Chapter 5, verses 25-34, when a woman seeking to be healed comes up behind Jesus and touches his cloak, he seems not to know who touched him. Apparently at a loss, he asks his apostles who it was that touched him. Matthew corrects this "error" in 9:20-22. Luke 2:52 says that Jesus advanced in wisdom. How can a person advance in wisdom who is already all-wise? In John 7:38, Jesus says, "He who believes in me, as the Scripture says, 'From within him there shall flow rivers of living water.'" No one can find this text in Scripture; apparently it does not exist in the Old Testament. In a word, Jesus made a mental error. In the Gospel of Mark, Jesus gives the wrong name for the high priest at a particular time in the life of David: "Have you never read what David did when he and those who were with him were in need, and hungry? how he entered the house of God, when Abiathar was high priest, and ate the loaves of propitiation . . . ?" (Mark 2:26) The high priest at that time was actually Abiathar's father, Ahimelech. Mistake after mistake.

Either there were many more cases of demonic possession in Jesus' time, or Jesus mistook epilepsy and delusional thinking for possession by devils. According to Richard P. McBrien, if the apostles had been convinced of Jesus' omniscience, they would not have been surprised by the crucifixion and resurrection, both of which he is reported in the gospels to have predicted.[24] Regarding the destruction of the Temple, Jesus said there would not be left a stone upon a stone, yet you can go to Jerusalem today and see plenty of Temple stones on top of other Temple stones, exactly as they were when Jesus made the prediction, despite the fact that the destroyed Temple was never rebuilt. Jesus was wrong about the effects of faith. He said (as earlier mentioned), "Whoever says to this mountain, 'Arise, and hurl thyself into the sea,' and does not waver in his heart, but believes that whatever he says shall be done, it shall be done for him. Therefore, I say to you, all things whatever you ask for in prayer, believe that you shall receive, and they shall come to you" (Mark 11:23-24). No mountains have been hurled into the sea, and billions of prayers of believers have gone unanswered. In his incorrect prediction of the end of the world, Jesus admits that he does not know the exact time of his second coming (Mark 13:32). Judas must have known that Jesus' knowledge was limited; otherwise, he would not have betrayed him. Jesus apparently didn't know that evangelists would eventually write gospels that would be riddled with obvious errors, at times about most important things such as the importance of the Law of Moses to Christians. If he had known this, and if he were divine, would he not have written down what Christians needed to know? Should Jesus' followers, for example, execute witches, homosexuals, bestialists, adulterers, and recalcitrant children, as prescribed by Moses? That Jesus did not leave clear written instructions tells me that he probably wasn't divine.

Jesus said to the multitudes, "You therefore are to be perfect, even as your heavenly Father is perfect" (Matt. 5:48). An all-knowing Jesus would have known that moral perfection is impossible for humans. Jesus seemed not to know that many birds starve to death: "Look at the birds of the air: they neither sow, or reap, or gather into barns; yet your heavenly Father feeds them" (Matt. 6:26). According to Jesus, the "Queen of the South" (the Queen of Saba, or Sheba) "came from the ends of the earth to hear the wisdom of Solomon" (Matt. 12:42). Sheba (Saba) was in the southwestern part of the Arabian peninsula, hardly the ends of the earth. Perhaps Jesus knew no more about geography than many others of his day. Jesus thought that the gospel would be preached in the whole world before the end of the world, which (as we have already seen) was predicted by Jesus to come within the lifetime of some of his contemporaries: ". . . and this gospel of the kingdom shall be preached in the whole world, for a witness to all nations; and then will come the end" (Matt. 24:14). This misjudgment is another indication of Jesus' geographical ignorance. Jesus believed in the tale of Noah and the Ark: "For as in the days before the flood they were eating and drinking, marrying and giving in marriage until the day when Noah entered the ark, and they did not understand until the flood came and swept them all away; even so will be the coming of the Son of Man" (Matt. 24:38-39).

Jesus prays in the Garden of Olives, "Father, if it is possible, let this cup pass away from me; yet not as I will, but as thou willest" (Matt. 26:39). Should Jesus not have known what the Father willed? When Judas arrives with a great crowd, Jesus, who had known at the Last Supper who would betray him, asks Judas, "Friend, for what purpose has thou come?" Did he really not know? And Jesus buys into the messianic nonprophecy of the Old Testament about the suffering servant. He must suffer, he explains, or else "How then are the Scriptures to be fulfilled, that thus it must take place?" (Matt. 26:54) On the cross, Jesus cries out, "My God, my God, why hast thou forsaken me?" An omniscient Son of God would have known that an all-loving Father would not abandon him.

In Chapter 4 of the Gospel of Luke, Jesus stands up in the synagogue, quotes a passage from Isaiah, and then claims that his preaching that day fulfills the prophecy. It seems rather obvious that the verses quoted by Jesus were said by Isaiah about himself. Here are the words that Jesus supposedly read: "The spirit of the Lord is upon me because he has anointed me; to bring good news to the poor he has sent me, to proclaim to the captives release, and sight to the blind; to set at liberty the oppressed, to proclaim the acceptable year of the Lord, and the day of recompense" (Luke 4:18-19). And here are the words found in the Book of Isaiah: "The spirit of the Lord is upon me, because the Lord hath anointed me. He hath sent me to preach to the meek, to heal the contrite of heart, and to preach a release of the captives and deliverance to them that are shut up: To proclaim the acceptable year of the Lord and the day of vengeance of our God: to comfort all that mourn" (Isaiah 61:1-2). Jesus reads nothing about healing the contrite but instead about bringing sight to the blind. Did Jesus not know, or did he misread, the original text?

In the Gospel of John, Jesus says, "And as Moses lifted up the serpent in the desert, even so must the Son of Man be lifted up, that those who believe in him may not perish, but may have life everlasting" (John 3:14). In the Old-Testament passage that Jesus alludes to, God has afflicted the Israelites with "fiery serpents" as a punishment for their having complained about conditions in the desert. The serpents having bitten and killed many, the repentant people come to Moses and ask him to pray that the serpents be removed. Moses prays and receives instruction from God to make a brazen serpent and place it where it can be seen. God says: "Whosoever being struck shall look on it shall live" (Numbers 21:8). Even though this story gives every indication of being fantasy, Jesus seems to think it relates a historic event. We see the same sort of credulousness on the part of Jesus in Matt. 12:40: "So even as Jonah was in the belly of the fish three days and three nights, so will the Son of Man be three days and three nights in the heart of the earth." The chances that a person named Jonah (or anyone) spent three days and three nights in a whale and survived are surely abysmally slight. But Jesus apparently thought he had. I realize that my rejection of the historicity of the Old-Testament stories referred to in this paragraph, and my conclusion that Jesus erred, will make no impression whatsoever on fundamentalists, who will simply, and understandably, respond that Jesus knew more than I know about this. Maybe they are right, but I doubt it. It is also possible that Jesus understood the stories as allegories, but I doubt that as well. Jesus lived before the age of science, when wonders were ubiquitous. Unless his knowledge was extraordinary (something for which we have no credible evidence),

Jesus had no reason to suspect that the brazen serpent and Jonah's whale were mythical.

The eminent theologian Karl Rahner attempts to show that a lack of knowledge is consistent with Jesus' divinity. His argument (and that of other avant-garde theologians) is that Jesus' human consciousness cannot be the same as his divine consciousness; otherwise he would not be fully human, which means that Jesus' human knowledge was limited. Although somewhere in his "unreflexive consciousness" Jesus knew that God was fully and immediately present in him, he was unable to express everything he knew. The theologians are aware that this view contradicts several pronouncements of the Church, but they reason that the teaching authority of the Church is below that of Scripture, whence they derive their information relative to Jesus' knowledge.[25] I marvel at the audacity of these theologians. But they overlook, in my opinion, the proven unreliability of Scripture.

If we allow Jesus to have been fully human intellectually, i.e., to have known no more than other intelligent people of his time knew, then we have to allow him to be fully human morally as well, do we not? In other words, we have to allow him to have sinned. Of course, the Epistle to the Hebrews tells us that Jesus was "tried in all things as we are except sin" (Heb. 4:15), but what did its unknown author really know? I imagine that the Jesus of history sinned like the rest of us. We read in the Bible that he got unreasonably angry (I'm sure you recall the cursing of the barren fig tree and the violent cleansing of the Temple), that he demeaned others mercilessly (think of his manner of interacting with the Pharisees). If he can do these sinful things and still be considered divine, then surely he can sin sexually as well. Perhaps Jesus had sex with Mary Magdalene, say, or even with John. Do these things preclude divinity? Where would one draw the line? How many human imperfections can a divine human have? If the divine human were not compellingly and consistently, indeed overwhelmingly, superlative, how could anyone be expected to believe in his divinity?

1. Bart D. Ehrman, *Jesus: Apocalyptic Prophet of the New Millennium*, p. 57.
2. "Pliny the Younger and Trajan on the Christians," on the website *Early Christian Writings*.
3. Tacitus, *Annals*, 15:44.
4. Flavius Josephus, *The Antiquities of the Jews*, Book 18.
5. Bart D. Ehrman, *Apocalyptic Prophet of the new Millennium*, p. 62.
6. Paul Hopper, "A Narrative Anomaly in Josephus," *Jewish Antiquities*, xviii: 63, p. 147, quoted in an Internet article by Neil Godfrey, "Fresh Evidence: The Forged Jesus Passage in Josephus."
7. Peter Kirby, "Josephus and Jesus: The Testimonium Flavianum Question,"

on the website *Early Christian Writings.*

8. (translated from the Brill edition by W. R. Schoedel).

9. Robert W. Funk and the Jesus Seminar, *The Acts of Jesus: The Search for the Authentic Deeds of Jesus*, p. 527. An earlier book gives the results of the Seminar's search for the authentic words of Jesus. John Dominic Crossan, one of the members of the Jesus Seminar, explains how the group decided which Bible quotations come from Jesus: "After extensive debate, we vote in secret, using colored beads to indicate our views about how likely it is that the particular words actually came for the historical Jesus. A red bead means that the saying 'most likely' came from Jesus, a pink bead means 'likely,' a gray bead means 'not likely,' and a black bead means 'very unlikely'" (*Who Is Jesus? Answers to Your Questions about the Historical Jesus*, p. xv). Mutatis mutandis, the Jesus Seminar used the same procedure to evaluate the authenticity of the deeds of Jesus.

10. L. Michael White, *Scripting Jesus: The Gospels in Rewrite*, p. 228.

11. Edmond J. Dunn, *What Is Theology?*, p. 69.

12. Ibid., p. 68.

13. Robert W. Funk and the Jesus Seminar, *The Acts of Jesus: The Search for the Authentic Deeds of Jesus*, p. 533.

14. Bart D. Ehrman, *The New Testament: A Historical Introduction*, p. 52.

15. Tom Brown, "Did Jesus Die on Good Friday?" from the website *Tom Brown Ministries.*

16. Robert Sheaffer makes the case that Jesus was not executed by the Romans in the Roman manner, crucifixion, but by the Jews in the Jewish manner, being stoned and then hung upon a tree. He claims that the Jews, who hated their Roman oppressors, would not have handed Jesus over to the Romans unless they had been required to do so; according to Sheaffer, a law denying the Jews permission to execute did not exist until 40 C.E. *The Making of the Messiah: Christianity and Resentment*, pp. 59-86.

17. Steve Allen, *Steve Allen on the Bible, Religion, & Morality*, p. 370f.

18. Dan Barker, *Losing Faith in Faith: From Preacher to Atheist*, p. 178.

19. Derreck Bennett, "Why I Am Not a Christian," on the website *Atheologica: Subjecting Religion to Critical Thought.*

20. Uta Ranke-Heinemann, *Putting Away Childish Things: the Virgin Birth, the Empty Tomb, and Other Fairy Tales You Don't Need to Believe to Have a Living Faith*, p. 131.

21. Kirby references an article by Amos Kloner, "Did a Rolling Stone Close Jesus' Tomb?," *Biblical Archaeology Review* 25:5, Sep/Oct 1999, pp. 23-29, 76.

22. Hans van Campenhausen, *Tradition and Life in the Church: Essays and Lectures in Church History*, p. 58.

23. Bart D. Ehrman, "Josephus's Clearest Claim about the Burial of Crucified Victims," on the website *Christianity in Antiquity: The Bart Ehrman Blog.*

24. Richard P. McBrien, *Catholicism*, p. 525.

25. This idea is explained in greater detail in McBrien's *Catholicism*, pp. 528-532.

Who do you think Jesus was?

PT (retired intensive-care nurse and educator): *I was raised in the Catholic faith that asserts Jesus' divinity. I took that on faith because I was taught it throughout my 16 years of Catholic education. As an adult and finally reading a little more of the New Testament, I was still not impressed, just couldn't accept the Bible as divinely inspired. To me, Jesus was a man, a prophet like other Jewish prophets. This belies the Christmas story and the miracles. People at that time were perhaps unsophisticated and easily led by Jesus' followers (handlers). Events were exaggerated, twisted for the specific effect to "prove" his divinity and to establish a new religion, which Jesus probably didn't intend. Plus there are numerous discrepancies among the gospel stories.*

Kim: *While Jesus most likely existed, it appears that much that is reported about him is subjective, often conflicted. Much of the Bible's Christmas story reads like a fairy tale. After Jesus died, he was buried; the rest is a story told for a polemical purpose. Writers with an agenda changed Jesus the itinerant preacher into Jesus the divine Son of God. Jesus believed in individual betterment that would better society; he did not intend to found a church. It is easy to admire the mostly good man that is Jesus, as reported. But is he any different, any better than, say, Gandhi?*

George: *A fictional character drawn from the totally unknown person Yeshua ben Miriam mentioned by Josephus in his history of Rome. The fiction or myth-making was elaborated by the early followers of Yeshua competing with other Jewish viewpoints. "Christianity" was started by Saul of Tarsus, who apparently was so frightened by an electrical storm that he had a seizure or hallucinatory episode that led him to change from a persecutor of Yeshua into a proselytizer on behalf of the Annointed One (the underlying meaning of "Christ"). His mission to the gentile world (after being unsuccessful with Judaica) altered Yeshua's teachings in order to be acceptable to the poor and enslaved in the Roman Empire. Ultimately, the religious fervor of Christians rose to the Roman leadership with Constantine, and Christianity began its dominance of the European world.*

Charlie: *Who really knows who Jesus was? I like biblical historian Bart Ehrman's ideas. I think Ehrman describes Jesus not as the loving, turn-the-other-cheek guy that the Gospels say he was.*

Was he a zealot? Very possibly. The Romans were subjugators, and occupied his land. They also weren't nice people, so I think it entirely possible he was a zealot. Maybe not unlike Che Guevera in Cuba? In any event, he wasn't the guy that the gospels portray him as. That he was ELEVATED to god-like status, is, in my view, true. What does it even mean in today's modern world to be a "god," or "the son of God"? All myth I believe. I think it does injustice to a guy who probably lived a good life and did the right thing as he understood it. Like all of us, he struggled.

Vince: Jesus, if he ever existed, was a moral and ordinary Jewish fellow. I believe that if he were living today, he would insist, as Deuteronomy 24:14-15 prescribes, that we not not abuse the needy and destitute laborer.

There is a labor song "Which Side Are You On?" It was adopted by the Civil Rights Movement as well. Jesus would have supported the song's message. And I believe he would applaud the Yiddish expression "Mit ein tokhes ken men nit tantsn af tsvey khasenes" (With one backside you can't dance at two weddings).

Sara (disability rights activist): As an atheist, I believe the Bible is fictional. However, I understand fiction is often based on real lives. It is absolutely possible that Jesus was a real, historical figure . . . I've not done the research. Jesus seems to have been an original hippie. His messages of peace, love, and forgiveness are idyllic. I think he and I could have been friends; he would be a calming influence on me! He was not the exclusionary or judgmental type of person that Christian religions seem to fall prey to . . . so much religion disturbs me with its "if you don't look like me and live as I do, you are not welcome. You are wrong. You'll go to Hell." Religion serves to divide.

Steve: Jesus was a Jewish person who reportedly lived and taught with great holiness. He was mythologized as a holy man; some of his teachings and those of others later established the Christian Church. This church includes many lofty norms of appropriate human behavior.

Chapter VI
Early Christianity

Although Matthew 16:18 has Jesus say to Peter, "[T]hou art Peter; and upon this rock I will build my church," it is all but certain that Jesus did not intend to found a church. When the Jesus Seminar voted on whether these words were the words of Jesus, most said either "I would not include this item in the primary database" or "Jesus did not say this: it represents the perspective or content of a later or different tradition."[1] Matthew uses the Greek word ἐκκλησία to represent that which Jesus supposedly intended to build. Most Bibles seem to translate it as "church," but the Jesus Seminar and other scholars prefer "congregation." Jesus, believing as he did that the end of the world would come during the lifetime of some of his contemporaries, would have had no reason to establish a complex, multi-structured institution. The job of his followers would have been simply to urge people to repent of their sins in preparation for the imminent return of the Lord in glory. If Christianity did not begin with Jesus, when did it begin? I think no one can answer that question with certainty. Which doctrines had to be in place? What kind of teaching authority had to be developed before Christianity could be said to exist? Instead of trying to answer these questions, I will introduce you to the fifth book of the New Testament, the Acts of the Apostles, whose principal actors are Peter and Paul, and to the foundational influence of Paul as expressed in his epistles. Finally, we will look briefly at the various factions of Christians of the first few centuries, one of which became orthodox Christianity.

The Acts of the Apostles

The Acts of the Apostles was written by the same person who wrote the Gospel of Luke, probably sometime between 80 CE and 90 CE, although a later date is possible. The Acts of the Apostles tells, or purports to tell, what the apostles did after Jesus' ascension into heaven. Like much of the rest of the Bible, Acts contains several passages that clearly contradict, or are inconsistent with, other parts of the New Testament. Chapter 24 of the Gospel of Luke indicates that the ascension of Jesus happened on Easter Sunday, whereas Acts 1:3 places it forty days after Easter. Also, in Acts 1:13, we get an apparent list of the apostles, which is slightly different from other such lists. In fact, no two of the four lists (one each in Matthew, Mark, Luke, and Acts) are exactly the same. In Acts 2:17, Peter quotes the prophet Joel to the effect that he and those listening to him were living in "the last days." This is just another of many erroneous references in the New Testament to the imminence of the end of the world. I wonder which of the following passages, if either, was spoken by Jesus: "Whosoever shall call on the name of the Lord shall be saved," according to Acts 2:21, or "Not every one that saith unto me Lord, Lord, shall enter into the kingdom of heaven," according to Matthew 7:21. Of course, both statements cannot be true. In Matthew 28:19, Jesus tells the apostles, "Go ye therefore, and teach all nations, baptizing them in the name of the Father, and of the Son, and of the Holy Ghost," whereas Peter tells a multitude of people in Jerusalem, "Repent, and be baptized every one of you in the name of Jesus Christ" (Acts 2:38). Which is it, baptism in the name of the Trinity or baptism in the name of Jesus? More than once in Acts there is an indication of the ugly doctrine of predestination. Here is an example: "And day by day the Lord added to their company such as were to be saved" (Acts 2:47).

In the first part of Chapter 5 of the Acts of the Apostles, Peter (or God) strikes Ananias and his wife dead because they withheld part of their money instead of laying everything at the feet of the apostles. Sounds mighty heavy-handed so me. By the way, if we can believe Acts, the earliest Christians had all possessions in common. Private ownership was forbidden. What does that do for the Christian enthusiasts of un-bridled capitalism? Not much, obviously. Acts is laden with unbelievable cures. A few faith healings I can certainly abide, but what about this exaggeration: "And there came also multitudes from the towns near Jerusalem, bringing the sick and those troubled with unclean spirits, and they were all cured" (Acts, 5:16)? Really? All? Every single one? Not just an occasional sick person like at Lourdes? What are we to make of the voice from heaven telling Peter that it was okay to eat food that he had previously considered unclean? (Acts 10:10-16 and Acts 11:4-10) Would not Jesus have so instructed the apostles during his lifetime? In fact, according to the Gospel of Mark, he did: "There is nothing outside a man that, entering into him, can defile him" (Mark 7:15). "Thus he [Jesus] declared all foods clean" (Mark 7:20). So why the voice from heaven in Acts? In Chapter 11 of Acts, Peter finally extends baptism to the Gentiles. Why had he not done so from the get-go? Why did Jesus not tell him to do so? Well, according to a famous passage in Matthew, he did just that: "Go, therefore, and make disciples of all nations, baptizing them in the name of the Father, and of the Son, and of the Holy Spirit" (Matt. 28:19).

The story of Paul's conversion is told three times in Acts (9:1-19, 22:6-16, and 26:12-18). Three discrepancies are obvious: (1) in Acts 9:7, when Paul is struck from his horse, those who are with him hear a voice, but when Paul retells the same story in Acts 22:9, it turns out that "they did not hear the voice of him that was speaking to me"; (2) in the first narrative, Paul is knocked to the ground, but his companions remain standing, whereas in Acts 26:12, they all fall to the ground; and (3) in the first and second accounts, Jesus sends Paul to Ananias for instruction, but in the third account he receives instruction from Jesus himself. In the first two accounts, Ananias restores Paul's sight, for Paul had been blinded by the vision. The third version makes no mention of blindness. It doesn't take a detective to see that all three accounts cannot be historically correct. One wonders if any is. In Acts 9:10-30, Paul spends a few days in Damascus after his conversion and then goes immediately to Jerusalem, where he meets with the apostles. Paul himself tells things differently in his Epistle to the Galatians. He makes a point of saying that after his conversion he did not go to Jerusalem. The implication is that he, Paul, has received his message directly from God. What need does he have of instruction from the apostles? Three years later he goes to Jerusalem (Gal. 1:15-18).

Peter escapes from jail with the help of an angel, as the chains drop from Peter's hands (Acts 12:6-8). Who does not long for the good old days when angels came to the aid of disciples in distress? I wonder where the angels went. We commoners are not supposed to say "Thou fool" to anyone lest we burn in hell for it, but saintly people like Paul seem to have been able to call people whatever they wanted. Paul addresses a false magician, who gets in the way of one of Paul's conversions, with "O full of all guile and of all deceit, son of the devil," and he then, to add injury to insult, strikes the man blind (Acts 13:7-11). In Lystra, Paul cures a man who had been crippled from birth (Acts 14:7-9). I don't think we see that kind of cure these days. And just when you thought the food restrictions had been lifted, we get this in a letter from the apostles in Jerusalem to the Gentiles in Antioch, Syria, and Cilicia: "For the Holy Spirit and we have decided [by the way, if the Holy Spirit really had decided something, what sense would it have made to add "and we"?] to lay no further burden upon you but this indispensable one, that you abstain from things sacrificed to idols [okay, I get that one] and from blood . . ." (Acts 15:28-29). Blood was not mentioned in Acts 10 and 11. And how can one eat meat without eating blood?

In Acts 16:6-8, Paul and associates are forbidden by the Holy Spirit to preach in the province of Asia (probably Asia Minor) and in Bithynia. Is God playing favorites? When Paul and Silas were imprisoned in Philippi, there came a great earthquake, the doors of the prison were opened and, of course, "everyone's chains were unfastened" (Acts 16:26). To the jailer, Paul says, "Believe in the Lord Jesus, and thou shalt be saved, and thy household" (Acts 16:31). Man of the house saved, whole family saved! Did the wife not have anything to say about her conversion? In Ephesus Paul had especially good luck curing people: "God worked more than the usual miracles by the hand of Paul, so that even handkerchiefs and aprons were carried from his body to the sick, and the diseases left them and the evil spirits went out" (Acts 19:11-12).

I think it is important to point out that not only zealous Christians are guilty of faulty scholarship; skeptics, too, are not always totally reliable. Here is an example. Acts 28:1-7 tells of Paul's being bitten by a poisonous snake on the island of Malta. Well, it turns out, as many have pointed out, that there are not and never have been poisonous snakes on Malta. Conclusion of some skeptics: the story was fabricated. But not so fast. It turns out that the island of Meleda, which happens to have a shallow harbor like the one described in Acts, was, before the introduction of the mongoose, loaded with poisonous snakes called vipera ammodytes. Such a snake might well have bitten Paul. It could be, therefore, that Acts got the name of the island wrong (still, of course, an error in an infallible document) but the story more or less right. Not all who are bitten by these snakes die. According to Acts, Paul suffered no harm. I think I would call this story pious hyperbole and let it go at that.

There are many Christians who know the Bible well, who are well aware of its problems, and who nevertheless believe in Christian doctrine. To me, Catholicism or any of the Protestant denominations are just as unbelievable as, say, Mormonism, which no traditional Christian has any problem disregarding, or Islam, which many Christians these days disdain. None of these scholarly, believing Christians will tell you that the reasons for their belief are historical or even based on reason. No, they are sure that their faith comes from God, who has given them the grace to believe. Of course, Mormons can maintain that they believe for the same reason, and so can Muslims. But this does not seem to matter. Faith in Christianity appears to be its own justification. The same can be said of belief in God. Most scholarly theists will admit that one cannot prove God's existence. It must be believed. Agnostics have no problem with other people believing in God. It is when these believers begin telling the rest of us what God's laws are and trying to get their sacred prescriptions and proscriptions turned into civil and criminal laws, that agnostics have problems with faith in God. If you cannot prove God's existence, is it not better simply to say "I do not know." Is that not more honest? And if God exists, she might like that better.

Paul of Tarsus (St. Paul)

Surely no one played a more important role in the spread of Christianity than Paul of Tarsus, the man who came to be known as St. Paul. It was Paul who insisted, against the will of Peter and James, who were in Jerusalem, that Gentiles should not have to become Jewish in order to become followers of Jesus. Paul never met Jesus, and although he had been an ardent persecutor of Christians, he became convinced, as the result of a profound psychological experience on the road to Damascus, that Jesus was the Messiah. In my opinion, Paul, influenced from childhood by the savior gods of his birth city of Tarsus, unconsciously metamorphosed the messianic miracle worker Jesus into the divine Son of God who died to make human salvation possible. And since it was important that Jesus, not Paul, be seen as the founder of Christianity, the doctrines of Paul (who wrote some twenty years before the first gospel writer, Mark) found their way into the mouth of the Jesus of the gospels. Whether or not, or to what extent, pagan deities contributed to the figure of Jesus as presented in the gospels is a hotly debated topic. As for Paul's role in the foundation of Christianity, Hyam Maccoby, a Talmudic scholar, writes that "Jesus did not found a new religion at all, but simply sought to play an accepted role in the story of an existing religion, Judaism. It was Paul who founded Christianity, and he did so by creating a new story, one sufficiently powerful and gripping to launch a new world religion. In this new story Jesus was given a leading role, but this does not make him the creator of Christianity, any more than Hamlet wrote the plays of Shakespeare."[2]

Let's examine some of Maccoby's ideas. After the death of Jesus, the Jerusalem Church, headed by James (not James the apostle but James the brother of Jesus) and Peter, came into conflict with Paul, often called the Apostle of the Gentiles, who was telling his converts that they did not need to follow the Jewish dietary laws and the law of circumcision. When James and Peter began to suspect that Paul himself no longer followed the Law, they summoned him to Jerusalem, where Paul "proved" that he still considered himself a Jew by participating in a Temple ceremony. Maccoby accuses Paul, who did not want to sever ties between his Gentile converts and the Jesus followers in Jerusalem, of evasiveness. According to Maccoby, when Peter, on a visit to Antioch, declined to eat with Paul's Gentile converts, he signaled his distrust of Paul and his rejection of Paul's movement. But it was Paul's movement that prevailed, for when Jerusalem was destroyed by the Romans in 70 CE, most followers of Jesus fled from Jerusalem, and the Jerusalem Church for all practical purposes ended. Now, the doctrine invented by Paul could find its way into the mouth of Jesus as portrayed in the gospels. Now, the Pharisees, who had been friendly to the Jewish Christians in Jerusalem but who disliked the new religion of Paul, were turned into the enemies of Jesus.

Maccoby argues cogently that the historical Pharisees were nothing like the pedantic hypocrites of the New Testament. They opposed the Sadducees and the high priest (who was a Sadducee) by ascribing only secondary importance to the Temple and the priesthood. They agreed with Jesus that healing on the Sabbath could be justified. According to Maccoby, Jesus was a Pharisee. The Pharisees were friendly to Jesus and, even after his death, to his followers in Jerusalem, who continued to worship in the Temple and to observe the Law; however, by the time the gospels were written, the close relationship between Pharisees and early followers of Jesus had changed. Through Paul, a new religion, Christianity, had come into being, with its own sacraments of baptism and Eucharist, and with it the abrogation of the Law of the Torah (the first five books of the Old Testament). This new religion won the internecine battle with the Jewish followers of Peter and James. The Pharisees became the enemies of Christianity; ergo, they had to become the enemies of Jesus in the gospels.

Many authors agree with Maccoby. According to Reza Alsan, "the Christ of Paul's creation has utterly subsumed the Jesus of history."[3] Thomas Jefferson considered Paul "the first corrupter of the doctrines of Jesus."[4] Carl Sagan wrote this: "My long-time view about Christianity is that it represents an amalgam of two seemingly immiscible parts, the religion of Jesus and the religion of Paul."[5] In Carl Jung's view, "Paul hardly ever allows the real Jesus of Nazareth to get a word in."[6] According to Soren Kierkegaard, "Paul made Christianity the religion of Paul, not of Christ. Paul threw the Christianity of Christ away, completely turning it upside down, making it just the opposite of the original proclamation of Christ."[7]

If Maccoby is right (and I think he is, by and large), one wonders why not all of Paul's theology made it into Jesus' mouth in the gospels. Nothing at all like these words of Paul, for example, are heard from the mouth of Jesus as the gospels present him: "For in one Spirit we were all baptized into one body, whether Jews or Gentiles, slaves or free; and we are all given to drink of one Spirit. For the body is not one member but many" (1 Cor. 12:13-14). And a few lines later: "Now you are the body of Christ, member for member" (1 Cor. 12:27). This is Paul's idea of the Church as the mystical body of Jesus, a concept foreign to the gospels. Or take these words of Paul: "Do you not know that we all who have been baptized into Christ Jesus have been baptized into his death? For we were buried with him by means of Baptism into death, in order that, just as Christ has arisen from the dead through the glory of the Father, so we also may walk in the newness of life" (Rom. 6:3-4). Never would the Jesus of the gospels have waxed so theological. And here is Paul's explanation of the resurrection of the body (you will not find this in any of the gospels either): "What is sown in corruption rises in incorruption; what is sown in dishonor rises in glory; what is sown in weakness rises in power; what is sown a natural body rises a spiritual body" (1 Cor. 15:42-44).

How, you might wonder, does Maccoby explain Paul's transformation from self-proclaimed Pharisee to founder of a rival religion, Christianity? Maccoby thinks Paul, whose name before his mystical experience on the way to Damascus was Saul, was only a Pharisee wannabee. As Maccoby pieces things together, Saul tried but failed to become a Pharisee (he could not meet the rigorous intellectual challenges). Deeply disappointed (for Paul wanted to accomplish great things in the world) but still wanting to play a role in the Jewish religion, he accepted a job as henchman of the high priest: he was to go out and round up heretics. In fact, he was on just such a mission when he was thrown from his horse, saw a bright light, and heard the voice of Jesus. Paul is probably not being altogether truthful when he says that he was a Pharisee, says Maccoby; a Pharisee would never have put himself in the employment of the high priest, an enemy of the Pharisees.[8] Maccoby thinks that Paul received little or none of his doctrine from the apostles, but almost everything from visions (the original vision and several more not mentioned in the Bible). Jesus taught him directly, or so Paul thought. He must have considered this information more accurate than anything he could learn from mere mortal eyewitnesses like the apostles.

An opposing view (a more traditional view) is presented by Bart D. Ehrman, who maintains that the most important ideas of Christianity were not invented by Paul but were in place before him. "People today," writes Ehrman, "often think of Paul as the second-founder of Christianity, after Jesus. Or even as the founder of Christianity. In my view that is assigning way too much importance to Paul. I don't know how much Paul himself came up with (based, in his view, on his encounter with Jesus). But he did not come up with the idea that Jesus' death brought salvation and that he had then been raised from the dead. That part he 'received' from others."[9] Ehrman refers to the First Letter to the Corinthians 15:3-5, which reads as follows: "For I delivered to you first of all, what I also received, that Christ died for our sins according to the Scriptures, and that he was buried, and that he rose again the third day, according to the Scriptures, and that he appeared to Cephas, and after that to the Eleven." I disagree with Ehrman. Paul's words are "what I also received," not "what I also received from others." I think

Paul was referring to the knowledge that he thought he had received directly from Jesus. In his Epistle to the Galatians 1:11-12, Paul says this: "For I give you to understand, brethren, that the gospel which was preached by me is not of man. For I did not receive it from man, nor was I taught it; but I received it by a revelation of Jesus Christ." Since I see no credible evidence that Paul truly was the recipient of divine revelation, I agree with Walter Kaufmann, who thinks that Paul invented "the central ideas of Christ's redemptive death and justification by faith."[10]

In his hometown of Tarsus, Paul, as a young man, would have been quite familiar with pagan deities who died and rose from the dead. Atonement was a major theme in these religions. The step from there to a risen Jesus who had died for the sins of mankind was an easy one. Whether or not the concept of eternal punishment was in place as a basic doctrine in the earliest years of the nascent Church (a topic not taken up by Maccoby), one thing is certain: Paul did not write about it. Either he knew of the concept and refused to acknowledge it, or it was a later idea that found its way into the gospels (all of which were written after the epistles of Paul). The word "hell" appears twenty-three times in the New Testament, but not a single time in Paul's epistles. He does speak of punishment for sin as death and condemnation, but he doesn't get more specific than that.

Paul did not know Jesus; the two men never met. He presumably would not have known Jesus' words about the Law of Moses as reported by Matthew: "Do not think that I have come to destroy the Law or the Prophets. I have come not to destroy but to fulfill. For amen I say to you, till heaven and earth pass away, not one jot or one tittle shall be lost from the Law till all things have been accomplished. Therefore whoever does away with one of these least commandments, and so teaches men, shall be called least in the kingdom of heaven" (Matt. 5:17-19). What does Paul say about the Law? "Therefore, my brethren, you also, through the body of Christ, have been made to die to the Law, so as to belong to another who has risen from the dead, in order that we may bring forth fruit unto God. For when we were in the flesh, the sinful passions, which were aroused by the Law, were at work in our members so that they brought forth fruit unto death. But now we have been set free from the Law, having died to that by which we were held down, so that we may serve in a new spirit and not according to the outworn letter" (Rom. 7:4-6).[11] That does not sound at all like the words of Jesus in the above passage from the Gospel of Matthew. In other places in the gospels, Jesus too is made to say that the Judaic Law has been superseded. Some Christian exegetes attempt to explain away this contradiction by claiming that Jesus' words in Matt. 5:17-19 do not refer to the Law of Moses but to the divine law. If so, why the reference to the prophets? Why does Jesus say "the Law or the Prophets"?

Regarding Paul's thoughts about the end of the world and the return of Jesus, one finds the following passage in the First Epistle to the Thessalonians, 4:16-17: "For the Lord himself with cry of command, with voice of an archangel, and with trumpet of God will descend from heaven; and the dead in Christ will rise up first. Then we who live, who survive, shall be caught up together with them in clouds to meet the Lord in the air, and so we shall ever be with the Lord." Walter Kaufmann attributes Paul's disinterest in social justice to his belief that the world would end soon.[12] Instead of exhorting Christians to moral courage in the face of despots, Paul writes to them: "Let everyone be subject to the higher authorities, for there exists no authority except from God, and those who exist have been appointed by God. Therefore, he who resists the authority, resists the ordinance of God; and they that resist bring on themselves condemnation" (Rom. 13:1-2). Two thousand years after Paul and his contemporaries, Jesus still hasn't come on clouds. Perhaps if Paul were writing today, responsible civil disobedience would resonate with him.

You have already seen that Paul, whose epistolary words are believed by Christians to have been inspired by the Holy Spirit, occasionally contradicts himself or is inconsistent with himself or with other passages of Scripture. To the Corinthians, Paul writes, "Do you not know that those who run in a race, all indeed run, but one receives the prize? So run as to obtain it" (1 Cor. 9:24). Compare this with Romans 9:15-16: "For he [God] says to Moses, 'I will have mercy on whom I have mercy, and I will show pity to whom I will show pity.' So then there is a question not of him who wills nor of him who runs, but of God showing mercy." Which is it? Does it matter if people run in order to obtain the prize, i.e. make an effort, or not? Paul seems to have struggled with the means of salvation: Does faith open the pearly gates? or is it good works? or is it both? Surely both of the following two passages cannot be true, can they? "For whoever have sinned without the Law, will perish without the Law; and whoever have sinned under the Law, will be judged by the Law. For it is not they who hear the Law that are just in the sight of God; but it is they who follow the Law that will be justified" (Rom. 2:13). Compare that with the words of Paul in the very next chapter of the very same letter: "For by the works of the Law no human being shall be justified before him [God], for through the Law comes the recognition of sin" (Rom. 3:20). Similarly, in Galatians 3:20, Paul writes that "Christ redeemed us from the curse of the Law." I'm sure that theologians have found a hair that they think Paul was trying to split, but I have not found it. We know what

Luther thought: Paul preached salvation by faith alone. If you ask me, Paul could have done a better job.

On another point, Proverbs 27:2 says, "Let another praise thee, and not thy own mouth: a stranger, and not thy own lips. In 2 Cor. 11:18, Paul says, "Since many boast of worldly things, I too will boast." Paul is, in fact, given to boasting and seems to justify his boasting by saying that he boasts "in the Lord" (2 Cor. 10:17). Paul boasts, "For I regard myself as nowise inferior to the great apostles" (2 Cor. 11:5). He goes on to say that, compared to the other apostles, he was "in many more labors, in prisons more frequently, in lashes above measure, often exposed to death" (2 Cor. 11:23). Yet elsewhere, in 1 Cor. 15:9, this same Paul says modestly, "For I am the least of the apostles, and am not worthy to be called an apostle, because I persecuted the Church of God." He seems to go to extremes both in humility and in boastfulness.

From Jesus to Christ

In my opinion, the historical Jesus was a faith-healing, itinerant preacher, whose mission was to prepare his fellow Jews for the imminent coming of the kingdom of God. He might have thought of himself as the Jewish Messiah but not as God. He did not change water into wine, he did not multiply loaves and fishes, he did not walk on water, and he did not raise the dead. Following an ignominious death, his followers began to think that he had risen from the dead. It seems to me that it is the belief in Jesus' resurrection that links the Jesus of history to the Christ of faith.

As you saw earlier in this book, you can count on the fingers of one hand the first-century extrabiblical references to Jesus. These sources do little more than provide evidence that Jesus probably existed. Our only option is to search for the historical Jesus in the pages of the New Testament, the entirety of which was written after faith in the Resurrection had solidified. The gospels, our primary source of information about Jesus, were written some 40 to 65 or more years after the death of Jesus. It soon becomes obvious to an astute reader that the writers of the gospels altered history when it served their theological or proselytistic purposes. Fact and fiction are intermingled. We know that this is true because of the many contradictions and inconsistencies apparent in the gospels. Three of the gospels, the so-called synoptic gospels (Mark, Matthew, and Luke), present a Jesus who is conscious of being the Messiah. Whether Jesus really had this self-image or whether Christians began to project this image onto him is debatable. One thing seems certain: By the time the first gospel, Mark's, was written, Christians believed that Jesus was much more than an itinerant preacher. The Gospel of John, written around the year 100 CE, presents a divine Jesus.

But what then are we to do with the epistles of Paul, which were written before the gospels and which, here and there, seem to speak of Jesus as divine? In his Epistle to the Philippians, Paul extols a Jesus "who though he was by nature God, did not consider being equal to God a thing to be clung to" (Phil. 2:6); moreover, the Epistle to the Colossians, albeit perhaps pseudonymous, says, "For in him [Jesus] dwells all the fullness of the Godhead bodily" (Col. 2:9). Still, other passages in Paul's epistles seem to deny Jesus' divinity. His First Epistle to the Corinthians states that "the head of every man is Christ ['the anointed one,' the Messiah], that the head of every woman is the man, and that the head of Christ is God" (1 Cor. 11:3). In the same epistle, Paul foresees the day when Jesus "delivers the kingdom to God the Father. . . . And when all things are made subject to him, then the Son himself will also be made subject to him who subjected all things to him, that God may be all in all" (1 Cor. 15:24, 28). Bart D. Ehrman, who confesses that for many years he was perplexed about how the divinity of Jesus could be absent from the synoptic gospels though present in the writings of Paul, which preceded them, says in an Internet blog that it finally occurred to him that Paul thought of Jesus as an angel.[13] But if that is what Paul thought, why did he not say so? I am far from convinced that Paul knew precisely what he thought about Jesus.

Early Christian Diversity

Christianity was splintered from the start; we just did not always know it. A collaborative article entitled "The Diversity of Early Christianity" on the website "From Jesus to Christ," by Frontline, contains articles by five scholars, all of whom make the point that early Christianity was anything but static and noncontroversial. I'll give you a relevant snippet from each person: (1) "Christianity, or one would rather say 'Christianities,' of the second and third centuries were a highly variegated phenomenon. We really can't imagine Christianity as a unified coherent religious movement" (Holand Lee Hendrix, Union theological Seminary); (2) "Christianity did not start out a unified movement. We have to remember that the disciples were probably dispersed at a very early time. . . . That is, at a time when there was no fixed formulation what the set of Christian beliefs should be" (Helmut Koester, Harvard Divinity School); (3) "Christianity was extremely diverse during this period [second and third centuries]" (L. Michael While, Religious Studies Program, University of Texas); (4) "The interesting thing about Christianity is that you have diversity form the beginning. . . ." (Wayne A. Meeks, Biblical Studies, Yale University); (5) "The Christian movement probably began not from a single center but from many different centers where different groups of disciples of Jesus gathered and tried to make sense of what they had experienced with him and what had happened to him at the end of his public ministry" (Harold W. Attridge, Yale Divinity School). If you think the various branches of early Christians had the same concept of Jesus, consider the words of Burton L. Mack, who claims that each type and sub-type of the Jesus movement "imagined Jesus differently."[14] Elaine Pagels and Karen L. King observe that we have only recently come to see "how hard countless church leaders had to work to create the impression that many of us used to take for granted--that Christianity actually was a single, static, universal system of beliefs." The authors explain: "Creating the impression was itself a remarkable achievement --one to which certain 'fathers of the church' were dedicated. But they did so precisely because they realized how diverse Christian groups were, and they feared that controversies over basic issues . . . might undermine the 'universal church' they were trying to build, along with the authority they were claiming for their church alone."[15]

One group of early Christians were the Ebionites. They were adoption-ists; that is, they believed that God adopted Jesus as his son when the latter was baptized by John the Baptist. The Ebionites regarded Jesus as the Messiah but insisted that he was not divine. According to them, followers of Jesus had to adhere to Jewish laws and rituals. They rejected Paul, who taught that Jesus had abrogated the Jewish Law. Ebionites accepted only one sacred book, the Gospel of Matthew, albeit without the first two chapters. Quite the opposite of the Ebionites were the Mar-cionites, who subscribed to the epistles of Paul, whom they considered the primary apostle. Marcionites believed that the all-loving God of the New Testament sent the divine savior Jesus, whose body was only an apparition, to earth to save humans from the wrathful God of the Old Tes-tament. The leader of the Marcionites was a second-century scholar by the name of Marcion, who rejected all of the books of the Old Testament and accepted only eleven books of the New Testament: an abbreviated version of the Gospel of Luke as well as ten modified epistles of Paul. And then there were the Gnostic Christians, themselves divided into many factions. Some, like the Marcionites, believed that Jesus was not at all human but entirely divine. Others thought that Jesus consisted of two separate parts: a divine Jesus and a human Jesus. Gnostics were polytheists, some believing that there were 365 different gods. According to many Gnostics, the god of the Old Testament was evil as was matter, which he created. Gnostics shared a belief that they themselves were spiritual beings who had become entrapped in matter. Escape from this entrapment was possible if one obtained the necessary knowledge (from the Greek word γνωσις, "gnosis"). This knowledge was secret, not available to all, only to Gnostics.

Of course, there was a group of Christians, the "proto-orthodox,"[16] who by and large held the views that would eventually prevail. When the Council of Nicea, called by the Roman Emperor Constantine in 325 CE, declared that Jesus Christ was fully divine and fully human, a universal church, the Catholic Church, was given quite a boost. For Christians, God was at he helm of his ship, guiding it safely through the narrows and past the reefs and icebergs of the first three centuries. I can imagine many a Christian today using a similar rationale: despite the multitude of competing versions of Christianity, God has brought my denomination, the true church, through safely. Well, but why in the world did an omnipotent, omniscient, omnibenevolent God allow so many different versions of Christianity to develop? Would he not have made his ship, the true church, so overwhelmingly attractive, that no one would have overlooked it and built their own? I say he would have.

1. *The Five Gospels: The Search for the Authentic Words of Jesus*, ed. Robert W. Funk et al, pages 36 and 207.
2. Hyam Maccoby, *The Mythmaker: Paul and the Invention of Christianity*, p. 184.
3. Reza Alsan, *Zealot: The Life and Times of Jesus of Nazareth*, p. 215.
4. Thomas Jefferson, Letter to William Short, April 13, 1820.
5. Carl Sagan, Letter to Ken Schei.
6. Carl Jung, "A Psychological Approach to the Dogma of the Trinity," quoted in Patrick Gray"s *Varieties of Religious Invention: Founders and Their Functions in History*, p. 123.
7. Soren Kierkegaard, *The Journals.*
8. Maccoby, pp. 85-99.
9. Bart D. Ehrman, from his blog entitled "Paul's Importance in Early Christianity."
10. Walter Kaufmann, *The Faith of a Heretic*, p. 225.
11. Robert Schaeffer explains that, according to Friedrich Nietzsche's *Morgenröte: Gedanken über die moralischen Vorurteile*, Paul was frustrated at his inability to master and comply with Jewish law; consequently, he looked for a way of destroying the law. Christianity provided him with the means. "Nietzsche's *Der Antichrist: Looking Back From the Year 100*," *Free Inquiry*, Winter, 1988/89, Vol. 9, No. 1.
12. Kaufmann, p. 222.
13. Bart D. Ehrman, in his blog entitled "Paul's Importance in Early Christianity."
14. Burton L. Mack, *Who Wrote the New Testament? The Making of the Christian Myth*, p. 6.
15. Elaine Pagels and Karen L. King, *Reading Judas: The Gospel of Judas and the Shaping of Christianity*, pp. 101-102.
16. Bart D. Ehrman, *The New Testament: A Historical Introduction to the Early Christian Writings*, p. 6.

Additional New-Testament Topics

Miracles

"Extraordinary claims require extraordinary evidence." - Carl Sagan, *Cosmos*

* * * * *

"Do you believe in miracles?" cried sports announcer Al Michaels at the end of the championship hockey game between the United States and the USSR in the 1980 Winter Olympics. If by miracles Michaels meant highly improbable events, I can, with everyone else, answer yes. Anomalies are a part of human existence. Even if the odds against something happening are a million to one, eventually a million-to-one shot happens. The odds against a particular jet liner crashing might well be a million to one, but every once in a while a particular jet liner crashes. If by miracles you mean things that violate the laws of nature, I do not believe in miracles. I do not think that nature's laws are ever suspended. Unexplained cures, for example, happen all the time, even to people who have no religious faith. Does God let people become lame and then, as it were, change his mind and cause some of them to be sound again? What a strange notion of God that idea evokes.

In his treatise "Of Miracles," the philosopher David Hume says the following: "The plain consequence is (and it is a general maxim worthy of our attention), 'that no testimony is sufficient to establish a miracle, unless the testimony be of such a kind that its falsehood would be more miraculous than the fact which it endeavors to establish; and even in that case there is a mutual destruction of arguments, and the superior only gives us an assurance suitable to that degree of force which remains after deducting the inferior.'" Hume then relates how he reacts when someone informs him that a dead man has been restored to life. He considers which is more probable: that the person has been deceived or is deliberately deceiving or that this person was actually restored to life. He weighs "the one miracle against the other" and always rejects the greater miracle. "If the falsehood of his testimony would be more miraculous than the event which he relates, then, and not till then, can he pretend to command my belief or opinion."[1]

In the gospels, Jesus cures lepers, restores sight to the blind, causes the lame to walk, changes water to wine, feeds thousands with a few loaves and fishes, and even raises the dead. Who can fail to be convinced of his divine powers? Well, I can, for one. To me, these wonders seem much less probable than the innocent repetition of false stories that had circulated for forty or more years since Jesus' death and, for that matter, much less probable than the deliberate distortion of history by men who were utterly convinced of the importance of attracting people to Jesus. In my opinion, the story of Christianity is the story of deceived deceivers and of overzealous followers, for whom pious falsehoods would be no more than white lies.

In his *Quest for the Historical Jesus,* Albert Schweitzer gives a synopsis of Samuel Reimarus's critique of the miracles of Jesus: "It is useless to appeal to the miracles, any more than to the 'Sacraments,' as evidence for the founding of a new religion. In the first place, we have to remember what happens in the case of miracles handed down by tradition. That Jesus effected cures, which in the eyes of His contemporaries were miraculous, is not to be denied. Their purpose was to prove Him to be the Messiah. He forbade these miracles to be made known, even in cases where they could not possibly be kept hidden, 'with the sole purpose of making people more eager to talk of them.' Other miracles, however, have no basis in fact, but owe their place in the narrative to the feeling that the miracle-stories of the Old Testament must be repeated in the case of Jesus, but on a grander scale. He did no really miraculous works; otherwise, the demands for a sign would be incomprehensible. In Jerusalem when all the people were looking eagerly for an overwhelming manifestation of His Messiahship, what a tremendous effect a miracle would have produced! If only a single miracle had been publicly, convincingly, undeniably, performed by Jesus before all the people on one of the great days of the Feast, such is human nature that all the people would at once have flocked to His standard."[2]

Some so-called miracles crumble not only because of the questionable reliability of their source, but also because of intratextual inconsistency. An example of this is the story of Jesus' causing devils to leave a man and take up residence in pigs. The evangelist known as Mark reports it this way: "[T]here met him [Jesus] from the tombs a man with an unclean spirit. This man lived in the tombs and no one could any longer bind him, even with chains, and he had rent the chains asunder and broken the chains into pieces. And no one was able to control him. And constantly, night and day, he was in the tombs and on the mountains, howling and gashing himself with stones. And when he saw Jesus from afar, he ran and worshipped him, and crying out with a loud voice, he said, 'What have I to do with thee, Jesus, Son of the most high God? I adjure thee by God, do not torment me!' For he was saying to him, 'Go out of the man, thou unclean spirit.' And he asked him, 'What is thy name?' And he said to him, 'My name is Legion, for we are many.' And he entreated him earnestly not to drive them out of the country. Now a great herd of swine was there on the mountain side, feeding. And the spirits kept entreating him, saying, 'Send us into the swine, that we may enter into them.' And Jesus immediately gave them leave. And the unclean spirits came out and entered into the swine; and the herd, in number about two thousand, rushed down with great violence into the sea, and were drowned in the sea" (Mark. 5:2-13). Could Jesus, as God, not foresee that the pigs would meet with a tragic end? If not, why not? If so, why did he act as he did? The story is inconsistent with the claim of Jesus' divinity. Either the story is false, the claim to divinity is false, or both. The same can be said of Jesus' cursing of a fig tree because it had no fruit, even though it was the wrong season for figs (Mark. 11:12-14). Surely a divine Jesus would not have acted so foolishly.

Bart D. Ehrman, professor at the University of North Carolina and author of several books on the New Testament and early Christianity, explains why it is impossible for the historian, as historian, to accept the miracles reported in the Bible.[3] As a historian, Ehrman knows that the people of biblical times understood miracles differently than we do today. Instead of viewing miracles as events that violate the normal workings of nature (events that demand acknowledgement of supernatural intervention), the ancients knew that miracles happened all the time. Their world included gods and godlike humans, as well as ordinary humans and animals. Amazing things like spectacular healings and resuscitations were part of their natural world, just like sunrises and lightning strikes. Therefore, according to Ehrman, if we agree that Jesus worked miracles when he healed the sick or raised the dead, we must also agree that the other wonder workers of Jesus' time, like Apollonius of Tyana and the emperor Vespasian, also worked miracles, for wonders were reported of them as well. Since miracles are, by definition, exceedingly rare, the weight of the evidence for a particular miracle would have to be exceedingly strong. Given the propensity of human witnesses to visual misjudgment, to exaggeration, and even to lying, how can we be certain that the testimony found in the Bible is accurate?

Ehrman points out that Jesus was not the only Jewish miracle-working son of God.[4] Of others that match this description, the two most famous were probably Honi "the circle-drawer" and Hanina ben Dosa. Honi, who lived about a century before Jesus, used to draw circles on the ground and stand in them until God caused it to rain. Apparently, he worked other miracles as well and referred to himself as the son of God. He and Jesus shared a place and time of execution (outside the walls of Jerusalem near the time of Passover). Hanina ben Dosa lived just after Jesus, in the middle of the first century CE. He is said to have healed the sick by his prayers and to have cast out demons. Like Honi, he was, through prayer, an accomplished rainmaker. Supposedly, a voice from heaven called him the son of God.

Not everyone agrees that miracles are exceedingly rare. Among Hindus in India, "miracles are innumerable, and go unchallenged."[5] They are thought to "spring quite naturally from the performance of ascetic rituals and the chanting of mantras." Although Gautama (the Buddha) played down his personal powers, it is said that he "walked from village to village and miracles happened all around him"[6]; furthermore, it is believed that his relics work wonders today. For Mohammed, the Koran was the greatest of miracles; he himself refused to perform miracles to prove his position as Allah's Prophet. Even today, some ultra-orthodox Muslims (for example, the Wahhabis) do not believe in miracles. On the other hand, according to Charles Panati, "popular Islam, particularly Sufi mysticism, abounds in miraculous cures."[7] If these claims of the prevalence of miracles in non-Christian religions are true, Christian proofs based on the miracles of Jesus or of his followers would seem to be seriously weakened if not invalidated.

John F. Haught, a professor at Georgetown University, proposes a liberal understanding of miracles: "Miracle stories and accounts of divine action are ways of expressing faith's conviction that something of special importance is going on in creation."[8] What I like about this statement is that it does not ascribe historicity to miracles, not even to Jesus' miracles. In Haught's view, one can be a Christian without believing that Jesus walked on water and raised the dead. If Haught were to change the words "faith's conviction," which imply certainty, to the single word "faith," and change "creation," which implies the existence of a creator, to "nature," the amended statement, which would read as follows, would satisfy agnostics like me while remaining true to the intent of the original: "Miracle stories and accounts of divine action are ways of expressing faith that something of special importance is going on in nature." For nonbelievers, the "something special" would simply refer to the wondrous, awe-inspiring phenomena of the natural world.

The Church

"Jesus came preaching the Kingdom, and what arrived was the Church" - Alfred Loise, excommunicated Catholic priest, *The Gospel and the Church*

* * * * *

The Catholic Church's claim that Jesus intended to found a church is based primarily on two passages in the Bible: (1) Matt. 16:18-19 has Jesus saying to Peter, "And I say to thee, thou art Peter, and upon this rock I will build my Church, and the gates of hell shall not prevail against it. And I will give thee the keys of the kingdom of heaven; and whatever thou shalt bind on earth shall be bound in heaven, and whatever thou shalt loose on earth shall be loosed in heaven." (2) In Matt. 18:15-17, we find these words of Jesus: "But if thy brother sin against thee, go and show him his fault, between thee and him alone. If he listen to thee, thou hast won thy brother. But if he do not listen to thee, take with thee one or two more so that on the word of two or three witnesses every word may be confirmed. And if he refuse to hear them, appeal to the Church, but if he refuse to hear even the Church, let him be to thee as the heathen and the publican." The Jesus Seminar evaluated all words attributed to Jesus in the New Testament by placing them in one of four groups with respect to perceived authenticity. The words just quoted (Matt. 16:18-19 and Matt. 18:15-17) were placed in the lowest group ("Jesus did not say this").[9] The Catholic theologian Edmond J. Dunn comments as follows: "Historical-critical studies today point out that Matthew's account of Jesus telling Peter that it was upon him (*Petrus, Rock*) that he was going to build his *church*, was reflective of the time Matthew was writing (about 85 CE) rather than of Jesus' own words."[10] It is beyond reasonable doubt that the evangelists Matthew, Mark, Luke, and John placed words in the mouth of Jesus that Jesus himself never spoke.

Perhaps Jesus did envision a loosely organized community of followers, but, believing (as the Bible says he did) that the end of the world would occur before some of those listening to him had died, he would have had no reason to found a complex, carefully structured mega-institution. The job of the apostles would have been to urge people to prepare for the arrival of the Kingdom by repenting of their sins. When Jesus returned upon the clouds of heaven, he would separate the good from the bad, the virtuous form the sinful, leading the former triumphantly into heaven and banishing the latter to the eternal fires of hell. A community of followers with Peter at their head, sure, why not? But the Jesus of the Bible simply did not have in mind anything like the Catholic Church of today with its pope, its cardinals, its archbishops, its bishops, its monsignors, its priests, its deacons, and its subdeacons, with its seven sacraments, its elaborate liturgy, its Vatican offices, its many thousands of buildings of worship large and small, its monasteries and convents, its Code of Canon Law. Richard P. McBrien agrees:

"Jesus did not intend to found a Church if by *found* we mean some direct, explicit, deliberate act by which he established a new religious organization."[11] McBrien goes on to say that Jesus founded a church indirectly by gathering disciples who were to preach the Kingdom of God and by expecting them to stay together after his death. However, this is far from the founding of a sophisticated, multi-faceted organization. To me it seems to be all but certain: If Jesus intended to establish anything, it was a kingdom, not a church.

New-Testament Prophecies

In Mark 13:30, Jesus says with reference to his second coming, "Amen, I say to you, this generation will not pass away until all these things have been accomplished." And virtually the same words are repeated in Matthew 24:34, and in Luke 21:32. According to Mark, Jesus had earlier spoken similarly: "For the Son of Man is to come with his angels in the glory of his Father, and then he will render to everyone according to his conduct [at the last judgment]. Amen, I say to you, there are some of those standing here who will not taste death, till they have seen the Son of Man coming in his kingdom" (Mk. 16:27-28). This simply did not happen. Paul expected Jesus' return to occur during his lifetime. His statement of this in the First Epistle to the Thessalonians can be regarded as a failed prophecy: "For the Lord with cry of command, with voice of archangel, and with trumpet of God will descend from heaven; and the dead in Christ will rise up first. Then we who live, who survive, shall be caught up together with them in clouds to meet the Lord in the air, and so we shall ever be with the Lord" (1 Thess. 4:16-17).

Some prophecies attributed to Jesus appear at first take to have been fulfilled. Matt. 12:40 quotes Jesus as saying, "For even as Jonas was in the belly of the fish three days and three nights, so will the Son of Man be three days and three nights in the heart of the earth." Jesus is reported to have been in the tomb from Friday afternoon until Sunday, thus more or less three days but in no way three nights. However, a bigger issue is whether or not Jesus actually said these words. We know that the evangelists wrote not only many things that did not actually happen but also many words that were not actually spoken. They simply invented material when it suited their proselytistic purposes. This prophecy of Jesus is probably one of those inventions. Similarly, Jesus supposedly predicted at the Last Supper that Peter would deny him before a cock crowed. The gospels of Matthew, Luke, and John say the cock will crow once; Mark's gospel says twice. Disregarding that minor discrepancy, Jesus seems to have been right, because all evangelists report that Peter did deny Jesus before a cock crowed. Here again, in my opinion, a gospel story is purely fictional, having been invented for the sake of enhancing the image of Jesus. Sometime between the death of Jesus in ca. 30 CE and the writing of the first gospel, the Gospel of Mark, in or shortly after 70 CE, this story began to be told, perhaps by Mark, perhaps by someone else. In any case, Mark liked the story and used it, whence it spread to the other evangelists. Truth appears to have taken a back seat to proselytizing. It seems that Mark and the other evangelists were willing to stretch the truth, even to alter it altogether. For them, for their soul-saving cause, the end justified the means.

When Jesus' disciples call his attention to the magnificent Temple in Jerusalem, Jesus says, "Amen I say to you, there will not be left here one stone upon another that will not be thrown down" (Matt. 24:2). While it is true that the Temple was destroyed in 70 CE, it is certainly not true that not one stone was left upon another. The Wailing Wall, a surviving wall of the Temple, remains standing to this day in Jerusalem, where it is of great significance to Jews, who visit it as a sacred place of prayer. As for being right about the destruction of the Temple, the prediction might have been a lucky guess (but not that lucky given the Roman occupation of Jerusalem at that time and the oppressed Jews' tendency to revolt), or it could have been an invented story that sprang up during or after the destruction of the Temple. In any case, it is unimpressive as a prophecy. If Jesus had been the divine Son of God, he might have written in the sand "$e=mc^2$," "differential equations," "Newtonian evolution," and "billions of galaxies," and demanded that these cryptic messages be preserved and propagated. Now that would be impressive. His prophecies in the Bible are not.

Additional Flaws of the New Testament

The New Testament also has its share of errors. A contradiction involving a doctrinal matter crucial to Christianity pits several epistles of Paul against the Epistle of James. Paul emphasizes salvation by faith alone: "For we reckon that a man is justified by faith independently of the works of the Law" (Rom. 3:28). "But to him who does not work, but believes in him who justifies the impious, his faith is credited to him as justice" (Rom. 4:5). "Having been justified therefore by faith, let us have peace with God through our Lord Jesus Christ" (Rom. 5:1). "Hence we also believe in Christ Jesus, that we may be justified by the faith of Christ, and not by the works of the Law; because by the works of the Law no man will be justified" (Gal. 2:16). "For by grace you have been saved through faith; . . . not as the outcome of works, lest anyone may boast"

(Eph. 2:8-9). But the author of the Epistle of James sees it differently: "You see that by works a man is justified, and not by faith only" (Ja 2: 24). How can there be a contradiction in the Bible on such an important issue if indeed the Bible is divinely inspired?

Let us take a look at some lesser New Testament contradictions. In the synoptic gospels (the gospels of Matthew, Mark, and Luke), much of the material is essentially the same. When details differ, we know that at least one of the writers is in error. "And they came to the other side of the sea, to the country of the Gerasenes; and as soon as he [Jesus] stepped out of the boat, there met him from the tombs a man with an unclean spirit" (Mark 5:1-2). Here is the parallel passage from Matthew: "Now when he [Jesus] had come to the other side, to the country of the Gerasenes, there met him two men who were possessed, coming from the tombs" (Matt. 8:28). Another example of this kind of error: "And he [Jesus] summoned the Twelve and began to send them forth two by two; . . . . And he instructed them to take nothing with them for their journey but a staff only--no wallet, no bread, no money in their girdle; but to wear sandals, and not to put on two tunics" (Mark 6:7-8). Compare that with Matt. 10:5-10: "These twelve Jesus sent forth, having instructed them thus: . . . Do not keep gold, or silver, or money in your girdles, no wallet for your journey, nor two tunics, nor sandals, nor staff." Were the apostles supposed to go with staff and sandals or not? But moving on, we have no trouble spotting a topological inaccuracy: In Matthew 4:8, Satan takes Jesus up to the top of a high mountain and shows him "all the kingdoms of the world." Not even close, and I do not care how high the mountain was; of course, the author of Matthew's Gospel thought the world was flat. There are other factual discrepancies like these and some chronological discrepancies as well; events take place in a different order. The Bible is far from inerrant. As Steve Wells, annotator of *The Skeptic's Annotated Bible*, says, referring to the Bible, "It is time for all of us to stop believing in, or pretending to believe in, a book that is so unworthy of belief."[12] Wells finds in the Bible 2178 absurdities, 462 contradictions, 428 conflicts with science and history, and 231 false prophecies and misquotes, among hundreds and hundreds of other reasons to reject the Bible, such as injustice, intolerance, divine violence, objectionable family values, and misogyny.[13]

Here are several more New Testament blunders:

- (Jesus speaks) "Not everyone who says to me, 'Lord. Lord,' shall enter the kingdom of heaven" (Matt. 7:21) vis-à-vis "And it shall come to pass that whoever calls upon the name of the Lord shall be saved" (Acts 2:21). Which is it? You would think Christians would be desperate to know.

- "All these things Jesus spoke to the crowds in parables, and without parables he did not speak to them" (Matt. 13:34) vis-à-vis the entire Gospel of John, in which Jesus speaks to the people directly, not in parables.

- (Jesus says) "And no one has ascended into heaven except him who has descended from heaven: the Son of Man who is in heaven" (John 3:13). But in the Old Testament we read this: "And as they went on, walking and talking together, behold a fiery chariot, and fiery horses parted them both asunder: and Elijah went up by a whirlwind into heaven. And Eliseus saw him and cried: My father, my father, the chariot of Israel, and the driver thereof. And he saw him no more" (2 Kings 2:11). Not only does John seem to forget that Jesus has not yet ascended into heaven, but he also describes Jesus as forgetting about Elijah.

- "For bodily training is of little profit" (1 Tim. 4:8). Are you listening, YMCAs and fitness centers of America? Heck, I was looking for an excuse to stop exercising.

- "But if anyone does not take care of his own, and especially of his household, he has denied the faith and is worse than an unbeliever" (1 Tim. 5:8). Hmm. But Jesus is reported to have said this: "Amen I say to you, there is no one who has left house, or brothers, or sisters, or mother, or father, or children, or lands, for my sake, who shall not receive now in the present time a hundredfold as much, houses, and brothers, and sisters, and mothers, and children, and lands--along with persecutions, and in the age to come life everlasting" (Mark 10:29-30). Put the two quotations together, and here is what you seem to get: Someone worse than an unbeliever will receive life everlasting.

- "For this Melchisedech was . . . King of Salem, that is, King of Peace. Without father, without mother, without genealogy, having neither beginning of days nor end of life, but likened to the Son of God, he continues a priest forever" (Heb. 7:1-3). If Melchisedech was never born and never died, he must never have lived, and he probably did not, along with many other Old Testament figures whose historicity is tenuous at best. Archaeology, as you have read on pages 44-47, has had much to say about this.

1. David Hume, "Of Miracles," in Linda Zagzebski and Timothy D. Miller, eds., *Readings in Philosophy of Religion: Ancient to Contemporary, p. 575.*
2. Albert Schweitzer, *Quest for the Historical Jesus*, p. 31.

3. Bart D. Ehrman, *The New Testament: A Historical Introduction to the Early Christian Writings,* pp. 209-210.
4. Ibid., p. 40.
5. Charles Panati, *Sacred Origins of Profound Things,* p. 501.
6. Ibid., p. 501.
7. Ibid., p. 503.
8. John F. Haught, *Science and Faith: A New Introduction,* p. 61.
9. Robert W. Funk, Roy W. Hoover, and the Jesus Seminar. *The Five Gospels: The Search for the Authentic Words of Jesus,* pp. 207 and 216.
10. Edmond J. Dunn, *What Is Theology?,* p. 85. I met Father Dunn quite by chance in the bookstore of a monastery in Iowa as I was buying his book.
11. Richard P. McBrien, *Catholicism,* p. 598.
12. Steve Wells, *The Skeptic's Annotated Bible,* page x.
13. Ibid., pp. xi-xv.

Do you think that Jesus intended to found a church?

Charlie: *Of course not. Jesus was a Jew who no doubt saw major problems with the practice of Judaism back then, but in my view, he had no desire to form a church based on "Christianity," whose concepts were foreign to him as a Jew. I believe it was Paul who founded Christianity and hitch-hiked on the life of Jesus (as the Gospels tell his life). In fact, supposedly Jesus' brother James, Peter, and others refused to accept Paul as a Jesus advocate and went their separate ways. If Jesus could see the results of things in the church, he would probably turn over in his grave.*

Part III: Hot Topics

Chapter VIII
Eschatology

"There is no continuous self who lives our lives, let alone one that could survive our deaths." - Susan Blackmore, "Why I Have Given Up"

* * * * *

One of life's important unanswered questions is what happens to us humans when we die. For my part, I hope I get to live on in a happy place or state with those whom I was close to on earth. But I'm not holding my breath. We have all heard of accounts of near-death experiences told by people who, having "died" for a short time, experienced things like passing through a tunnel toward light, meeting with loved ones, and feeling joyful. Several years ago a neurosurgeon, Eben Alexander, wrote a book about his near-death experience. He describes riding happily on the back of something like a large butterfly with a beautiful human female. Only later, so he says, did he realize that the woman's face belonged to his deceased sister whose picture he had never seen prior to his near-death experience. He claims that the experience was supernatural because his brain had been unable to function at all during surgery. And he ought to know a lot about brains. Still, "ought to" might be the key words. Both Dr. Alexander and his book have apparently been discredited by an investigation by *Esquire* magazine.[1] According-ing to the same source, scientists including neuroscientist Sam Harris have criticized the book. Harris, an atheist, is quoted as saying that "the evidence he [Alexander] provides for this claim . . . suggests that he doesn't know anything about the relevant brain science."[2] Others, too, claim to have found holes in Dr. Alexander's story. Still, there have been thousands of reports of near-death experiences, and most have been pleasant. While I am not convinced by these reports (it seems altogether possible that near-death experiences are creations of the dying brain), I cannot say with certainty that such phenomena have nothing to tell us about a possible afterlife.

The Catholic Church has taken no official position on near-death experiences; however, it has over the centuries made official pro-nouncements about various eschatological matters. About death itself the Church has offered little of an official nature, only that Adam, the first man, was not created mortal and that Adam's sin brought death to himself and to his descendants.[3] Catholic theologians and philosophers have, of course, expressed opinions about death. Thomas Aquinas, the renowned 13th-century Catholic philosopher, considered death the separation of a reasoning soul from its material body,[4] while the respected 20th-century theologian Karl Rahner maintained that "every moment of life participates in death" and thus that "death as a personal and spiritual phenomenon is not identical with the cessation of biological processes."[5] Important to all Catholics is what, according to the Catholic Church, comes after death: a particular judgment followed immediately by heaven (perhaps preceded by purgatory) or hell, and then later, at the end of the world, the reuniting of all human bodies with their souls prior to a general judgment. What the Catholic Church teaches about these matters constitutes in large measure the content of this chapter. My sources include, among others, Denzinger's authoritative *Enchiridion Symbolorum* (a collection of pronouncements by popes and church councils throughout the history of the Church) and the *Catechism of the Catholic Church* (the most recent Catholic catechism, published originally in Latin by the Vatican, with an imprimatur by Cardinal Joseph Ratzinger, the future Pope Benedict XVI). As a former Catholic seminarian who completed the four years of theological studies required for the priesthood, I can assure my readers that they are getting an accurate presentation of Catholic doctrine even though I long ago left the Church and became an agnostic.

Heaven

Scripture is remarkably silent about heaven, and what it does say hardly makes heaven attractive to me. In Chapter 22 of the Gospel of Matthew, the Sadducees ask Jesus this question: Which of seven brothers will have, in heaven, the one wife to whom each was married, consecutively, on earth? Jesus answers that "at the resurrection they will neither marry nor be given in marriage, but they will be as angels of God in heaven" (Matt. 22:30). If this implies what I think it implies, you can forget about sex in heaven. How then are those who make it to heaven rewarded? In 1336, Pope Benedict XII answered this question definitively: "By virtue of our apostolic authority, we define the following: According to the general disposition of God, the souls of all the saints . . . and other faithful who died after receiving Christ's holy Baptism (provided they were not in need of purification when they died, . . . or, if they then did need or will need some purification, when they have been purified after death, ...) already before they take up their bodies again and before the general judgment--and this since the Ascension of our Lord and Savior Jesus Christ into heaven--have been, are, and will be in heaven, in the heavenly

Kingdom and celestial paradise with Christ, joined to the company of the holy angels. Since the Passion and death of our Lord Jesus Christ, these souls have seen and do see the divine essence with an intuitive vision, and even face to face, without the mediation of any creature."[6] How did Benedict know that those in heaven see the divine essence (God) face to face (whatever that might mean since God, as a spirit, is surely faceless)? He knew, or thought he knew, from these three passages in Scripture: (1) "We know that, when he [Jesus] appears, we shall see him just as he is" (1 John 3:2). (2) "We see now through a mirror in an obscure manner, but then face to face" (1 Corinthians 13:12). (3) "And they shall see his [Jesus'] face and his name shall be on their foreheads" (Revelation 22:4). Since two of these biblical passages point to Jesus and the third is ambiguous, why didn't Benedict say, "Those in heaven will see Jesus"? That at least would be consistent with Scripture. For enlightenment I turned to the *Catechism of the Catholic Church*. My question, it seems, is answered there: "Because of his transcendence, God cannot be seen as he is, unless he himself opens up his mystery to man's immediate contemplation and gives him the capacity for it. The Church calls this contemplation of God in his heavenly glory 'the beatific vision.'"[7] It's important to keep in mind that the Catholic Church considers itself the only reliable interpreter of Scripture. If you ask me, Benedict should have just gone with Paul: "No eye has seen, nor ear heard, nor the heart of man conceived, what God has prepared for those who love him" (1 Cor. 2:9). *Mutatis mutandis*, almost everyone can agree with these words, even agnostics. I think I hear an agnostic now: "I don't know what God, if he exists, may or may not have prepared for people who lead good lives." Ah, the comforts of agnosticism.

Hell

"The God that holds you over the pit of hell, much as anyone holds a spider, or some loathsome insect, over the fire, abhors you and is dreadfully provoked; his wrath towards you burns like fire." - Jonathan Edwards, "Sinners in the Hands of an Angry God"

* * * * *

A concept that has caused me a great deal of grief in my lifetime is that of hell, traditionally a place of eternal punishment by fire. When I was a child and a teenager attending St. Benedict's Church in Evansville, Indiana, an all too frequent topic of the Sunday sermon was the horrors of hell. I can tell you that these sermons scared the hell out of me, even as a youngster with (I think) normal prepubescent sexual curiosity, and especially as a teenager when I began masturbating, as most teenage boys do. I believed that my actions, unless confessed to a priest, would send me to hell. And I was too embarrassed to mention sexual sins in the confessional, so I lied each month when forced by the nuns or by my mother to go to confession. "Bless me, father, for I have sinned. My last confession was one month ago. I was disobedient twenty times, I was angry ten times . . ." I just made up numbers. When as a junior in high school I finally made a "good confession," I felt that the weight of the world had been lifted from me. Now I know that nothing had really changed. If God is just, even just a little just, there can be no hell. For hell to exist, God would have to be a monster! God, god, or the gods (if any of the above exist) may not care about humans or even know that humans exist, but I see no reason to think that he, she, or it is a monster, or that they (should there be more than one) are monsters.

Lest you think that hell is not a concept affirmed by Jesus, let me refer you to several passages in the Bible. In Mt. 13:41, Jesus is reported to have said, "The Son of Man will send forth his angels, and they will gather out of his kingdom all scandals [i.e., people who offend or shock moral feelings] and those who work iniquity, and cast them into the furnace of fire, where there will be the weeping, and the gnashing of teeth." And in Mt. 25:41, Jesus says, "Then he will say to those on his left hand, "Depart from me, accursed ones, into the everlasting fire which was prepared for the devil and his angels." And then there's Mark 9:41-42, where Jesus, having just given the curious advice that if one's hand is an occasion of sin, one should cut it off, adds: "It is better for thee to enter into life maimed, than, having two hands, to go into hell, into the unquenchable fire." The Bible, as if to reinforce its direct references to hell, gives us the parable of the wedding feast, where a king orders the burning of the cities and towns of those who, having been invited to the feast, decline the invitation. The king then sends out his servants to invite anyone and everyone to the feast. When the guests arrive, one is found to be without a proper wedding garment. Here are the king's words: "Bind his hands and feet and cast him forth into the darkness outside, where there will be the weeping and the gnashing of teeth." And the moral of the story: "For many are called but few are chosen." Not only is hell an unimaginably horrible place, but most people will end up there (Mt. 22:1-14). The same message seems to be expressed in Mt. 7:13-14: "Enter by the narrow gate. For wide is the way and broad is the gate that leads to destruction, and many there are who enter that way. How narrow the gate and close the way that leads to life! And few there are who find it."

The Catholic Church through the pronouncements of its popes and councils could hardly make clearer its doctrine of hell. Pope Vigilius in 543 condemned anyone who says that the punishment of the wicked would be temporal (that is, would end sometime).[8] Pope Pelagius I in 557 declared that unrepentant sinners are punished in "eternal and inextinguishable fire."[9] The Fourth Lateran Council in 1215 pronounced that evil humans would receive an "eternal punishment with the devil."[10] The Council of Lyon in 1245 declared that "if anyone dies in the state of unrepented mortal sin, that person will doubtlessly be tormented constantly in the flames of an eternal hell."[11] As if that is not enough, the Council of Florence (1438-45) adds its weight most disgustingly to this already disgusting doctrine by declaring that all non-Catholics will go to hell: "[The Catholic Church] firmly believes, professes, and warns that no one outside the Catholic Church--not only pagans but also Jews and heretics and schismatics--will participate in eternal life but will go into the eternal fire 'that was prepared for the devil and his angels.'"[12]

In a section entitled "Of the Relations of the Saints towards the Damned," whoever wrote the Supplement to the *Summa Theologica* of Thomas Aquinas (it is thought to have been gathered by Rainaldo da Piperno from Aquinas's commentary on the *Fourth Book of the Sentences* of Peter Lombard), poses the question "Whether the blessed in heaven will see the sufferings of the damned?" He answers as follows: "Wherefore in order that the happiness of the saints may be more delightful to them and that they may render more copious thanks to God for it, they are allowed to see perfectly the sufferings of the damned."[13] It seems the author tries to mitigate the repulsiveness of his answer somewhat by answering the question "Whether the blessed rejoice in the punishment of the wicked?" in this way: "A thing may be a matter of rejoicing in two ways. First directly, when one rejoices in a thing as such: and thus the saints will not rejoice in the punishment of the wicked. Secondly, indirectly, by reason namely of something annexed to it: and in this way the saints will rejoice in the punishment of the wicked, by considering therein the order of Divine justice and their own deliverance, which will fill them with joy. And thus the Divine justice and their own deliverance will be the direct cause of the joy of the blessed: while the punishment of the damned will cause it indirectly."[14] I don't buy it, do you? Let's say that a dear friend of yours murdered someone and that the state gave him or her a life sentence of excruciating torture. Would you be able to put aside all compassion for your friend and rejoice that justice has prevailed? Now change "life sentence" to "eternal sentence." To an intervening question about the possibility of the pity of the elect toward the damned, Aquinas answers as follows: "Mercy or compassion may be in a person in two ways: first by way of passion, secondly by way of choice. In the blessed there will be no passion in the lower powers except as a result of the reason's choice. Hence compassion or mercy will not be in them, except by the choice of reason." But, explains the author, the sufferings of the damned are not able to be dispelled, which means that compassion towards them would not be reasonable; thus "the blessed in glory will have no pity on the damned."[15] Reason is often abused in defense of religious error; in this explanation from the Supplement of the *Summa Theologica*, the abuse of reason is taken to the level of the inhumane.

Several years ago, one of my Innsbruck classmates, who had become a bishop, was trying to bring me back into the fold. I told him that one of the huge stumbling blocks for me was the idea of hell. He couldn't deny the existence of hell, of course, because that is a defined doctrine of the Catholic Church. What he did say was that no one knows if anyone is actually there. Wow! Forget the fact that the Bible tells us that most people will end up there. If the bishop's view is shared by many of his colleagues, what a long way towards sanity this church has come since the days of my youth! Now all the Church has to do is admit that it was fallible when it declared itself to be infallible, and then it will have extricated itself from the corner it has painted itself into (this idea is not original with me; it comes essentially from the Swiss theologian Hans Küng).

I was pleasantly surprised when I opened McBrien's *Catholicism*, and read his three-page section on hell. Father McBrien says in essence the same thing my bishop friend said: "Neither Jesus, nor the Church after him, ever stated that persons actually go to hell or are there now."[16] While I wish this view represented the current thinking of the Catholic Church, I fear it doesn't. Here is what Wikipedia has to say about McBrien's book: "It was officially disapproved by the United States Conference of Catholic Bishops on the grounds that many of its statements are 'inaccurate or misleading,' that it exaggerates 'plurality' within the Catholic theological tradition, and that it overemphasizes 'change and development' in the history of Catholic doctrine, even though official dogmas of the Catholic Church are, according to the Magisterium, unchangeable truths."[17] A website called "Catholic Answers" says that McBrien's *Catholicism* "is highly erroneous and an unreliable guide to the Church's teachings." At least it's good to know that there are some Catholics these days who prefer to think of God as something other than an oxymoronic all-loving father who puts some of his children in a place of torture for all eternity.

Predestination

One of the least savory ideas to rear its head in the history of Christianity is predestination, the idea that God chooses in advance of human volition whom he will save and whom he will damn. We humans have no choice in the matter. Several quotations from Scripture seem directly to affirm predestination. Here are two; both are written by Paul to communities of Christians whom he considered predestined: "Blessed be the God and Father of our Lord Jesus Christ, who has blessed us with every spiritual blessing in the heavenly places in Christ, just as He chose us in Him before the foundation of the world, that we would be holy and blameless before Him. In love He predestined us to adoption as sons through Jesus Christ to Himself, according to the kind intention of His will, . . ." (Eph. 1:3-5). To another group of Christians, Paul writes similarly: "And we know that God causes all things to work together for good to those who love God, to those who are called according to His purpose. For those whom He foreknew, He also predestined to become conformed to the image of His Son, so that He would be the firstborn among many brethren; and those whom He predestined, He also called; and those whom He called, He also justified; and those whom He justified, He also glorified" (Rom. 8:28-30).

Albert Schweitzer points out in Chapter 19 of his *Quest for the Historical Jesus* that the only message Jesus gives his disciples when he sends them forth is "Repent, for the Kingdom of God is at hand." According to Schweitzer, "all that goes beyond that simple phrase must be publicly presented only in parables, in order that those only, who are shown to possess predestination by having the initial knowledge which enables them to understand the parables, may receive a more advanced knowledge, which is imparted to them in a measure corresponding to their original degree of knowledge."[18] Schweitzer sees the Beatitudes as "predestinarian in form." They are not meant, he maintains, "as an injunction or exhortation, but as a simple statement of fact."[19] In someone's being poor, meek, peace-loving, etc., it is "made manifest that they are predestined to the Kingdom," says Schweitzer. In redemptive terms, "The Lord is conscious that He dies only for the elect. For others His death can avail nothing, not even their own repentance."[20] I think highly of Albert Schweitzer, both as a scholar and as a person; however, I do not understand how he can choose to follow a spiritual leader whose God predestines only certain humans to salvation. Schweitzer was a lifelong Lutheran.

According to St. Augustine, while all people deserve to go to hell,

God in his mercy selects some to be saved. Martin Luther seemed to espouse predestination. Modern Lutherans apparently believe in a predestination (of some) to salvation but not a predestination (of the rest) to damnation. Figure that one out! Calvinists believe that God predetermined the exact number of those to be saved and of those to be damned before the creation of the world. All people are considered unworthy of salvation. God in his mercy selects a certain number to be saved. For me, the idea that God should have a hell in the first place staggers the mind, and that he should assign to this hell whomever he chooses with no regard to individual merit is beyond ridiculous. How do Calvinists "know" that they are not going to hell? All look to the same signs: faith, participation in the sacraments, and/or good works. Catholics see these things as effecting their salvation; Calvinists see them as signs that God has chosen them.

1. Luke Dittrich, "The Prophet: An Investigation of Eben Alexander, Author of the Blockbuster 'Proof of Heaven,'" *Esquire*, August 2013, pp. 88-95, 125-126, 128.
2. "Eben Alexander: American neurosurgeon," Wikipedia.
3. Second Council of Orange (529), Denzinger, 175.
4. "The Nature of Death - St. Thomas Aquinas," on the website *Catholicism without Compromise*.
5. "Karl Rahner," on the website *Encyclopedia of Death and Dying*.
6. Benedict XII, *Benedictus Deus,* in *Catechism of the Catholic Church* - Libreria Editrice Vaticana, Doubleday: New York, 1995, p. 289. The complete text in Latin can be found in Denzinger's *Enchiridion Symbolorum,* No. 530.
7. *Catechism of the Catholic Church*, No. 1028, p. 290.
8. Denzinger, 211.
9. Denzinger, 228a.
10. Denzinger, 429.
11. Denzinger, 457.
12. Denzinger, 714.
13. Thomas Aquinas, *Summa Theologica*, Suppl., 34, 1.
14. Ibid., 34, 3.
15. Ibid., 34, 2.
16. Richard P. McBrien, *Catholicism*, p. 1152.
17. "Richard P. McBrien," Wikipedia.
18. Albert Schweitzer, *Quest for the historical Jesus*, p. 352.
19. Ibid., p. 353.
20. Ibid., p. 388.

Any thoughts about an afterlife?

Charlie: *I like reincarnation. The great equalizer. What fairer way to balance the scales of life and give everyone who lives or has ever lived, a fair chance at equality. In the end, we all end up the same after many an effort to get things right. To me, this makes more sense than all religious belief. It's all about people, not control or power, or fear, or guilt. Religion judges. Who are they to judge? Especially the Catholic religion.*

I'm perfectly willing to accept the fact that there's another dimension out there that we can't prove scientifically. Like the mystery of the multiverse, where much of these answers may lie. In fact, such a potentially exciting afterlife exploring the unknowns out there, learning new and different things and people and ways of doing things. Better than sitting on a cloud in a white robe, playing the harp, and being bored to death.

As I get older I muse about these things. And hope. The alternative is nothing and the sadness of nothingness even though we won't be aware. I look at all the people I've known and know, and think how great it would be to enjoy pursuits and interactions at some later date in existence. No one has ever come back, though. A scientific reality.

Do you look forward to heaven? Do you fear hell?

Sara: *Heaven and hell are real, but not in an eternal afterlife sense. People and situations create heavens and hells. Victims or torture and abuse live in hell; an animal succumbing to its predator and being eaten alive dies in hell. Falling in love is heaven. A beautiful day with a perfectly enjoyed event with perfectly enjoyed people is heaven.*

Vince: *I fear human exploiters, many if not most of them religious. However, if there be a God and he/she/it is omniscient, then he/she/it can see through me. As my daddy used to say: here's hoping that hell is as pleasant as the road that leads to it.*

George: *No and No. They are mythical and lack any evidence of having a physical existence in our universe.*

Larry: *I don't want to go to heaven because I won't know anyone there.*

Chapter IX
Does Prayer help?

"The poor wretches lifted their clasped hands toward heaven and prayed for justice, for liberty--but their god did not hear. He cared nothing for the sufferings of slaves, nothing for the tears of wives and mothers, nothing for the agony of men. He answered no prayers. He broke no chains. He freed no slaves" - Robert Green Ingersoll, "Myth and Miracle"

"Then Miss Watson she took me in the closet and prayed, but nothing come of it. She told me to pray every day, and whatever I asked for I would get it. But it warn't so. I tried it. Once I got a fish-line, but no hooks. It warn't any good to me without hooks. I tried for the hooks three or four times, but somehow I couldn't make it make it work. By-and-by, one day, I asked Miss Watson to try for me, but she said I was a fool." - Huck Finn in Mark Twain's *Huckleberry Finn*

"The man who prays is the one who thinks that god has arranged matters all wrong, but who also thinks that he can instruct god how to put them right." - Christopher Hitchens, *Mortality*

* * * * *

Today I saw the following post on Facebook: "If God has ever answered your prayers, click 'like.'" And Facebook readers were told that 161,000 people had already so clicked. Are you impressed by the large number? I'm not impressed at all. I wouldn't be impressed if the number were 161,000,000. There is something called coincidence operative in the world. All of us have wanted things. Some of us have prayed for these things. My guess is that those who didn't pray and those who did pray got, on average, what they wished for with similar frequency. You may know of someone who prayed to win a lottery and won. How many people in the same lottery prayed to win but lost? How many religious people have prayed to win lotteries that were won by atheists? Coincidences happen.

I do not believe in the power of prayer, not at all. In my opinion (yes, I may be wrong, of course), God never answers prayers--never has, never will. If someone you prayed for gets well, does this in any way prove divine intervention? Even if you pray for a most unlikely thing, and that thing happens, so what? Coincidence can explain the outcome, can it not? What if you are hiking in a remote region of an infrequently visited foreign country and you meet a person who turns out to be your long-lost twin brother, from whom you were separated shortly after birth? Coincidence explains the meeting, does it not? Now let's say you often prayed to be reunited with your brother, and the above meeting occurs. Were your prayers answered by God? Not that I can tell; in my opinion, the meeting was still a coincidence. Now, if you pray for the most improbable events time after time, and time after time these events occur, you have my attention. Let's say that you stop at the local convenience store today, buy one lottery ticket, pray to win the $100,000,000 lottery, and win; and let's say that the same thing happens next month and the following month and the following month, indeed for twelve months in a row. I am now a believer. But that will not happen, and you know it. Assuming odds on a one-dollar bet to be less than one in one hundred million and trusting my shaky knowledge of statistical math, I reckon that the odds of your winning twelve times in a row are far less than one in one hundred million to the power of twelve, or one over 10 followed by 95 zeros. Yet why couldn't and wouldn't an all-powerful, all-loving God cause such a miracle to happen? You did pray for it, right?

A 2006 article in the *New York Times* about "the most scientifically rigorous investigation of whether prayer can heal illness, begun almost a decade ago and involving more than 1,800 patients," found that "prayers offered by strangers had no effect on the recovery of people who were undergoing heart surgery."[1] The study's coauthors were Dr. Herbert Benson, a cardiologist and director of the Mind/Body Medical Institute near Boston, and Dr. Charles Bethea, a cardiologist at Integris Baptist Medical Center in Oklahoma City. In the six years prior to 2006, we are told, there had been at least ten investigations of the efficacy of prayer, the results of which were mixed. The Benson study was "intended to overcome flaws in the earlier investigations."[2] Predictably, one professor criticizes the study because it reduces religion "to basic elements that can be quantified, and that makes for bad science and bad religion."[3] Of course, believers can hunker behind such an objection, which cannot be proved or disproved. I have little doubt that, if the study had resulted in evidence supportive of the power of prayer, its finding would be loudly touted from pulpits and in Christian journals.

Each year millions of people journey to shrines in various parts of the world, many of them hoping for a cure. I don't know why they do this. If they really believed Jesus, they would just stay at home and pray. After all, the Bible reports that Jesus said, "And all things whatever you ask for in prayer, believing, you shall receive" (Matt. 21:22). But they come to the shrines nevertheless. A subset of these pilgrims consists of the lame, a few of whom are able to leave behind the crutches they came with. They came to be healed, they prayed to be healed, and they feel they are healed. Something comes over them and they find they can walk without crutches. Surely these healings are miracles, you say? I cannot prove that they are not (which is not at all the same thing as saying that anyone can prove that they are), but I can point out a fact of life at these holy shrines: no one leaves behind artificial limbs. No prayers have ever caused a human arm or a leg to regrow. Why would God answer prayers that lameness be cured and not prayers that limbs be regrown? Does that kind of God make sense?

In Matthew 21:21, Jesus is reported to have said, "Amen, I say to you, if you have faith and do not waver, not only will you do what I have done to the fig tree [Jesus had cursed the tree and it had withered], but even if you shall say to this mountain, 'Arise, and hurl thyself into the sea,' it shall be done." I don't know about you, but I have not heard reports of tree-withering prayers or of prayers causing mountains to be hurled into the sea. Matt. 18:19 has this: "I say to you further, that if two of you shall agree on earth about anything at all for which they ask [I guess we can overlook the poor grammar], it shall be done for them by my Father in heaven." I think we need to get two Christians to pray together for an end to all war. The Epistle of James says that "the prayer of faith will save the sick man, and the Lord will raise him up." If John 14:14 reports Jesus' words accurately, it should not even take two supplicants; one ought to do: "If you ask anything in my name, I will do it." So, one supplicant or two, why has starvation not been eliminated, why has cancer not been cured, and why do we still have wars? Well, say the theologians, Jesus meant that our prayers would be answered with what we requested *or* with something better, even though the upgrade may not be apparent to us. It is an irrefutable answer; nevertheless, it is worthless because its veracity cannot be proved either. Answers like that keep religions in business.

I never cease to be amazed at the people who thank God for answering a prayer which would never have been necessary if God had answered their previous prayer. Consider the following fictional case. A teenager, who was seriously injured in a car accident, gradually improves and, after a long and arduous hospital stay, returns home with only a few facial scars and a limp. The teen's parents, who have prayed repeatedly since the accident for their child's recovery, praise God for answering their prayers. They seem to forget that, before the accident, they had prayed daily that God keep their child safe. If God had answered those prayers, the later prayers would have been unnecessary. They likewise forget that the all-powerful God they believe in could have returned their child in perfect condition, i.e., *sans* scars and limp. If anyone asked these parents, pious Christians, whether God answers prayers, they would point unhesitatingly to their child's "miraculous" recovery. For them, that is all the proof they will ever need. Some of us need more proof than that.

1. Benedict Carey, "Long-Awaited Medical Study Questions the Power of Prayer," *New York Times*, March 31, 2006. I was unable to find more recent studies.
2. ibid.
3. ibid.

Chapter X

Free Will

"Man is rational and therefore like God; he is created with free will and is master over his acts." - *Catechism of the Catholic Church*, No. 1730.

"It seems to me now that free will is an illusion, and even our precious selves are not solid persisting entities but ephemeral constructions that change all the time." - Susan Blackmore, "Why I Have Given Up"

* * * * *

The Catholic Church affirms the existence of free will in the following three passages from authoritative sources: (1) "God thus operates in the hearts of men and in the free will itself, so that a holy thought, a pious plan, and every motion of good will is from God, because we can do anything good through Him, without whom we can do nothing."[1] (2) "Freedom of will weakened in the first man cannot be repaired except through the grace of baptism; once it has been lost, it cannot be restored except by Him by whom it could be given."[2] (3) "The freedom of will which we lost in the first man, we have received back through Christ our Lord; and we have free will for good, preceded and aided by grace, and we have free will for evil, abandoned by grace."[3]

I have a long list of maybes. Here is one that may surprise you: Maybe we do not have free will. Maybe our decisions happen at a subconscious level before the conscious mind "decides." In that case, the conscious mind merely expresses what the subconscious mind has already decided. Neuroscientist Sam Harris, in his book *Free Will*, calls attention to recent research of brain activity that actually seems to bear this out. If this is ever proved to be true, what a game changer that will be. You will know that your decision to believe or not to believe is not a conscious decision. It might feel like the conscious mind is deciding, but you will know it is not. What will become of moral responsibility? How can people commit sins if their conscious mind has no role in decision making? How differently we will have to view thieves and robbers! As Bertrand Russell says in *Why I Am Not a Christian*, "If, when a man writes a poem or commits a murder, the bodily movements involved in his act result solely from physical causes, it would seem absurd to put up a statue to him in one case and to hang him in the other."[4] As for responsibility, Russell says, "When a man acts in a way that annoys us, we wish to think him wicked, and we refuse to face the fact that his annoying behavior is a result of antecedent causes which, if you follow them long enough, will take you beyond the moment of his birth and therefore to events for which he cannot be held responsible by any stretch of the imagination."[5] I would like to agree enthusiastically with this statement but find myself able only to admit the possibility of its being true.

In a book published in 2015, University of Chicago evolutionist Jerry A. Coyne writes that "the notion of pure 'free will,'--a linchpin of many faiths--now looks increasingly dubious as scientists not only untangle the influence of our genes and environments on our behavior, but also show that some 'decisions' can be predicted from brain scans several seconds before people are conscious of having made them." Coyne continues, "Most scientists and philosophers are now physical 'determinists' who see our genetic makeup and environmental history as the only factors that, acting through the laws of physics, determine which decisions we make."[6] I am not yet certain that our actions are determined by a part of our brain over which we have no control. But I do think it possible. If we admit that we *might* not be free agents, should that admission not make us more tolerant, more compassionate human beings? Of course, responsible or not, thieves and murderers would still have to be imprisoned to protect society from harm, and perhaps also to make an impression on the subconscious, decision-making minds of the rest of society.

1. "Bishops of the Holy See Concerning the Grace of God," Henricus Denzinger, 135.
2. Council of Orange, *Enchiridion Symbolorum, Definitionum et Declarationum de Rebus Fidei et Murum*, Denzinger, 186.
3. Council of Quiersy, Denzinger, 317.
4. Bertrand Russell, *Why I Am Not a Christian*, p. 38.
5. Ibid., p. 40.
6. Jerry A. Coyne, *Faith vs. Fact: Why Science and Religion are Incompatible*, p. 15.

Chapter XI

Religion, Morality, Politics

Religion and Criminality

"One is often told that it is a very wrong thing to attack religion, because religion makes men virtuous. So I am told; I have not noticed it." - Bertrand Russell, *Why I Am Not a Christian*

"It is often claimed that religion is the protector of morals and that the breakdown of the former inevitably leads to a breakdown of the latter. While there may be some correlation or coincidence between periods of moral change and periods of religious change, there is no evidence at all for the assumption that the abandonment of any established religion leads to an enduring decline in morality. There is more evidence to the contrary." - Morris Cohen, *The Faith of a Liberal*

* * * * *

Samuel Butler's novel *Erewhon Revisited* tells of a man by the name of Higgs who arrives in a remote section of the fictional country of Erewhon. At the end of his stay there, Higgs leaves in a hot-air balloon. Twenty years later he returns to find that a new religion has sprung up in which he, the one who ascended into heaven, is worshipped as the "Sun Child." Distraught, Higgs finds the high priests of the religion, Hanky and Panky, and tells them he intends to expose their fraud. They advise him not to act rashly, for the morals of the people are part and parcel of the religion. If the religion goes, they say, the morals of the people will go as well. Convinced by this argument, Higgs leaves. The same reasoning holds sway today among many people in our country. We have all heard the idea--whether expressed or implied--that without religion, the United States would be an immoral country. But is this true? It is difficult to take the pulse of a nation's morality. How can one compare the morality of two countries, for example, country A, which has a majority population of Christians, and country B, in which most people are atheists and agnostics?

Surely one indicator of the morality of a society is the pervasiveness of criminality. Most of us would probably agree that, in a democratic society, a high level of criminality points to a high level of certain kinds of immorality. At least in the area of criminality, the results of research are available to us. Social conditions might also say something indirectly about morality. Are the moral standards of a particular country sufficiently high that the wealthy are willing to sacrifice for the health, education, and safety of the poor? In an on-line article entitled "Is Faith Good for Us?" Phil Zuckerman examines several studies and concludes that "the United States has far higher homicide, poverty, obesity, and homelessness rates than any of its more secular peer nations. It is also the only Western industrialized democracy that is unwilling to provide universal health coverage for its citizens. The fact is that extremely secular nations such as Japan and Sweden are much safer, cleaner, healthier, better educated, and more humane when compared to the United States, despite the latter's exceptionally high levels of theism."[1]

Several studies have found that religion reduces criminality. Colin J. Baier and Bradley R. E. Wright (2001) discovered that, in general, "religious beliefs and behaviors exert a moderate deterrent effect on individuals' criminal behavior."[2] Highly religious people and people who attend religious services regularly are less likely to be involved in criminality, with the exception of property damage. What concerns me more, however, is a comparison of the morality of religious people with the morality of non-religious people. It is possible, for example, that religion is indeed associated with less criminality, and that atheism is as well. To try to explain this relationship, I will use Phil Zuckerman's article "Atheism, Secularity, and Well-Being: How the Findings of Social Science Counter Negative Stereotypes and Assumptions" as the source of all statistical information contained in the remainder of this section, "Religion and Criminality." The article is accessible on the Internet.

Phil Zuckerman, an atheist, begins his article with "People who don't believe in God are filthy, corrupt fools, entirely incapable of doing any good."[3] This shocking statement is actually a paraphrase of the first two verses of Psalm 14: "The fool says in his heart, 'There is no God.' They are corrupt, they have done things that must be abhorred; there is not one who does what is good." Even today, more than 2000 years later, a negative view of atheists pervades the United States. It is too often assumed that someone who does not believe in God has no values. Fortunately, studies disprove this negative characterization. In Zuckerman's words, "When we actually compare the values and beliefs of atheists and secular people to those of religious people, the former are markedly less nationalistic, less prejudiced, less anti-Semitic, less racist, less dogmatic, less ethnocentric, less close-minded, and less authoritarian."[4] These sound like positive moral values to me.

Zuckerman cites several studies that find that religiosity inhibits criminality; he also cites several that find it does not. In any case, according to Benjamin Beit-Hallahmi (as quoted by Zuckerman), "the claim that atheists are somehow more likely to be immoral has long been discredited by systematic studies."[5] Zuckerman admits that secular people do break the law more often than religious people in the areas of underage alcohol use and of illegal drugs. "But when it comes to more serious or violent crimes, such as murder, there is simply no evidence suggesting that atheistic and secular people are more likely to commit such crimes than religious people." Indeed, only 0.2 percent of prisoners in the United States (two out of every thousand) are atheists. A poll taken in 2005 showed that five percent of Americans are atheists (50 out of every thousand), which means that atheists are underrepresented in our prisons impressively, indeed by a factor of 25. Referencing Kimberley Blaker (*The Fundamentals of Extremism: The Christian Right in America*), Victor J. Stenger writes that "child and spouse abuse is highest among the most fundamentalist Christians and Muslims."[6]

If it were true that religion deterred crime, and that atheism fostered it, we would expect to find that the most religious countries have the lowest murder rates, and that the least religious countries have the highest. What one actually finds is the opposite: the murder rate is lower in the more secular countries and higher in the more religious countries. In our own country, highly religious states tend to have the highest violent-crime rates, while the least religious states tend to have the lowest. If these statistics are accurate, they are worth being put in America's proverbial pipe and smoked.

Bertrand Russell wrote in the 1950s, "You find as you look around the world that every single bit of progress in humane feeling, every improvement in the criminal law, every step toward the diminution of war, every step toward better treatment of the colored races, or every mitigation of slavery, every moral progress that there has been in the world, has been consistently opposed by the organized churches of the world. I say quite deliberately that the Christian religion, as organized in its churches, has been and still is the principal enemy of moral progress in the world."[7] Many American Christians see things quite differently; they assume that without Christianity we humans would be immoral. Worldwide, there is moral prejudice against atheists, who, it is often thought, are more likely to commit immoral acts than are religious people. University of Connecticut anthropologist Dimitris Xygalatas finds that no evidence supports this kind of thinking. According to him, now that researchers have examined various aspects of moral conduct, "from charitable giving and cheating in exams to helping strangers in need and cooperating with anonymous others," it is clear that "no matter how we define morality, religious people do not behave more morally than atheists, although they often say (and likely believe) that they do."[8]

Politics and Religion

"An infinite God ought to be able to protect himself, without going in partnership with State Legislatures. Certainly he ought not so to act that laws become necessary to keep him from being laughed at. No one thinks of protecting Shakespeare from ridicule, by the threat of fine and imprisonment."- Robert Green Ingersoll, "Some Mistakes of Moses"

* * * * *

There they are in one heading, the two words that divide families and alienate friends: religion and politics. In general, it is not the dogmatic aspects of religion that find their strident way into politics and around the Thanksgiving dinner table. Things like the Trinity, the divinity of Jesus, the real presence in the Eucharist, predestination, the virgin birth, even the resurrection of Jesus do not bedevil politicians, tear families apart, and cause friends to part ways. Of course, there are exceptions, such as the existence of God and the efficacy of prayer. But most of the destructive differences of opinion lie in the realm of morality. Among the relevant topics that seem to evoke the most intransigent misunderstandings these days are abortion, race relationships, the environment, gender equality, and the distribution of wealth. All hell can break loose when the government becomes involved with these issues, or when Uncle Jack introduces them as topics for discussion during Thanksgiving dinner. Let us examine these topics one by one.

Abortion

Despite the fact that the Romans in Jesus' time practiced abortion, the New Testament has nothing to say about this practice. The Old Testament, on the other hand, clearly indicates that the killing of an unborn child is a less serious offense than the killing of an adult: "If men quarrel, and one strike a woman with child, and she miscarry indeed, but live herself, he shall be answerable for so much damage as the woman's husband shall require, and as arbiters shall award. But if her death ensue thereupon, he shall render life for life" (Ex. 21:22-23). As I see it, the main reasons why the Catholic Church and some evangelical Protestants oppose abortion so adamantly are, first, their belief in the existence of an immortal human soul and, second, their belief that the soul might be present when the fertilized egg divides for the first time.

That tiny speck might be a human being, and if so, killing it would be murder. Actually, I am quite sympathetic to this argument. If I were a Christian, I think I would argue similarly. But I am not, and much of society is not; therefore, while anti-abortionists have every right to their anti-abortion position, they cannot expect me, an agnostic, and others like me to adopt their position. Unlike Christians, I am far from convinced that humans have an immortal soul, and even if they do, I have no idea when it joins the body. My position is this: If the fetus is viable, thou shalt not kill it. Pre-viability abortion, when undertaken for the mother's mental or physical health, or because of other serious concerns or hardships of the mother, is moral in my estimation so long as every effort is made to eliminate fetal pain. All abortions for trivial reasons are morally questionable, some more questionable than others. Still, if there is an all-merciful deity, I assume that souls, if there are such, of unbaptized aborted embryos or fetuses will be dealt with mercifully. One of the problems with Christianity is that it does not really believe, despite assertions to the contrary, that its God is merciful. If he were, he would not have a hell.

Of course, abortion is not only a moral issue; it is very much a political issue as well, an important one these days. I know someone who votes abortion, period. If a candidate is pro-choice, that candidate does not get this person's vote no matter what fine qualities he or she might have. In Roe vs. Wade (1973), the Supreme Court decided that abortion is legal in the United States until viability. Many conservative Christians think the court's decision should be overthrown in favor of a ban on all abortions. Among other things, such a ruling would result in the proliferation of back-alley abortions. Some women are so desperate to end their pregnancy that they will risk their life to accomplish it. Often such desperate women die. Other women, afraid to die perhaps, will carry the fetus to term despite unimaginable sacrifice and suffering. Is that what we as a society want? On the other end of the continuum, extreme liberals will want all abortions legalized. Even viable fetuses will be aborted. Of course we can (many will say should) continue to debate Roe vs. Wade; however, such debate is healthy only if we, all of us, are able to say of people on the other side of the debate that they are well-intentioned. You, an intelligent, conscientious person, may feel certain that humans have an immortal soul, and you may feel that you know when human life begins, but many equally intelligent, equally conscientious people do not feel this certainty. Surely both sides must be given their due.

Race relationships

One would think that our country would have its racial problems behind it by now; instead, 150 years after the Civil War, we still have much work to do. One of the forces responsible for the slow pace of acceptance of black people as altogether equal to whites, has to be the Bible and, with it, Christianity. Here is what Paul, in Galatians 4:30-31, says about slaves: "But what does the Scripture say? 'Cast out the slave-girl and her son, for the son of the slave-girl shall not be heir with the son of the free woman.' Therefore, brethren, we are not children of a slave-girl, but of the free woman." The reference is to Genesis 21:10, where Sarah, the wife of Abraham, upon seeing Ishmael (Abraham's son by the Egyptian Hagar) playing with her son Isaac, says, "Cast out this bondswoman and her son; for the son of the bondswoman shall not be heir with my son Isaac." That is the kind of attitude that once underlay the social structure of the American South. It has always amazed me that the slaves of American owners adopted the religion of their owners. Of course, slaves had neither the leisure nor the education to read the Bible and discover its many contradictions and absurdities. Now that they have both the leisure and the education, it is too late; they have been indoctrinated. For meaningful change to happen, the bonds of "deceived-deceiverism" must be broken. A mass exodus of African Americans from the ranks of Christianity will probably not happen soon.

I've heard--we all have, I suspect--that everyone looks for someone to feel superior to. If that is true, it explains, I guess, some racial prejudice. Poor, uneducated whites can feel superior to poor, uneducated blacks. I'm not sure why, but they can, and some do. Still, the problem is surely more complex than that. There are so many more black males in prison than white males. For some whites, that imbalance bespeaks black inferiority. Some white people hate Barack Obama just because he is black. They say he is uppity. It is true that he is brighter and better educated than most other Americans of all colors, and he does not try to hide his intelligence and his knowledge. If he were white, I doubt he would be called "uppity." As a white man, his intelligence and education would likely elicit praise from many who now deride him.

I was lucky. Although my father had the usual prejudices of his day (he used the N-word, for example), he did not hate black people. My first black friend was a coworker in a sporting goods store. We were both seniors in high school, he in an all-black public school, I in an almost all-white Catholic school. He was a star basketball player and a great guy. Later, as a teacher, I felt as comfortable with my black students as with those of any other race. The very few students whom I can truly say I could not stand were white. I think we all, well, most of us, truly want equal opportunities for people of all races. For some reason, black males are being left behind. And I do not think it has much to do with intelligence. If black women can compete with whites intellectually as a group, black men should be able to also. Many black men are kind, friendly, hard-working. It is our moral obligation, as individuals and as a society, to help them succeed. Success is contagious; as unsuccessful black males see their fellow blacks stepping into respected positions in the community, they will find the hope and strength to do what they need to do to join their ranks. All churches and religions need to express, in word and deed, their unequivocal support for the equal treatment of all people regardless of race.

What does improving interracial relationships have to do with politics? A lot. It means supporting the 15th Amendment to the U.S. Constitution (1870), according to which no one can be denied the right to vote based on race, and it also means maintaining the spirit of the Voting Rights Act of 1965, parts of which were recently overturned by the Supreme Court. It means supporting government programs that promote the advancement of minorities. It might mean supporting higher taxes to make such programs possible. It might mean volunteering for political candidates who appreciate people of all colors. It might mean writing letters to political representatives in support of inner-city programs. It means political kindness, openness, and trust in our country's relationship with the people of Africa, for example. We Americans have traditionally been proud of our support of the underdog. The words "Give me your tired, your poor, your huddled masses yearning to breathe free" appear at the base of the Statue of Liberty. Yes, morality and politics are, for better or for worse, bedfellows. One of the primary purposes of every religion ought to be to teach high moral standards. If a particular church or religion promotes racial discrimination, we should abandon that church or that religion. We should know that such an institution is un-American, and immoral.

The environment

It is encouraging to see that some churches and religious leaders are beginning to take positions in defense of the environment. Many politicians, however, afraid of offending some of their wealthy industrial supporters, are dragging their feet on this issue, maintaining (often disingenuously, I think) that the conclusions of climate science are unconvincing. The same scientific method that produced the modern conveniences that all of us, including politicians, trust and love, yes, the same scientific method that has taken men to outer space, is somehow defective, they suggest, when applied to the atmosphere, even though most do not have a clue what the scientific method is. To get reelected, unscrupulous politicians support antiquated nonsense sponsored by big donors. The one thing that will change this corruption is public insistence that political reelection depend, in part, on being in stride with twenty-first century science. The World Council of Churches has taken a strong position in favor of environmentalism. Where was this enlightenment when our society was thoughtlessly polluting the atmosphere and the waterways? But better late than never in this case. If pastors preach protection of the environment, if they preach the reality of global warming, then the attitude of many voters, who were heretofore uninterested in the environment, will begin to change. We can hope that Pope Francis's recent encyclical, "Laudato Si," in which he exhorts all people to care for our common home, the earth, will bring many more Catholics aboard the good ship Environment.

Gender equality

We've come a long way in the struggle against gender inequality. With the 19th Amendment to the U.S. Constitution in 1920, women's suffrage became the law of the land. Can you believe it was so long in coming? You will recall from a separate section of this book the social ranking accorded to women by the Bible. Women were subject to their husbands. They were not permitted to speak in church. If they wanted to know anything, they were supposed to ask their husbands. When I was a kid in the 1940s, a woman's place was thought to be in the home, especially if she had children. Nowadays, most women, like most men, are gainfully employed outside the home. More women than men are enrolled in and graduate from our colleges and universities these days, and they have higher GPAs. More and more women are finding their way into the military, and some are participating in combat. But, in many workplaces, they still do not receive equal pay for equal work, and they are still underrepresented in the highest levels of management. Nevertheless, the handwriting is on the wall. It is only a matter of time--not much time, I hope--until the gender wage gap and the gender management gap are closed. This is one moral-political issue that is about to reach a happy end, it seems to me. Congratulations to us if that be true.

Distribution of wealth

Another gap, however, is widening: the gap between rich and poor. The main political reason for this is that the super rich pay far too small a percentage of their incomes in taxes. Between 1945 and 1981, the income tax rate of the richest Americans averaged 70 percent. Under President Eisenhower it reached 91 percent. And under Eisenhower the greatest interstate highway system in the world was constructed. In 2014, the tax rate of the wealthiest Americans was under 40 percent. Today many of our roads and bridges are in desperate need of repair or reconstruction. More importantly, what does it say about our society that so many people languish while others luxuriate, flying their private jets to get to their private yachts? We're talking about money they don't need at all and which many millions of people in the world desperately need for lowering infant mortality and providing basic medical assistance to the sick and injured. You would think it would bring unadulterated joy to the billionaires of the world to oversee the distribution of their fortune among the world's needy. But no; it seems that most cannot abide the thought of no longer being among the world's wealthiest. Happily, Bill Gates and Warren Buffet have taken up the flag of altruism. Would that all of the world's affluent individuals followed their lead!

What are the various Christian religions doing about the problem of income disparity? Not much, it seems. If they were, the wealth of the churches themselves would shrink appreciably as they set an example for their faithful to follow. The worst of the worst, as I see it, are some of the mega-churches that preach a prosperity theology. According to them, Jesus wants Christians to be wealthy. Really? Wasn't it Jesus who advised a wealthy would-be follower to divest himself of his riches and then come follow him? The present pope, Francis I, has taken a few baby steps in the direction of ecclesiastical poverty, but he and his church still have miles to go. Let's try to do better, you and I. In the meantime, maybe we can get the government to increase the taxes of those who can afford to pay more (I, a retired teacher, include myself) in order more equitably to distribute the riches of the country and of the world.

Christians say that they follow the teachings of Jesus. But do they? In Luke 14:33, Jesus is reported to have said that "everyone of you who does not renounce all that he possesses, cannot be my disciple." In Mark 10:17-22, a young man comes to Jesus and asks what he needs to do to be saved. Jesus tells him to keep the commandments, to which the young man replies that he has done this since childhood. Jesus adds: "One thing is lacking to thee; go, sell whatever thou hast, and give to the poor." The young man goes away dejected because he has many riches. Then Jesus addresses his disciples: "With what difficulty will they who have riches enter the kingdom of God!" (Mark 19:23) In Matt. 6:19-21, Jesus says: "Do not lay up for yourselves treasures on earth

. . . but lay up for yourselves treasures in heaven . . . for where thy trea-
sure is, there also will thy heart be." If Christians really believed Jesus,
if they really believed that it is hard for the wealthy to enter heaven, that
the wealthy risk spending eternity in horrible suffering, would they not
scramble to disencumber themselves of their possessions?

Mark Twain, a religious iconoclast, wrote in a letter to his older brother
Orion, "I have a religion--but you will call it blasphemy. It is that there
is a God for the rich man but none for the poor."[9] What Twain surely
meant is that the benevolence of Christianity's God seems to be inconsistent with the existence of poverty. What he might have added is that
the failure of Christians to address adequately the problem of poverty
belies the sincerity of their faith. The well-known atheist Bertrand Russell, who died in 1970, points out in his book *Why I Am Not a Christian*,
four moral precepts of Jesus which, if they were not largely ignored by
Christians, would change our world radically. Two of these precepts
address the issue of poverty: "To him who asks of thee, give" (Matt.
5:42); and "If thou wilt be perfect, go, sell what thou hast, and give to
the poor" (Matt. 19:21).[10] What a different social and political world we
would have if all Christians lived up to these maxims.

I have never liked the story in the Gospel of John about Mary, the
sister of Lazarus and Martha, who uses a pound of ointment "of great
value" on the feet of Jesus. Judas's objection is a good one as far as
I am concerned: "Why was this ointment not sold for three hundred
denarii, and given to the poor?" (John 12:4-5) Jesus defends Mary,
saying, "Let her be. . . . For the poor you have always with you, but
you do not always have me" (John 12:7-8). A similar sentiment has
underlain ostensibly most of the Catholic Church's expenditures
throughout the bulk of its history, even though self-aggrandizement
has all too often been the most likely driving force. Oh sure, we find
a handful of Christians (monks, nuns, ascetics, among others) who
possess nothing of their own. But the vast majority ignore Jesus' ad-
monition to poverty. The Catholic Church as a whole certainly does.
Look at its tremendous wealth. Its possessions--cathedrals, elaborate residences, jeweled chalices, ornate vestments, to say nothing
of immense land holdings --are worth many billions of dollars. Very
few priests, bishops, cardinals, and, yes, even popes live in poverty.
Many are quite wealthy.

What would you do if you won, let us say, $100,000,000? I know what
I would do: put no more than $1,000,000 in the bank, give perhaps
$2,000,000 to each of my three children, and joyfully hand the rest, after
taxes, to various charities. If it sounds like I am tooting my own horn,

please read the following poem, which I wrote years ago and whose
sentiment still resonates with me today:

> A neophyte dabbler in social concerns,
> I find myself wondering why
> The rich do not mollify poverty's pain
> From their treasures that reach to the sky.
>
> Still, even a teacher is rich when compared
> To the billions in poverty's snare.
> And I could give more--aye, there is the rub,
> For to them I'm a rich millionaire.

I do not excuse myself. Most of the requests for contributions that arrive
in the mail go unanswered. I could give more and not suffer greatly.
But I do not have the ridiculously superfluous income that the super-
wealthy enjoy. Nowhere close. I could increase my annual giving by
a few thousand dollars. Any of the world's richest people could do a
hundred thousand times more than that.

* * * * *

Friendships have been destroyed because of the growing American
phenomenon of increased political certainty. More and more of us are
utterly convinced that our views about politics are correct. I probably
follow politics more closely then most people, and I am comfortable
with my political views, but I am far from absolutely certain that mine
are the only correct views. We, all of us, need to get rid of absolute
certainty in the realm of politics. What in the world are we basing it on?
Okay, full disclosure: I am a Democrat. As a Democrat, I tend to favor
the little guy, the disadvantaged person who needs help to live a comfortable life. Those of us who have more than the amount of wealth
necessary to enjoy our lives should, in my opinion, happily share our
wealth with those who have little. We should, it seems to me, favor a
graduated tax scale that assigns a very high tax rate to the wealthiest
among us (80% seems altogether appropriate for the super rich). In
my opinion, pure capitalism is pure greed. Capitalism must be tem-
pered by socialism, as it is in Europe. Free health care for all seems to
me to be a no-brainer. These political ideas are important to me, but
they are based on concepts whose rightness or wrongness cannot be
proved. I cannot prove that we humans should help others. Logically,
selfishness makes just as much sense as altruism. Awareness of this
increases my tolerance of people of different political views. If you are
a Republican, you can be my friend, and I hope I can be yours. As

friends, we can speak openly to each other about our political views. And surely that is the way it should be with religion.

Homosexuality and Masturbation

"Homosexuality as a 'clinical' entity cannot be seriously upheld in the face of evidence that human behaviour shows an imperceptible graduation from the wholly heterosexual to the wholly homosexual. The variety of the experience which is statistically normal to the male population concerned is far greater than could have been guessed." - Alex Comfort, "The Kinsey Report," *Freedom*, May 1,1948

"Masturbation: the primary sexual activity of mankind. In the nineteenth century it was a disease; in the twentieth, it's a cure." - Thomas Szasz, fellow of the American Psychiatric Association

* * * * *

The Catholic Church makes no distinction between male and female homosexuality. According to the *Catechism of the Catholic Church*, all homosexuality is condemned: "Basing itself on Sacred Scripture, which presents homosexual acts as acts of grave depravity, tradition has always declared that 'homosexual acts are intrinsically disordered' [*Persona Humana 8*]. They are contrary to the natural law. They close the sexual act to the gift of life. They do not proceed from a genuine affective and sexual complementarity. Under no circumstances can they be approved. [...] Homosexual persons are called to chastity. By the virtues of self-mastery that teach them inner freedom, at times by the support of disinterested friendship, by prayer and sacramental grace, they can and should gradually and resolutely approach Christian perfection."[11] The Bible condemns active male homosexuality in several passages (Leviticus 18:22, Leviticus 20:13, Romans 1:26-27, 1 Corinthians 6:9-11) and active female homosexuality in at least one passage (Romans 1:26-27). If the Bible is right, then the Catholic Church and fundamentalist Christians are right; however, that is a big "if." As you may realize, there are a multitude of reasons to distrust the Bible. What does common sense tell us? Does it not say that if a good God created us (as Christians maintain), surely he wants us to satisfy our God-given urges as long as doing so is not harmful to others. Science tells us that homosexuality and heterosexuality are innate urges; some of us have the one, some have the other, and some have both. Surely it is not wrong to satisfy these urges as long as no one is harmed in the process. When, if ever, will the Catholic Church and the fundamentalist Christian churches catch up with the sexual moral consciousness of the twenty-first century?

Genesis 38:6-10 tells what happened when Onan, having been ordered by his father, Judah, to impregnate the widow of Judah's son
(and Onan's brother) "spilled his seed upon the ground" because
he could not abide the thought of siring children who would bear his
brother's name (as Jewish law prescribed). For this action, God slew
Onan. Although this story has often been cited as an indication of the
sinfulness of masturbation, it seems the story is better understood as
an indication of God's displeasure at the disobedience of Onan. In
the rest of the Bible, no passage can be found that directly proscribes
masturbation. The passage that comes closest is Matthew 5:27-28,
where Jesus is said to have said, "I say to you that anyone who so
much as looks with lust at a woman has already committed adultery
with her in his heart." Since a large part of male masturbation is mental and can involve lusting after a woman, it would seem that Jesus
condemned masturbation, at least in some cases. Of course, these
words can also be seen as Jesus's condemnation of pornography. If
you are a Christian male who practices masturbation or who enjoys
pornography, you would seem to be walking a fine line. Oh, by the
way, one wonders why Jesus did not say anything about women who
lust after men.

Physical Punishment and Religion

"Pope Francis believes it is fine for parents to smack their children
as punishment for bad behaviour. He made the remarks, which were
condemned by campaigners for child protection, in front of thousands
of people at his weekly general audience in St. Peter's Square during
a homily about the responsibilities of fatherhood. The Pope recalled
a conversation he had had with a father, who told him that on occasion he hits his children if they have been naughty. The Pope, smiling
and miming the action of slapping a child on the bottom, said: 'One
time, I heard a father say, "At times I have to hit my children a bit, but
never in the face so as not to humiliate them." That's great. He had a
sense of dignity. He should punish, do the right thing, and then move
on,' he told around 7,000 people gathered in the Pope Paul VI Hall on
Wednesday." - Nick Squires, Feb 5, 2015

* * * * *

Yes, I spanked my children, always with the hand, but sometimes quite
forcefully, and I am not proud of it. I certainly understand, and agree
with, modern parents who eschew corporal punishment altogether (and

not with Pope Francis, who says it can be okay). You have probably heard the old saying "Spare the rod and spoil the child." Many parents believed this, hook, line, and sinker. Adrian Peterson did. Peterson, a star running back for the Minnesota Vikings, was suspended in the 2014 season for hitting his four-year-old son so hard with a switch that the blows broke his son's skin and left multiple ugly marks up and down his legs. What Peterson did, has been done (not always so violently, of course), by millions of Christian parents, who wanted to raise their children to be God-fearing adults. They certainly managed to raise them as parent-fearing children. I did not know this until recently, but the Bible weighs in on the matter of parental discipline. In the Book of Proverbs 23:13-14, we read: "Withhold not correction from the child: for if thou beatest him with the rod, he shall not die. Thou shalt beat him with the rod, and shalt deliver his soul from hell." So there you go, Christian parents. Which will it be: Do you go with the Bible (the word of God), or do you use common sense and follow the accumulated wisdom of society? I know what I would do if I had young children today. Steve Allen would seem to agree: "Most parents have given their children an occasional swat . . . ; nevertheless, the many modern parents who do not beat their infants at all provide another example of the generally civilizing influence of those modernist, humanist philosophies that have had such beneficial effects during the past few centuries."[12]

1. Phil Zuckerman, "Is Faith Good for Us" (Internet article).
2. Colin J. Baier and Bradley R. E. Wright, from the Internet abstract of an article entitled "'If You Love Me, Keep My Commandments': A Meta-Analysis of the Effect of Religion on Crime."
3. Phil Zuckerman, from his Internet article "Atheism, Secularity, and Well-Being: How the Findings of Social Science Counter Negative Stereotypes and Assumptions."
4. Ibid.
5. Ibid.
6. Victor J. Stenger, *The New Atheism: Taking a Stand for Science and Reason*, p. 150.
7. Bertrand Russell, *Why I Am Not a Christian*, p. 21. I think this is overstated, but I also think it is worth thinking about. To reinforce his words, Russell refers to the cruelties practiced in the ages of faith (the Inquisition, the burning of witches) and to the Catholic Church's insistence that Catholic couples remain married even though one partner is syphilitic (in Russell's time, before the discovery of penicillin, syphilis, a highly contagious venereal disease, which can be passed on even to an unborn child, was fatal).
8. Dimitris Xygalatas, "True North: Is religion vs. atheism really an indicator of morality?" *The Courier-Journal*, October 29, 2017.
9. Mark Twain, Letter to Orion Clemens, October 19-20, 1865.
10. Bertrand Russell, *Why I Am Not a Christian*, pp. 14-15.
11. *Catechism of the Catholic Church*, 2357, 2359.

12. Steve Allen, "Corporal Punishment," *More Steve Allen on the Bible, Religion, and Morality*, p. 67.

Any thoughts about the intersection of religion and politics?

Sara: *The Golden Rule implies respect for other people's differences. But things get hung up and torn apart when politics and religion are concerned. Take the big issue of abortion; nothing more divisive than that! I am not pro-abortion, but I am pro-choice, because it's none of my damned business what another woman does with her uterine contents! I have my opinions, certainly. But I do not have a right to impose my opinions on other people's bodies. Yet that is exactly what pro-lifers aim to do, typically in God's name! Why can't they simply not have abortions themselves? Their attitude is hateful and boastful, I think. It's why a separation of church and state must be maintained, even strengthened (as I feel the lines are extensively overlapping currently). To me, if the religious world would embrace the core teachings of Jesus, our world would be a better place.*

What should be the role of religion in politics?

PT: *The role of religion in American politics today is complex. Are we "one nation under God" or one built on separation of church and state? Fundamentalist judges try to install creches and the Ten Commandment tablets on county courthouse lawns. It was assumed that John F. Kennedy's presidency would be directed by the Catholic pope! He made it clear that his faith would not interfere with the law. What seems to be common among most sincere people of faith, among humanists, atheists and agnostics is a willingness to accept the idea that we are in this together, and that we should act as if we love one another.*

Part IV: Later Church History

Chapter XII
Popes and Church Councils

Anathemas

In theological parlance, to anathematize is to pronounce an anathema (a condemnation, an excommunication) against someone. The word "anathema" appears five times in the New Testament, in Romans 9:3; 1 Cor. 12:3; 1 Cor. 16:22; Gal. 1:8 and Gal. 1:9. According to non-Catholic Christians, those five are the only anathemas by which Christians are bound. Anathemas have been imposed by the Catholic Church hundreds of times throughout the twenty centuries of its existence. The first such pronouncements I can find come from the Council of Rome in the year 382. Here is the first of that council's eight anathemas:

- "We anathematize those who do not altogether freely proclaim that he [the Holy Spirit] is of one power and one substance with the Father and the Son."[1]

Contrary to what I thought previously, Catholics who do not "freely proclaim" the dogma to which an anathema has been attached are not automatically out of the Church and presumably on their way to hell. Excommunication, it seems, happens "only when the rejection of the dogma is culpable, obstinate, and externally manifested."[2]

Since I think my readers would be bored by a lengthy sojourn in the dreary land of anathemas, our tour will be short. Here are several of the more interesting anathemas:

- "If anyone believes that the devil made certain creatures in the world and also makes lightening and storms and draughts by his own authority, . . . let him be anathema" (the Council of Braga, 561).[3] Believing this should help to keep you on the straight and narrow.

- "If anyone does not confess in accordance with the holy Fathers, accurately and truthfully, that the Father, the Son, and the Holy Spirit are a Trinity in a unity and a unity in a Trinity, that is, one God in three consubstantial persons and of equal glory, that one and the same deity, nature, substance, virtue, power, rule, command, will, and operation of the three are unmade, without beginning, immutable, the creator and protector of all, let him be condemned" (the First Lateran Council, 649).[4] The Latin here is "condemnatus sit" instead of "anathema sit," a difference without a distinction perhaps.

- "If anyone disdain the dogmas, mandates, interdicts, sanctions, or decrees salubriously promulgated by the guardian of the Apostolic See for the Catholic faith, for church discipline, for the improvement of the faithful, for the correction of crimes, or for the interdiction of imminent or future evils, let him be anathema" (the Council of Rome of 860).[5]

- "If anyone saith, that nothing besides faith is commanded in the Gospel; that other things are indifferent, neither commanded nor prohibited, but free; or, that the ten commandments nowise appertain to Christians; let him be anathema" (the Council of Trent, 1545-1563).[6] This anathema appears to apply to those Catholics who culpably and obstinately proclaim the idea of justification by faith alone, which is a foundation stone of many Protestant religions.

- "If someone denies that in the sacrament of the most holy Eucharist are contained the body and blood, with the soul and divinity, of Our Lord Jesus Christ and hence the whole Christ, but says that he is in it merely as a sign or a figure, or virtually, let him be anathema" (the Council of Trent, 1545-1563).[7] According to the doctrine of the real presence, the consecrated host might look like bread and taste like bread and be analyzed in a laboratory as bread, but it is not bread; it is Jesus himself. All Catholics are supposed to believe this.

- "If anyone says that the one true God, our creator and Lord, is not able to be known with certainty, by the light of natural human reason, from the things that have been made, let him be anathema" (the First Vatican Council, 1870).[8] I get the impression that many modern Christian thinkers would take exception to the phrase "with certainty" of this anathema. Does that mean they have been, gasp, anathematized?

- "If anyone says that human disciplines ought to be treated with such freedom that their assertions, although they are opposed to revealed doctrine, be retained as true and not be able to be proscribed by the Church, let him be anathema" (the First Vatican Council).[9] You would think the Church would have learned by the nineteenth century not to do battle with science.

The Church of Rome would have all Catholics line up like ducks behind the Roman Pontiff, bound not only by his pronouncements but also by the pronouncements of all the popes and councils in all of church history. How could God, who supposedly promised that the gates of hell would not prevail against his church, allow the Catholic Church, if it is the true church, to err in any of its canons, given the anathemas attached to them? Therefore, all of these canons must be true--the few that I have included above and the many that I have skipped. Who can believe that? Not I. I wonder how many priests and theologians do.

Pius X's Errors of Modernism

In 1909, Pius X published a list of sixty-five chief tenets of Modernism and then prohibited the defense of the condemned propositions under the penalty of excommunication. I think at some point I was required to take the Pope's "Oath Against Modernism"; perhaps it was part of the vow-of-celibacy horror just before ordination to the subdeaconate. If so, the oath means nothing to me now, for I left the Catholic Church more than forty years ago. I did recently wonder what some of the propositions of the Modernists were, so I availed myself of the wonderful resources of the Internet. Here are several. As you read them, keep in mind that these eminently defensible statements were condemned by the Pope.

Here's Error No. 9: "They [i.e., those people] display excessive simplicity or ignorance who believe that God is really the author of the Sacred Scriptures."

Along the same line, Error No. 11: "Divine inspiration does not extend to all of Sacred Scriptures so that it renders its parts, each and every one, free from every error." Those of us who have read the Old Testament and the New Testament know that there are many contradictions, inconsistencies, absurdities, and factual errors in the Bible.

Error No. 14: "In many narrations the Evangelists recorded not so much things that are true, as things which, even though false, they judged to be more profitable for their readers." This does indeed seem to be what the Evangelists did. For them, the end must have justified the means: In their minds, the end (bringing people to Jesus) was so important that they could overlook the disingenuous means (invention, exaggeration).

Error No. 22: "The dogmas the Church holds out as revealed are not truths which have fallen from heaven. They are an interpretation of religious facts which the human mind has acquired by laborious effort."

Error No. 29: "It is permissible to grant that the Christ of history is far inferior to the Christ who is the object of faith." As we have seen, even the biblical Jesus had quite a few character flaws.

Error No. 38: "The doctrine of the expiatory death of Christ is Pauline and not evangelical." Paul wrote before the Evangelists did. It seems at least possible that the doctrine of redemption began with Paul and found its way to the Evangelists.

Error No. 63: "The Church shows that she is incapable of effectively maintaining evangelical ethics since she obstinately clings to immutable doctrines which cannot be reconciled with modern progress."

You may want read all of them. They are on the Internet; just search for "65 errors of Modernism."

The Second Vatican Council (Vatican II)

The Second Vatican Council (1962-1965) was convened by the saintly, and progressive, Pope John XXIII and reconvened, after his death by another admirable pope, Paul VI. Vatican II was thought by progressive Catholics of the time to bring a promise of liberal innovations. In the end, there was reason for elation as well as disappointment. With respect to the latter, one thinks of artificial birth control and the ordination of women, neither of which, to this day, has been accepted by Rome and which, to many, seem further from acceptance now than they did fifty years ago. Progressive hopes were raised when the present pope, Francis I, began mingling with the people, doing non-traditional things like paying his own hotel bills and scolding capitalists for their lack of concern for the poor; however, Francis, despite his widely disseminated response to a question about the gays in the Vatican ("A gay person who is seeking God, who is of good will--well, who am I to judge him?"), quickly made it clear that he has no intentions of altering the Church's position on female priests. But I digress; back to Vatican II.

In some ways, Vatican II did make a difference, even though its suggested reforms did not mushroom but were in large measure ignored as more conservative popes began to reign. One reform that did survive is the use of the vernacular in the Mass. Most Catholics consider this a big step in the right direction. Also, with Vatican II, the Catholic Church finally admitted that the Catholic Church bore some of the responsibility for the division of Christianity during the Reformation. And perhaps most important of all, Vatican II reversed the many papal condemnations of the principle of religious freedom. Richard P. McBrien puts it this way: "The distance between Pope Pius IX's *Syllabus of Errors* (1864) and Vatican II's *Declaration on Religious Freedom* (1965) is more than chronological. They inhabit two different theological universes."[10]

Vatican II rejected coercion in the profession of religious faith and at least nominally encouraged ecumenism. Rome would be willing to move slightly in matters it considers non-essential. For example, some originally Protestant hymns are now sung in Catholic churches, and Catholics are now permitted to attend Protestant services and to read from Protestant bibles. But, of more importance, the council recommended attitudinal changes. John W. O'Malley, a Georgetown University professor who has written extensively about Vatican II, comments as follows about these changes: "Now, for the first time, Catholics were encouraged to foster friendly relations with Orthodox and Protestant Christians, as well as Jews and Muslims, and even to pray with them. The council condemned all forms of anti-Semitism and insisted on respect for Judaism and Islam as Abrahamic faiths, like Christianity."[11] But changes like these, significant as they are, do not get at the fundamental doctrinal differences between Catholicism and other denominations and religions; dogmatically, the gap is still wide. In any case, according to Vatican II, Catholics are to acknowledge "whatever truth and grace are to be found among the nations." The council stresses that "the Church is the whole people of God."[12] It elevates the role of lay people in the Church. Finally, of potentially major significance for ecumenism, Vatican II "sets aside the pre-Vatican II concept that the Roman Catholic Church alone is the one, true Church, and that other Christian communities (never called 'churches' before Vatican II) are somehow 'related' to the Church but are not real members of it. This is not to say, however, that all churches are equal."[13]

The Second Vatican Council included as its participants more than 2600 bishops from around the world as well as some 300 theologians and other experts. It was by far the largest church council ever; the largest up to that time, Vatican I, had consisted of 737 participants. As another first, the European bishops at Vatican II were outnumbered by the bishops from the rest of the world. Of course, this demographic expresses the situation of Catholicism as its membership wanes in Europe and increases in some third-world countries. Vatican II also surpassed previous councils in numbers of lay and non-Catholic observers. In this sense, as well as in the sense previously mentioned in this section, Vatican II can be called ecumenical. Pope John XXIII, canonized in 2014, insisted that the role of the council was not to condemn (as many previous councils had done with their endless anathemas), but to move the Church in the direction of Christian unity and world peace. Pope Francis seems to second these two purposes while adding an important one of his own: concern for the poor, which means for him a movement away from the unconscionable disparity of wealth that we find in some places of the world, including the United States. I think that wealth disparity, among social issues, is the issue that moves me most deeply--the one that determines, in large measure, how I vote, especially in national elections.

1. *Enchiridion Symbolorum, Definitionum et Declarationum de Rebus Fidei et Morum*, Edition 21-23, 1937, p. 36.
2. Richard P. McBrien, *Catholicism*, p. 888. I learned recently that the 1983 Code of Canon Law "abolished the penalty of anathema" ("Are YOU anathema? How about Your Protestant Friend?" *National Catholic Register*). This actually changes little since the punishment for heresy is still excommunication.
3. *Enchiridion Symbolorum, Definitionum et Declarationum de Rebus Fidei et Morum*, Edition 21-23, 1937, p. 112.
4. Ibid., p. 121.
5. Ibid., p. 160.
6. Ibid., p. 297.
7. Ibid., p. 309.
8. Ibid., pp. 498-499.
9. Ibid., p. 500.
10. Richard P. McBrien, *Catholicism*, p. 677.
11. John W. O'Malley, "Opening the Church to the World," The New York Times, Oct. 10, 2012.
12. Richard P. McBrien, *Catholicism*, p. 684.
13. Ibid., p. 685.

Dark Corners of Church History

"The strongest case against religion is its unbroken history as a major source of the most horrible evils that the world has seen." - Victor J. Stenger, *The New Atheism*

* * * * *

Many years ago, as a Catholic seminarian, I tried to dispel my doubts about my religion by thinking of the holiness of the Catholic Church. I focused on the apparent selfless lives of many saints, on the courage of the martyrs, on the sacrifices of cloistered monks and nuns, on the dedication of missionaries, even on the good lives of some of the Catholics whom I knew personally. But it did not work for me. The Church is simply too flawed to lay claim to a supernatural founding by someone who was both God and man, who promised that the gates of hell would not prevail against his church. (Of course, as I know now, it is quite possible that Jesus never said these words or anything like them, that he, in fact, never intended to found a church.) The Inquisition, in which thousands of people, mostly women, were executed on trumped-up charges of witchcraft, is a thoroughly disgusting part of church history. The lives of several popes have been morally abysmal; the infamous Alexander VI by no means stands (or wallows) alone. The corrupt morals of many cardinals, bishops, and abbots, of priests and monks, are historically well documented. The Church today is immensely wealthy while poor people die of preventable sickness and of starvation around the world. So, if you cannot believe what is in the Bible, and if important people within the Church have not been consistent exemplars of a high level of morality, what is left to validate the Church's claim to be the one true church? Miracles? Putting aside the question of whether miracles happen at all, we see that wonders happen not only among Catholics or, more broadly, among Christians. Other religions too can point to their miracles. I left the seminary (and eventually the Church), married, had children, and never regretted my decision.

The Crusades

"The Crusades - the most signal and most durable monument of human folly that has yet appeared in any age or nation." - David Hume, *The History of England*

* * * * *

The goal of many of the military campaigns, or crusades, proclaimed by various popes over a period of three centuries was to free the Holy Land from the control of the Muslims, thereby reopening it as a pilgrimage destination. Pope Urban II, who summoned the First Crusade in 1095, is thought to have had a secondary motive: a reunion with the Eastern Churches, which had broken with Rome less than a century earlier in an event called the Great Schism. Karen Armstrong believes that the popes were motivated also by a desire for political power. According to her, popes and emperors "were competing for political supremacy in Europe, and that meant gaining the monopoly of violence."[1] Convinced that his crusade would be an act of love, Urban likened it to a pilgrimage, "except," as Armstrong puts it, "that these pilgrims would be heavily armed knights, and this 'act of love' would result in the deaths of thousands of innocent people."[2] Motives of the laity for joining a crusade ranged from financial or political profit to papal indulgences, from a craving for adventure to feudal loyalty. The First Crusade captured Jerusalem, massacred Muslims and Jews, and destroyed Muslim holy places. According to Armstrong, "it was said that they [the Crusaders] killed more than a hundred thousand people at Antioch."[3] Still, despite its initial success, the First Crusade ultimately failed. Eight more crusades to the same part of the world followed over the next two hundred years and were likewise unsuccessful. By 1303, the last crusader-held area of the Holy Land had been lost. Estimates of fatalities in the attempts by Crusades to capture the Holy Land vary from a low of 10,000 to a high of nine million. Wikipedia says 1.9 million. And this slaughter can be laid at the feet of Vicars of Christ on Earth. Or of violent Roman men in white robes. Take your pick.

Several other papal crusades, unnumbered, were going on during these same years as well as later. One goal of these crusades was the conquest and conversion of pagans and heretics in Europe. During a crusade ordered by Pope Innocent III in 1208 against the Cathars (called the Albigensian Crusade), crusaders invaded the French town of Béziers, killing everyone--perhaps 15,000 or more men, women, and children. Crusaders, motivated to fight by the Pope's promise of indulgences and by his permission to appropriate Cathar land, invaded many Cathar towns over the next twenty years. What had the Cathars done to merit such a horrendous action by the Pope? It seems that one of their number had murdered a papal emissary as he returned from an attempt to convert them. Yes, such an act was inexcusable. Did it justify the brutal slaughter of many thousands? Of course not. The murder of the emissary was an excuse for a crusade, not the reason. Innocent III wanted to eradicate what he considered to be a heresy. Cathars considered the riches of this world evil; therefore, to them, the Roman Catholic Church was evil. An intolerant pope had them killed.

The Papal Inquisition

In an attempt to deal with heretics in a more systematic manner, Pope Gregory IX created the first Inquisition in 1231. Inquisitors were appointed from the ranks of Franciscan and Dominican monks to search out and try suspected heretics. Those who were convicted of heresy and remained steadfast in their heresy, were handed over to civil authorities for punishment, which sometimes meant execution. The two groups of special interest to the inquisitors at that time were the Waldensians in Germany and northern Italy, whose heresy was the rejection of a special priesthood and of the veneration of saints, and the aforementioned Cathars, who believed in two gods, one who created the material world and one who created the spiritual world. Cathars who refused to convert and to disclose the names of other heretics were killed or imprisoned. It was not unusual for the property of guilty heretics to be confiscated by the state and shared with the Church.

In all, the Inquisition in various forms continued for more than 600 years. In time, it extended its reach to include witches; as a consequence, some 50,000-60,000 women and men accused of witchcraft were put to death. Overall, in researching the Inquisition in its various phases, I was surprised that the number of the executed did not extend into the millions, as is sometimes estimated. Still, horrible is horrible, whether done once or a million times. Jesus is reported by Matthew to have said that the gates of hell would not prevail against the church that he would found (Matt. 16:18-19). If hell exists, have its gates not prevailed against a church whose leaders do horrible things?

Catholics, in a single day, August 23, 1572, slaughtered between five thousand and ten thousand Protestants (Huguenots) in an attack called the St. Bartholomew's Day Massacre. And how do you think the Pope received news of the massacre? Historian Yuval Noah Harari writes, "When the pope in Rome [Pope Gregory XIII] heard the news from France, he was so overcome by joy that he organized festive prayers to celebrate the occasion and commissioned Giorgio Vasari to decorate one of the Vatican's rooms with a fresco of the massacre."[4] Nice guy, this pope!

Christian Intolerance Toward Jews

Christian intolerance toward Jews started in the early years of Christianity. According to the Gospel of John, Jesus said to a group of Jews, "If you are the children of Abraham, do the works of Abraham. But as it is, you are seeking to kill me, one who has spoken the truth to you which I have heard from God." Jesus continues: "The father from whom you are, is the devil, and the desires of your father, it is your will to do" (John 8:39-40,44). These words, probably never spoken by Jesus, have brought untold suffering to the Jews over many subsequent centuries, as have the words reportedly said by the Jews at the trial of Jesus: "His blood be on us and on our children" (Matt. 27:25). Serious problems began for the Jews when the Roman Emperor Constantine converted to Christianity and made Christianity, heretofore persecuted, an approved religion (312 CE). "[W]ith the conversion of Constantine, Christians began openly to relish and engineer the degradation of world Jewry," writes Sam Harris.[5] In the last year of his life (337 CE), Constantine decreed that marriage of a Jewish man to a Christian woman would be punishable by death. Not long thereafter, under Emperor Theodosius, Christianity became *the* state religion (380 CE), and Christians were granted permission to destroy synagogues. Christian mobs did just that in Antioch, Daphne, and Ravenna.[6] Various Church authorities made their anti-Jewish voices heard. Church Fathers--Origen (d. 254), St. Athanasius (296-373), John of Antioch (d. 441), St. Jerome (d. 420)--rebuked the Jews for having killed Jesus. St. Cyprian labeled Jews a "breed of evildoers, lawless children." "Your father is the devil," said St. Cyprian (d. 258), echoing the Gospel of John. Of St. Ambrose (d. 397) and his famous student St. Augustine (354-430), a Wikipedia article says this: "Patristic bishops of the patristic era such as Augustine argued that the Jews should be left alive and suffering as a perpetual reminder of their murder of Christ. Like St. Ambrose, he defined Jews as a special subset of those damned to hell."[7] The article goes on to say that Ambrose "sanctified collective punishment for the Jewish deicide and enslavement of Jews to Catholics." According to Wikipedia, St. John Chrysostom (ca. 349-407) went further than other Church Fathers when he declared the sins of the Jews to be criminal and endless; he even asserted that, because Jews rejected Jesus, they deserved to be killed.

With the Justinian Code of 528 CE, the eastern emperor Justinian I forbade Jews from assembling in public and reading the Bible in Hebrew, among other things. Most popes did not rush to denounce the Jews; nevertheless, the situation of the latter became worse and worse until, in the year 772, Pope Leo III outlawed Judaism entirely. In 855 Jews were forced to leave Italy. In 1096, before leaving for the Holy Land, members of the First Crusade massacred a huge portion, perhaps as many as one-third, of the Jewish population in northern France and Germany. While Catholic officials, including many popes, condemned acts of violence against Jews, their words seem to have fallen, by and large, on deaf ears.

Many popes reaffirmed the papal bull of Pope Calixtus II (around 1120) which forbade Christians from forcing Jews to convert to Christianity, from harming Jews, from taking their property, etc., on pain of excommunication; nevertheless, in 1180, King Philip II of France seized the property of Jews and expelled them from France. In 1205, Pope Innocent III announced that "the Jews by their own guilt are consigned to perpetual servitude because they crucified the Lord."[8] Throughout the Middle ages and beyond, the Jews were forced to live in ghettos and to wear something that identified them as Jews. Popular antisemitism persisted, fueled by fictitious charges of poisoning wells and spreading Black Death. Jews came to be accused of using Christian blood to restore the blood lost by menstruation and through hemorrhoids, to alleviate labor pains, to restore lost vision, to replace consecrated oil in circumcision, to insure fertility when smeared on both male and female genitalia, and, in case the Messiah really had come, to guarantee eternal life to the dying. This blood was supposedly obtained by kidnapping and murdering Christian children.

In 1215, the Fourth Lateran Council required Jews to wear special attire as well as a "badge of shame" in all Christian countries. The same council defined the doctrine of transubstantiation, according to which consecrated bread and wine became the real body and blood of Jesus. Christians then came up with the imagined crime of host desecration, which apparently brought about the execution of thousands of Jews. The same council forbade Jews from owning land, from becoming civil officials, and from entering the military. Jews were pushed into lowly occupations such as tax collecting, rent collecting, and moneylending (Christians in the Middle Ages considered moneylending to be usury, a sin). Under penalty of death, Jewish men were forbidden to have sex with Christian women. Disbelief in the resurrection of Jesus and in the Last Judgment became a capital offense. Pope Gregory IX, in 1236, ordered church officials in England, France, Spain, and Portugal to confiscate all copies of the Talmud (the compilation of Jewish law) from Jews.

The infamous Spanish Inquisition began in 1478 when Pope Sixtus IV authorized Ferdinand and Isabella to appoint inquisitors. The primary reason for the Spanish Inquisition was to prevent the many Jews who had been baptized (called *conversos*) from reverting to their Jewish practices. In 1555, Pope Paul IV issued a papal bull which "revoked all rights of the Jewish community" in the papal states.[9] It required all Jews in those states to live in the Roman ghetto. Paul's successor, Pope Pius IV, had Jewish ghettos built in other Roman towns, and his successor, Pope Pius V, recommended the expansion of the Roman ghettos to border towns. Pope Pius VII (1800-1823) had the walls of the Roman ghetto rebuilt after Napoleon had emancipated the Jews. The ghetto endured until 1870, when the Papal States ended. A Jesuit ban of candidates who were of Jewish descent (unless their father, grandfather, and great-grandfather had belonged to the Catholic Church) remained in effect until 1946.

Catholics were not the only persecutors of Jews. Antisemitism was endemic to the Middle Ages. Martin Luther, disappointed that the Jews had not converted to his reformed Christianity, said that their synagogues should be burned, their homes destroyed, their prayer books confiscated, and their passports revoked. Luther was ruthless toward the Jews, calling them "venomous beasts, vipers, disgusting scum, cancers, devils incarnate."[10] According to Luther, it was permissible for Christians to destroy the Jews' private houses and to lodge Jews in stables. "Let the magistrates burn their synagogues and let whatever escapes be covered with sand and mud," said Luther, who added, "We are not at fault in slaying them."[11] Luther seems to have retracted this extremism in his final sermon shortly before his death: "We want to treat them [the Jews] with Christian love and to pray for them, so that they might become converted and would receive the Lord."[12] John Calvin also spoke derisively of the Jews of his time: "I have had much conversation with many Jews: I have never seen either a drop of piety or a grain of truth or ingenuousness--nay, I have never found common sense in any Jew."[13]

No one knows the number of Jews who have died at the hands of Christian persecutors; estimates vary widely. A list of European countries in which massacres of Jews occurred includes Germany, France, England, Spain, Austria, Poland, Hungary, and Portugal. Many people are surprised to learn that fewer than 2,500 people were actually executed by the Spanish Inquisition. They forget that some 5,000 Jews were massacred in Germany in 1096, that as many as 20,000 Jews were slaughtered in Poland in 1648, and that some 2,000 Jews were murdered in Kiev in 1768. On and on, in place after place, in century after century, European Jews were massacred by Christians. Then, of course, there was the unimaginable Holocaust of 1938-44, in which an estimated six million Jews perished. Opinions differ as to the responsibility of Christians for this horror. I would not insult Christianity by calling Hitler and his Nazi henchmen Christians. Still, much responsibility must be borne by the thousands, perhaps millions, of Christians (including some in the United States) who knew or should have know what was being done to the Jews and who chose nevertheless to look the other way. We would all like to know that we, Christian or not, would have acted more bravely than some of these people. But we do not know this, do we? At least I do not.

Papal Immorality

It is hard to be overly impressed with a church whose leaders--some, by no means all--have led anything but exemplary lives. In the Bible, Jesus is reported to have said to the apostle Peter, "thou art Peter, and upon this rock [the Greek word πέτρα (petra) means "rock"] I will build my Church, and the gates of hell shall not prevail against it" (Matt. 16:1,19). A truly divinely guided institution ought to be like a bright light shining on a mountain for all to see, but this has not been the case with the Catholic Church as far as I have been able to ascertain. There have been simply too many ordinary popes, bishops, and priests, and even some very bad ones. Most lists of scandalous popes would surely include the following five: Sergius III (904-911), John XII (955-964), Benedict IX (1032-1048), Alexander VI (1492-1503), and Julius III (1550-1555). As a group, their offences included murder, rape, shameless debauchery (holding sexual orgies in the Lateran Palace), and using papal wealth for family aggrandizement.[14] Other disgraceful popes about whom I have read several accounts are Innocent VIII (1484-1492), a worldly man, who ordered that witches in Germany be punished with utmost severity; Sixtus IV (1471-1484), who established the Spanish Inquisition and later appointed the notorious Tomás de Torquemada as Grand Inquisitor; and Calixtus III (1455-1458), who revived harsh anti-Jewish laws and forbade social interaction between Christians and Jews. Stephen VI (896-897) exhumed the rotting corpse of his predecessor, Pope Formosus, clothed the corpse in papal vestments, and propped it up on a throne. A trial ensued, in which Formosus was found guilty, As a punishment, the fingers of the corpse were cut off, and it was thrown into the Tiber River.

What does all this mean? It seems to mean that God did not watch carefully over the church that claims to be his church. What impartial observer would recognize as the true church an organization under the leadership of such corrupt men? If you are an ultraconservative Catholic, you can rationalize the damning facts away, I guess. Otherwise, no.

1. Karen Armstrong, *Fields of Blood: Religion and the History of Violence*, p. 209.
2. Ibid., p. 210.
3. Ibid., p. 216.
4. Yuval Noah Harari, *Sapiens: A Brief History of Humankind*, p. 216.
5. Sam Harris, *The End of Faith: Religion, Terror, and the Future of Reason*,

p. 97.

6. On the website *Religious Tolerance: Two millennia of Jewish persecution*.

7. "Christianity and antisemitism," Wikipedia.

8. "Deicide: The execution of Jesus: Who is/was responsible, according to the Roman Catholic Church?" on the website *ReligiousTolerance.org*.

9. "Roman Ghetto," Wikipedia.

10. Martin Luther, "On the Jews and Their Lies," quoted in "Fundamentals of Monotheism: Antisemitism in history," on the website *Lights of Faith & Glory*.

11. "Martin Luther: Reformer, man of God, antisemite," on the website *Christian Today*.

12. "Luther and the Jews," on the website *lutherreformation.org*.

13. "John Calvin," Wikipedia.

14. More specific information can be found in these books: Sir Nicholas Cheetham, *Keepers of the Keys: A History of the Popes from St. Peter to John Paul II*; John Julius Norwich, *Absolute Monarchs: A History of the Papacy*; Richard P. McBrien, *Lives of the Popes*.

What do you consider the darkest corners of Christian history?

George: *(1) Pervasive persecution of Jews--by fabricating the fictions involved in the creation of Christianity; (2) the complicity between the Inquisition and the local governments in executing persons who in good conscience disagreed with the authority of the Church; (3) the suppression of Galileo's and Copernicus' discoveries; (4) collaboration with the National Socialist and Fascist regimes of Hitler and Mussolini; (5) inventing dictates of Natural Law to interfere with human sexuality and reproductive freedom while ignoring that the imposition of celibacy is contrary to such Natural Law and ignoring that, by "causing" miscarriages, God is the cause of more abortions than all human abortionists--both legal and illegal; and (6) accumulating treasures, wealth and properties in order to increase the prestige and appearance of power of the Church.*

Vince: *Most corners of Christian history are dark, from the Auto-da-fé to the Catholic Church's collaboration with Hitler. Yet religious people, many of them Christian, resisted Hitler (e.g., Angelo Roncalli, the future Pope John XXIII). Others were active in the Civil Rights Movement (e.g., Delta Ministry of the National Council of Churches). They were motivated by their faith to do good works. As a dialectician I recognize this.*

Chapter XIV

The Reformers

Martin Luther

In 1517, in the German town of Wittenberg, an Augustinian monk by the name of Martin Luther (1483-1546), a professor of biblical studies, issued ninety-five theses intended to bring about debate on ecclesiastical matters that troubled him. In so doing, he unwittingly took the first step along a path that would radically change the course of history. In 1511, Luther had traveled to Rome, where he was horrified by the rampant immorality he found among the clergy. Some priests there even mocked the doctrine of transubstantiation, saying from the altar, "Bread thou art, and bread thou shalt remain."[1] One important issue addressed by Luther in his Ninety-five Theses was the sale of indulgences. To understand what indulgences are, one has to understand the concept of purgatory. Purgatory is said to be a place where deceased Christians whose sins have been forgiven make satisfaction for their offences. Indulgences are remissions of time in purgatory, either one's own future time there or the time of a deceased person who is already in purgatory. Indulgences presuppose repentance for sins committed. In Luther's day, indulgences were attached to donations made for the rebuilding of St. Peter's Cathedral in Rome. Some unscrupulous hawkers lied about the power of indulgences, telling potential buyers that they also took away sins. Luther, appalled by the sale of indulgences, the immoral life of some clergy, and other perceived abuses within the Catholic Church, penned his Ninety-five Theses. He had no way of knowing that these theses would become the nucleus of a giant snowball that would come to be called the Reformation.

Luther intended his theses as topics for scholarly debate. Thesis 5 denies to the pope the full power of indulgences: "The pope has neither the will nor the power to remit any penalties beyond those imposed either at his own discretion or by Canon Law." Popes then and now issued and issue so-called plenary indulgences, i.e., full remission of temporal punishment due to sin. Thesis 50 states that "Christians should be taught that if the pope knew the greedy crookedness of the indulgence preachers, he would prefer to let St. Peter's Cathedral be burned to cinders than have it erected with the skin, body, and bones of his flock."[2] Luther must have suspected that the opulent reigning pope, Leo X, cared little about where the construction money came from. Eventually Luther's theses brought him into conflict with Johann Tetzel, a Dominican seller of indulgences. The Dominicans pushed charges of heresy against Luther, who was called to meet in Augsburg with Cardinal Cajetan. The latter agreed in advance not to send Luther to Rome to be tried for heresy (the memory of the Inquisition was still fresh in the minds of Europeans). Thus reassured, Luther appeared before the cardinal but refused to make concessions. Cajetan dismissed him with an imposition of silence; however, Luther would soon ignore the order. In a famous series of debates in Leipzig with the theologian Johann Eck, in which the central topic became papal jurisdiction, Luther argued, heretically, that Christ, not the pope, was the head of the Church; real authority on earth resided in a consensus of the faithful, he said. In the course of the debate, Luther asserted that a church council could err. After Leipzig, it was known publicly that Luther's views stood in opposition to Catholic doctrine. A series of unorthodox treatises written by Luther in the year 1520 resulted in his being summoned to the German city of Worms for a meeting with Emperor Charles V. Here Luther refused to recant anything unless a conflict with Scripture could be shown; as he put it, "I do not believe in the authority of either popes or councils by themselves, for it is plain that they have often erred and contradicted each other."[3] The emperor, who disagreed with Luther, nevertheless granted him safe passage home, where he was protected by Frederick the Wise in the castle of the Wartburg. Here Luther accomplished what may have been his greatest achievement, a translation of the Bible into German. Now, for the first time ever, even laymen could read the Bible and reach their own conclusions. Finally an enlightened laity was possible, and the rest, as they say, is history.

In his commentary on the Epistle to the Romans, Luther wrote, "All things whatever arise from, and depend on, the divine appointment; whereby it was foreordained who should receive the word of life, and who should disbelieve it; who should be delivered from their sins, and who should be hardened in them; and who should be justified and who should be condemned." Although Lutherans these days argue that their founder subscribed to "single predestination" (i.e., the preordainment of some to heaven but not of others to hell), there are nevertheless indications in the writings of Luther that seem to show that the reformer did indeed mean "double predestination," which includes predestination to hell. In response to an objection by the renowned Catholic humanist Erasmus, who disagreed diametrically with Luther on the matter of predestination, Luther wrote words you may find hard to believe: "Thus God conceals His eternal mercy and loving kindness beneath eternal wrath, His righteousness beneath unrighteousness. Now, the highest degree of faith is to believe that He is merciful, though he saves so few and damns so many; to believe that He is just, though of His own will He makes us perforce proper subjects for damnation, and seems (in Erasmus' words) 'to delight in the torments of poor wretches and to be a fitter object for hate than for love.'"[4] Luther's "highest degree of faith" strikes me as utter nonsense. He continues, "If I could by any means understand how this same God, who makes such a show of wrath and unrighteousness, can yet be merciful and just, there would be no need for faith. But as it is, the impossibility of understanding makes room for the exercise of faith when these things are preached and published; just as, when God kills, faith in life is exercised in death." I find it hard to imagine that Luther saw predestination as the only apparent obstacle standing between him and a completely rational understanding of Christianity.

In Luther's view, all men are evil as the result of original sin and cannot attain everlasting life on their own but only through the grace of God, through which they are saved from their sins. Mysteriously, Luther, who throughout his adult life was tormented by a fear of death, somehow derived at least some peace from the idea of divine predestination. He finds support for his ideas in the epistles of Paul and the Gospel of John as well as in the writings of Augustine; thus, Paul, John, and Augustine become his favorite authorities. God's grace results in faith, and it is by faith, not by works, that man is saved. Among the first doctrines to go are the primacy of the pope and the importance of tradition. Everything a Christian needs is found in Scripture, according to Luther. The Catholic Church claims that the Pope and tradition are guidelines to the interpretation of Scripture. Luther ends up by saying, not in word but in deed, that he (Luther) is the only one who can interpret Scripture correctly. In a word, he casts out the Pope and becomes a pope himself. He rejects everyone who stands in the way of his truth. Several early allies, themselves reformers, become, once they have shown an unwillingness to accept all of Luther's religious views, his bitter enemies; among them are Erasmus, Thomas Murner, Andreas Karlstadt, and Thomas Müntzer.

John Calvin

John Calvin (1509 to 1564) broke with the Catholic Church in 1530 and took up the work of church reformation. He spent most of his life thereafter in Geneva, Switzerland, where he became highly influential. It is telling that when another reformer, Michael Servetus, who had criticized some of Calvin's ideas, came to Geneva, Servetus was arrested and burned at the stake as a heretic (1553). Seven years before Servetus' execution, Calvin wrote to William Farel, that "If he [Servetus] comes [to Geneva, I shall never let him go out alive if my authority has weight . . . ." [5] In 1561, he wrote in a letter to Marquis Paet, high chamberlain to the King of Navarre: "Do not fail to rid the country of those scoundrels [Anabaptists and others] who stir up the peoples to revolt against us. Such monsters should be exterminated, as I have exterminated Michael Servetus the Spaniard." The French philosopher

Voltaire directed his satiric wit at Calvin, as well as at Luther and Ulrich Zwingli, as follows: "If they [the three reformers] condemned celibacy in the priests, and opened the gates of the convents, it was only to turn all society into a convent. Shows and entertainments were expressly forbidden by their religion; and for more than two hundred years there was not a single musical instrument allowed in the city of Geneva."[6] To be sure, Calvin functioned as a strict guardian of public morality. I am not aware that Luther and Zwingli adopted similar roles.

Historiographer Susan Jacoby has nothing good to say about John Calvin. According to her, he "could be as brutal and repressive as Torquemada [the Grand Inquisitor of the Spanish Inquisition]" once he had attained political power.[7] To support her charge of brutality, Jacoby offers the following data: "During the first five years after Calvin's triumphalist return to Geneva [he had been expelled from the city because of his strict discipline], ten people were beheaded, thirty-five burned at the stake, and seventy-six driven from their houses after their property had been seized."[8] Regarding Calvin's repressiveness, Jacoby writes as follows: "Calvin cared not only about doctrine--especially predestination--but also about strict social discipline, maintained not only by civil magistrates and ecclesiastical pooh-bahs but by a network of neighborhood informers united in their determination to ferret out anyone who did not subscribe to strict Calvinist practices and beliefs about everything from the basic sinfulness of humanity to any pleasure that might be derived from such inventions of the devil as colorful clothes, music, sweet foods--in short, anything that might please any of the human senses."[9]

What interests me especially about Calvin is his idea of absolute predestination. Here it is in Calvin's own words: "By predestination we mean the eternal decree of God, by which he determined with himself whatever he wished to happen with regard to every man. All are not created on equal terms, but some are preordained to eternal life, others to eternal damnation; and, accordingly, as each has been created for one or other of these ends, we say that he has been predestinated to life or to death."[10] According to Calvin, all events "are governed by the secret counsel of God. Nothing happens but what he [God] has knowingly and willingly decreed."[11] Calvin observed that, among those who had heard him preach, some had been moved and others not. The explanation for the dissimilar reception, Calvin thought, was that God freely gave his grace to some and withheld it from others. This reminded him of Jesus' parable of the sower in which some seed falls among thorns and on stones. The clincher for Calvin might have been these words of Jesus: "No one can come to me unless it has been granted him by my Father" (John 6: 65).

Calvin, along with Zwingli, John Knox, and others, was influential in the development of a branch of Christianity called Reformed tradition (Presbyterian, Congregationalist, and, in some cases, Episcopalian). Although *The Westminster Confession of Faith*, a Reformed confession, states that "by the decree of God, for the manifestation of his glory, some men and angels are predestinated unto everlasting life, and others foreordained to everlasting death,"[12] the Anglican Church seems to have moved away from absolute predestination. These days, one is more likely to find Anglicans who, with some Presbyterians, Lutherans, and others, affirm the possibility of a predestination to heaven but not to hell. A little progress is still progress.

1. Richard Marius, *Martin Luther: The Christian Between God and Death*, p. 82.
2. Ibid., p. 140.
3. Ibid., p. 294.
4. Martin Luther, *The Bondage of the Will*, on the website *Christian Classics Ethereal Library*.
5. "John Calvin," Wikipedia.
6. Ibid.
7. Susan Jacobi, *Strange Gods: A Secular History of Conversions*, p. 110.
8. Ibid., p. 150.
9. Ibid., p. 151.
10. John Calvin, *Institutes of the Christian Religion*, Bk. 3, Ch. 21, Sect. 5.
11. Ibid., Bk. 1, Ch. 16, Sect. 3.
12. *The Westminster Confession*, Ch. 3, III.

What has Christianity contributed to the world?

Kim: *Christianity, like almost all religions, has a civilizing influence on humankind. In addition, it provides some hope for people concerning what happens to us when we die. However, I view Christianity as I do most of the religions, even those religions about which we know nothing. It seems to me very likely that even ancient humans, as soon as they were able to walk and communicate, or maybe even earlier, created some kind of religion. Thinking humankind, or, at least, most of it, needs some kind of religion to provide answers. The down side of religion, the negative side, is that many/most people tend to think that their religion is the only "real" or "true" one. This has unfortunately led to religion playing a large role in war, massacres, executions, etc. Has much really changed today, 2,000 years after Christ? I truly believe that if Christ walked the earth today, he would be very disappointed, although maybe not shocked or surprised.*

Part V: Popular Delusions

Chapter XV

The Shroud of Turin and the Sudarium of Oviedo

"But, according to research by British scholar and author Charles Freeman, to be published in the journal *History Today*, the truth is that the shroud is not only medieval, just as the radiocarbon dating suggests, but that it is likely to have been created for medieval Easter rituals--an explanation that flies in the face of what he called 'intense and sometimes absurd speculation' that coalesces around it." - Charlotte Higgins, "Turin shroud was made for medieval Easter ritual, historian says," *Religion*, October 23, 2014

* * * * *

The Shroud of Turin is intriguing. The famous shroud, believed by many Christians to be the burial cloth of Jesus, is approximately 14 feet long and three and one-half feet wide, imprinted with a faux-photonegative image of a naked man. Although the first historical record of the Shroud is from the 14th century, when it appeared in the small French town of Lirey; although the bishop of the nearby city of Troyes proclaimed that it had been "cunningly painted"; and although Pope Clement VII required that a public display of the Shroud be preceded by an announcement that it was a painting or a picture, many Christians today believe it to be the authentic burial cloth of Jesus. In fact, Pope Benedict XVI visited the Shroud and knelt in prayer before it. If the scholars and scientists are right who maintain that the famous shroud is the burial cloth of Jesus upon which has been supernaturally imprinted an image of his body as it lay in the tomb, the Shroud of Turin offers strong evidence for the divinity of Jesus. Yet much evidence from elsewhere belies this divinity: the multiple egregious errors of the Bible in both Old and New Testaments, including the impossibility of Noah's Ark and Jesus' failed prediction of the immediacy of the end of the world; Jesus' flawed moral character; the less-than-impressive credentials of popes, clergy, and Christian laity; the atrocities of the Crusades; the horrors of the Inquisition; the problem of suffering (the theodicy question); and more. In 1988, when the Shroud was carbon-14 dated by three independent laboratories--Oxford University, the University of Arizona, and the Swiss Federal Institute of Technology--and found to have originated around the middle of the 14th century, I thought that the controversy had been settled once and for all. It turns out that I greatly underestimated the tenacity of the Shroud enthusiasts. The first objection I remember hearing was that, since the Shroud had been in a fire, the results of the carbon-14 testing were rendered inaccurate. Although experts countered that carbon-14 testing would be only minimally affected by smoke, the debate continued.

In my opinion, one of the strongest arguments against the authenticity of the Shroud of Turin comes from the Bible itself, from the raising of Lazarus in the Gospel of John: "And at once he who had been dead came forth, bound feet and hand with bandages, and his face was tied up with a cloth" (John 11:44). Later in John's gospel we are told what Peter and John saw when they entered the tomb of the risen Jesus: "Simon Peter therefore came following him [i.e., 'the other disciple whom Jesus loved'], and he went into the tomb, and saw the linen cloths lying there, and the handkerchief that had been about his [Jesus'] head, not lying with the linen cloths, but folded in a place by itself" (John 20:6-7). Of course, the Lazarus text cannot be used as proof that Jesus was entombed wearing a separate head cloth (and thus not draped completely with a shroud like the Shroud of Turin, which covers both head and body), and the plurality of cloths in the post-resurrection text seems to be explainable with one shroud and one or several ties. Still, the presence of a separate "handkerchief that had been about his head" argues for a shroud or shrouds that would not cover the face. A website entitled *Burial Customs During the Time of Christ* states that "preparation of the corpse for burial consisted mainly in washing it and wrapping it in shrouds."[1]

I recommend an Internet article from 2012 disputing the authenticity of the Shroud of Turin: "The Shroud of Turin and the Image of Edessa: A Misguided Journey," by Charles Freeman, whose erudition is evident. In the following passage, he attacks the scholarship of one of the major defenders of the Shroud, Ian Wilson: "I am writing this in the hope that those who read Ian Wilson's immensely enjoyable but essentially fictional account of the history of the Turin Shroud accept it as such, fiction not history. He has too little understanding of the wider world of medieval relics, in which the Shroud is one of thousands associated with the crucifixion and tomb alone. He quotes selectively and ignores too many obvious objections to his narrative. His focus on the Shroud to the exclusion of many other much [more] prestigious relics leads him to confuse the different shroud relics not only with each other but with images that show Christ alive. If the Shroud has a history that extends beyond the fourteenth century he certainly has not found it. I don't think he has found a single clear reference prior to that date to the cloth we know as the Turin Shroud."[2]

Proponents of Shroud authenticity claim that no one has been able to produce an image like the one on the Shroud; however, Joe Nickell, well-known investigator of paranormal phenomena, maintains that comparable images have been produced using several different methods. A CNN article from 2009 reports that an Italian scientist claims to have reproduced the Shroud: "Luigi Garlaschelli created a copy of the shroud by wrapping a specially woven cloth over one of his students, painting it with pigment, baking it in an oven (which he called a 'shroud machine') for several hours, then washing it." The result "looks like the cloth that many Christians through the centuries have believed is the actual burial shroud of Jesus, he told CNN." The CNN article goes on to explain that Garlaschelli's research "shows the pigment may simply have worn off the cloth over the centuries since it was 'discovered' in 1355, but impurities in the pigment etched an image into the fibers of the cloth, leaving behind the ghostly picture that remains today." According to Garlaschelli, "his work disproves the claims of the shroud's strongest supporters."[3] Nickell points out that one of the problems with the Turin shroud is that it should show signs of being wrapped around a body (an unnaturally wide face, for example), but it doesn't. The CNN article does not say how, or even if, Garlaschelli obviated this difficulty; however, Nickell, in an article about Garlaschelli's accomplishment, says that the Italian worked with "a bas-relief substituted for the face to avoid wrap-around distortions."[4] But what about the body? Would it not show "wrap-around distortions"?

Another problem, originally noted by L. A. Schwalbe and Raymond Rogers, is that, although there would be much more pressure on a cloth resting under the dorsal side of a corpse than on a cloth covering the frontal side of the same corpse, no significant difference in pressure can be noted on the Shroud.[5] This is an important consideration, it seems to me. Garlaschelli, of course, would have painted the back side of his cloth with the model's dorsal side up. Other problems noted by Nickell are these: the "blood" flows are "unnaturally picturelike"; the "blood" is "suspiciously red"; the "body" is "unnaturally elongated," à la Gothic art; although "blood" on the right foot seems to indicate that the right leg was bent, there is an imprint of the right calf on the Shroud.[6] Dr. Michael M. Baden, whom Nickell calls "one of the United States' most distinguished medical-legal experts," commented as follows about the image on the Shroud: "In no way do I hold myself out as an expert on the shroud, but I do know dead bodies. Human beings do not produce this kind of pattern."[7] Moreover, Walter McCrone, an international expert in blood analysis and winner of the National Award in Analytical Chemistry, testified long ago that there was no blood at all on the Shroud.

I recently became aware of yet another argument of the Shroud enthusiasts, this one based on a cloth called the Sudarium of Oviedo. The Sudarium is supposed to be a cloth that was put over the face of Jesus shortly after he died. It is stained but has, unlike the Shroud of Turin, no "supernatural" markings. The Sudarium has no recorded history until the 7th century, when it supposedly arrived in Spain in a chest along with other relics. The chest remained unopened until 1075. The late Monsignor Giulio Ricci, whom Joe Nickell calls "a lifelong shroud zealot," claimed that he found on the Sudarium a pulmonary fluid that indicated death by suffocation (which occurs in crucifixion). And a biologist by the name of Max Frei, "the same person whose work regarding pollens on the shroud was severely criticized--even by the Shroud of Turin Research Project [a pro-Shroud group],"[8] reports finding pollen on the Sudarium compatible with the flora of Palestine in the first century. Dr. Pierluigi Baima-Bollone, according to Joe Nickell "a zealous shroud partisan,"[9] claimed that the blood of both the Shroud and of the Sudarium is type AB, which is quite rare except in the Middle East. According to Nickell, who thinks neither cloth contains blood, Bollone's finding of type AB blood on the Shroud was "utterly negated by the tests of the forensic serologists of the secret commission."[10]

Mark Guscin, a Shroud and Sudarium enthusiast, writes as follows: "If the face of the image on the Shroud is placed over the stains on the sudarium, perhaps the most obvious coincidence is the exact fit of the stains with the beard on the face.[11] According to Joe Nickell, Guscin "touts the initial work of Monsignor Giulio Ricci, followed by that of Dr. Alan Whanger, whom he describes as a 'highly respected scientist'; he also praises what Whanger calls the polarized image overlay technique." Nickell continues: "Actually, Whanger is a retired geriatric psychiatrist and former missionary who took up image analysis as a hobby. He is the Shroud of Turin enthusiast . . . who perceived a hammer, a Roman thrusting spear, a pair of sandals, and other ridiculous imagings on the shroud. [...] Mary Whanger explains that her husband used a superimposition technique involving polarized filters and two projectors to compare two images . . . being 'able to observe the two images fading in and out of one another.' Dr. Whanger would 'first superimpose two images, using what he came to consider "best possible alignment": eyebrows, tip of nose, and mouth.' Then he and Mrs. Whanger would do comparisons, tracing 'points of congruence' on clear plastic sheets."[12] Nickell calls the Whangers' conclusion "pseudoscientific nonsense."[13] Retired scientist Colin Berry has also compared the stains on both the Shroud and the Sudarium and finds "no correspondence . . . just wish thinking and the pushing of pet theories that suit a proselytising agenda."[14] Berry even juxtaposes on his blog an image of the face from the Shroud of Turin and an image of the stains from the Sudarium of Oviedo. I also don't see a match; you might want to take a look. Carbon-14 testing has been done on the Sudarium, which indicated a 7th-century origin. Predictably, this result was rejected by the Sudarium enthusiasts because of "the excessive pollution of the samples."[15]

Despite reading extensively in the writings of both proponents and adversaries of the Shroud of Turin and the Sudarium of Oviedo, I am unable to prove to anyone the fraudulent nature of either of these cloths, although I do think that both are frauds.[16] You are perhaps familiar with the literature of creationists, some of whom use science to a degree well beyond my ability to understand. A six-thousand-year-old earth! Dinosaurs and men living at the same time! Or else imaginary dinosaurs! A God who put large bones in the ground and made them appear to be ancient in order to test our belief in the Bible! I think it is utter nonsense; yet I cannot refute scientific arguments that I cannot follow. Something akin to this creationist phenomenon is operative in the world of sindonology (yep, that's what Shroud scientists call their speciality). I have no expertise in the properties of blood, in carbon-14 dating, or in the superimposition of images. I think that a few of the sindonologists may be deliberately deceptive, knowingly perpetuating a fraud. They may be doing this for the "noble" motive of bringing more people to Jesus, by hook or by crook. The rest, I imagine, are innocent, deceived deceivers. I don't know. As I've said before, I may be a deceived deceiver. Maybe we all are.

1. S. Safrai, "Home and Family," *The Jewish People in the First Century*, on the website *Burial Customs in the Time of Christ*.
2. Charles Freeman, "The Shroud of Turin and the Image of Edessa: A Misguided Journey" (Internet article).
3. Richard Allen Greene, "Scientist re-creates Turin Shroud to show it's fake," CNN
4. Joe Nickell, *Relics of the Christ*, p. 145.
5. Ibid., pp. 142-143.
6. Ibid., pp. 148-149.
7. Ibid., pp. 149-150.
8. Ibid., p. 163.
9. Ibid., p. 176.
10. Ibid., p. 176.
11. Mark Guscin, "The Sudarium of Oviedo: Its History and Relationship to the Shroud of Turin" (Internet article).

12. Joe Nickell, *Relics of the Christ*, pp. 160-161.

13. Ibid., p. 161.

14. Colin Berry, from his blog "The Shroud of Turin: lightly-toasted flour imprint? The blog that separates the science from the pseudo-science."

15. "Clues to the Resurrection of Jesus: The Sudarium of Oviedo," on the Christian website *30Days*.

16. One of those arguing against Shroud authenticity is Robin Lane Fox, an atheist historian who once remarked that he believed in the Bible but not in God. In his book *The Unauthorized Version: Truth and Fiction in the Bible*, Fox includes a beautiful two-page summary of evidence against the authenticity of the Shroud of Turin. Fox mentions the radiocarbon dating, of course, but then adds this: "The remarkable fact is that 'science' was not intellectually necessary: historically, the evidence was already overwhelming that the Shroud was a late fake." For example, Fox calls attention to the contradiction between the unwashed and untended image on the Shroud and John 19:39-40, which tells that Jesus' body had been washed and annointed with spices prior to its being wrapped (pp. 250-251). An Internet article entitled "Burial customs during the time of Christ" includes this information: "The Mishnah states that the corpse is annointed and rinsed. The body was first annointed with oil to clean it and this was followed by a bath of water."

What do you think about the Shroud of Turin?

George: *Carbon-14 dating of the Shroud indicates that the material originated centuries after the time of Yeshua, yet the "miracle" persists in that the image is claimed to be that of Jesus. How could anyone know what he looked like? Certainly the men of historic Israel did not have the blond hair and northern looks assigned to many depictions of Jesus.*

Chapter XVI

Famous European Apparitions

"I think I can see many similarities between Marian apparitions and alien abductions--even though the witnesses in the former cases are not promptly taken up to Heaven and don't have their reproductive organs meddled with." - Carl Sagan, *The Demon-haunted World*

Lourdes

Lourdes is a town of approximately 18,000 inhabitants. It lies in southwestern France in the foothills of the Pyrenees mountains. Today, Lourdes has a population of some 15,000, with 270 hotels (more hotels than any other city or town in France except Paris). What accounts for these demographics? About a mile from the town, in 1858, the Virgin Mary is said to have appeared eighteen times to a 14-year-old peasant girl, Bernadette Soubirous. Word and reputation spread over the years, and a large church was built at the site of the alleged apparitions. These days, Lourdes is visited by around five million people each year. Many visitors go there to be cured.[1] Some report that they are cured. A few of the cures have been recognized by the Catholic Church as miraculous. In the early years of the shrine, the annual number of recognized miraculous cures was much higher than it is today. One website reported 57 per year before 1917, a total of 56 from 1947 to 1990, and only four since then.[2] Clearly the Church has become more circumspect when it comes to miracles. It is said that cures involving diseases that have a history of spontaneous remission are not considered for miracle status. But who knows if even the last four recognized miraculous cures are truly miraculous. I suspect that they, too, will be scientifically explainable someday as natural phenomena. My question remains: Where among the crutches that pilgrims leave behind are the prostheses?

The first of eighteen apparitions happened on February 11, 1858. Bernadette, her sister, and a friend were gathering firewood. Bernadette described the apparition as "a small young lady." Her sister and the friend saw nothing. Three days later, armed with holy water, Bernadette and her friend returned to the grotto. When Bernadette threw holy water at the vision to see if it were demonic, the lady only smiled. The lady spoke for the first time at her third appearance, telling Bernadette that she should return to the grotto every fifteen days, assuring the girl that she would be happy in the next world. The number of people present at the appearances increased steadily from three at the first three appearances to eight at the fourth, . . . to 9000 at the fifteenth. Bernadette said that at the fifth appearance the lady taught her a prayer, which she recited for the rest of her life but kept secret from others. At the sixth appearance, the apparition told Bernadette to pray for sinners and at the seventh appearance told her a secret that she never revealed to anyone. I guess the disclosure could have been too personal. The lady's words at her eighth appearance were "Penance! Penance! Penance! Pray to God for sinners. Kiss the ground as an act of penance for sinners!" Kiss the ground as an act of penance? In her ninth appearance the lady instructed Bernadette to enter the grotto, drink at the fountain, and wash herself. Bernadette entered as instructed and, by scratching at the earth, brought forth some muddy water, so muddy that she could hardly drink it. She was also told to eat grass that was growing there, although she did not know why. Reportedly, a spring flowed in that spot the next day. At her thirteenth appearance, the lady instructed Bernadette to go to the priests and tell them to come in procession and build a chapel at the grotto. The reply from the priests was that they would do nothing until they knew the identity of the apparition. Bernadette reported, after the fourteenth appearance, that when she asked the lady for her name, the lady only smiled. At the fifteenth appearance, Bernadette once again asked for the lady's name. Again the lady only smiled. At the sixteenth appearance, after four additional requests for her name, the lady said, "I am the Immaculate Conception." This is supposed to mean that the Virgin Mary was conceived without original sin. But what a strange way to express this idea. Have you ever referred to yourself as a conception? Would you ever, except in jest? After the seventeenth appearance, a local physician reported that Bernadette suffered no ill effects from a flame that should have burned her hand. After this appearance, the local officials closed the grotto to the public and even to Bernadette. As a result, the girl had to kneel outside a fence for the eighteenth appearance of the lady, who, according to Bernadette, seemed to be at the same distance as always. After this, Bernadette received no more apparitions and reportedly no longer desired to return to the grotto. She became a nun in 1866 and died at the age of 35. I'm comfortable saying that Bernadette probably thought she saw the Virgin Mary. I doubt that the latter was actually present.

Fatima

On May 13, 1917, two shepherd children, ten-year-old Lucia Santos and her younger cousin, seven-year-old Jacinta Marto, beheld a beautiful lady, in brilliant white, standing among the leaves of an oak tree. Another cousin, nine-year-old Francisco Marto, was present but saw nothing. The apparition instructed the children to return to the same site on the thirteenth day of each month. The lady instructed Lucia, the spokesperson for the small group, to have Francisco pray the rosary. He did, whereupon he could see but not hear the vision. In her July appearance, the lady revealed something which she forbade them to disclose. (The element of secrecy hearkens back to Lourdes.) On October 13, at the final appearance, the lady revealed her name (Our Lady of the Rosary), expressed a desire that a chapel be built on the site of the apparitions, and exhorted people to repent. The children also experienced undisclosed visions. Then, as the sun emerged from behind a cloud, Lucia, who had promised the people that the lady would give them a sign on that day, looked to the sky and said, "The sun!" As the 70,000 or so people present looked to the sky, many saw the sun dance, spin colorfully like a pinwheel, move through the sky, and/or fall toward the earth. Some reported that their clothes, which had become wet from a recent rainfall, dried miraculously. This incident is referred to as the Miracle of the Sun.

What is a poor skeptic to make of all this? Joe Nickell, well-known investigator of parapsychological phenomena, tells us that Lucia "was a petted and spoiled child. Her sisters fostered in her a desire to be the center of attention by teaching her to dance and sing. At festivals, Lucia would stand on a crate to entertain an adoring crowd. Among her other talents was a gift for telling stories (fairy tales, biblical narratives, and saints' legends--which made her popular with village children) as well as an ability to persuade others to do her bidding."[3] Tellingly, on two previous occasions, Lucia had claimed to have seen apparitions. According to Nickell, she had a "fantasy-prone personality." Stephen Mason maintains that "even Lucia's mother said it was all 'childish nonsense' and that her daughter was 'nothing but a fake. . . leading half the world astray'."[4] I saw several indications that Lucia could not be trusted to tell the truth. Philip Coppens writes as follows: "Questioned by canon Formigao, only six days after the October 13, 1917 apparition, she [Lucia] was asked: 'The 13th of this month, did you ask that the people would look at the sun?' Lucia: 'I don't remember having done that.' Formigao: 'Did you ask them to close their umbrellas?' Lucia: 'The last time, I cannot remember whether I asked them.' Formigao: 'Did she tell you that the people would be punished if they did not repent their sins?' Lucia: 'I do not remember whether she said that; I think not.' Formigao: 'The 13th, you did not have such doubts as you have today about what the Virgin has said. Why do you have such doubts today?' Lucia: 'That day I could remember better; it was closer to the events.' Lucia clearly had a rather short-term memory."[5] It is sometimes said that the apparition correctly predicted the premature deaths of Francisco and Jacinta; they died in the great flu epidemic of 1918. Since Lucia recorded the "prediction" in 1929, one cannot be too impressed. It is notoriously easy to predict accurately after the fact.

Lucia said that the apparition at Fatima had disclosed three secrets to the children in July in 1917. The first secret was that they had been shown a vision of hell. The second secret, written by Lucia in 1941, was that World War I would end, but that a worse war would begin in the reign of Pope Pius XI if people did not stop sinning. Pius XI died in February of 1939. By that time Germany had already annexed Austria and occupied the Sudetenland. From her vantage point of 1941, it was easy for Lucia to "predict" the beginning of World War II. The third secret, written as a letter in 1944 and sent to Rome, was finally disclosed by Cardinal Joseph Ratzinger, the future Pope Benedict XVI, in the year 2000. The visionary told of "an angel with a flaming sword in his left hand; flashing, it gave out flames that looked as though they would set the world on fire; but they died out in contact with the splendor that Our Lady radiated towards him from her right hand: pointing to the earth, the angel cried out in a loud voice: 'Penance, Penance, Penance!'"[6] She told of a "bishop dressed in white," who "prayed for the souls of the corpses he met on his way; having reached the top of the mountain, on his knees at the foot of the big Cross he was killed by a group of soldiers who fired bullets and arrows at him, and in the same way there died one after another, the other bishops, priests, men and women Religious." Some see in this vision a prediction of the attempt on the life of Pope John Paul II in 1981. In that assassination attempt, the Pope was injured (but not killed) by a single individual, not by a group of soldiers, and none of the other stuff happened at all. No arrows were fired, and no bishops, priests, etc. died. I think it is safe to say that, while Lucia and the other children might have seen a vision, the experience was entirely subjective; moreover, it seems to me, Lucia's rendition of whatever she thought she saw and heard cannot be trusted.

Medjugorje

I just watched on the Internet a video of Mirijana Dragicevic, one of the five visionaries who, beginning in 1981, are said to have witnessed apparitions of the Virgin Mary in the Bosnian town of Medjugorje. The video shows Mirijana on October 2, 2014, making her way through a crowd of hundreds of people. She smiles, greets people along the way, then arrives at her destination and kneels. During the next several minutes, we see her as she smiles in apparent ecstasy as the apparition arrives; she seems to concentrate on words she hears, moves her lips from time to time, sheds a few tears, and even frowns as if distraught now and again. Then she sits and dictates to two scribes what the vision has said to her. One of the scribes then reads the transcript to the crowd, first in Bosnian, I assume, and then in English. The other scribe then reads her transcript in what seemed to me to be Italian. While the transcript is being read in English, video viewers are able to read it superimposed on the screen. After the reading, Mirijana makes her way back through the crowd, once again greeting people along the way. As I watched the visionary during the would-be apparition, I was confident that she was sincere; however, after I had heard and read the transcript, I was doubtful, because I neither heard nor saw anything in the words that should have led Mirijana to frown or appear sad. So what is it? Does she experience something subjectively that others present do not experience, or is she faking? I just don't know. What I do seriously question is the objectivity of the apparitions at Medjugorje.

It can be quite difficult to disprove an apparition. One of the best ways, I guess, is to disprove the credibility of the visionary. Here is a story that, if true, does just that. A Frenchman, Jean Louis Martin, having read a book that convinced him of the veracity of the Medjugorje apparitions, packed up and moved to that town. After some months, however, he began to have doubts. The visionaries had begun asserting that, during the apparitions, they were aware of nothing else. To test this, a certain Dr. Joyeux had placed a sheet of cardboard before the eyes of two of the visionaries during a vision. Asked afterwards if their vision had been interrupted by the cardboard, the visionaries claimed that they had seen nothing but the vision. Jean-Louis had noticed that in Medjugorje almost everyone tried to deny the fact that, in the first months, the visionaries had heard what was said by the people present and had reacted with words of their own. Assisted by Canadian parapsychologist Louis Bélanger, a professor at the University of Montréal, Jean Louis carried out a test on the unsuspecting Vicka, one of the visionaries. During the purported vision, he brought two fingers close to her eyes to see if she would react, and she definitely did. I have seen the video, which was made by Professor Bélanger. You can see it too by going to the website "Medjugorje Without a Mask." Visionaries need to establish strong credibility. Vicka seems to have failed.

A Medjugorje inquiry commission has concluded its investigative work and passed its findings on to the Congregation for the Doctrine of the

Faith. Various Internet sites report that this congregation has found the apparitions to be false. The Catholic News Agency writes as follows: "If reports in Italian media outlets are to be believed, the Congregation for the Doctrine of the Faith met June 24 [2015] to discuss the alleged Marian apparitions in Medjugorje, reaching the conclusion that they are inauthentic, but recognizing the site as a place of prayer."[7] Reportedly, Pope Francis will make the final decision on the matter.

1. According to James Randi, Lourdes is "the most famous of 15 similar shrines that were already located in that area of France and were all visited regularly by the ailing before the Bernadette story was told." Randi examines two reported Lourdes cures recognized by the Catholic Church as miraculous and finds the evidence unimpressive, *The Faith Healers*, pp. 23-30.
2. Robert Todd Carroll, "Lourdes," on the website *Skeptic's Dictionary.*
3. Joe Nickell, "The Real Secrets of Fatima," on the website of the Committee for Skeptical Inquiry.
4. Stephen Mason, "The Miracle of Fatima: What was the Virgin Mary's secret message to the Pope?" on the website *Psychology Today.*
5. Philip Coppens, "The Lies of Fatima," on the website *Philip Coppens.*
6. On the website of Marianland.com.
7. Internet article "CDF reportedly judges Medjugorje apparitions false, but permits pilgrimage."

> *What do you think about reported apparitions of the Virgin Mary?*
>
> **Steve**: *Hopeful apparitions are common to human perception; people often see what they want to see. The apparitions at Lourdes, Fatima, and Medjugorje are examples. I remember one such example in south Texas years ago, when a woman saw Jesus' face in her screen door. Lots of people from all over the nation flocked to see for themselves. For a while it was a popular viewing site and place of prayer.*

Chapter XVII
The Image of Guadalupe

If you grew up as a Catholic in the United States, there is a good chance you have heard of Our Lady of Guadalupe and perhaps also of Juan Diego, a young Aztec man to whom the Virgin Mary allegedly appeared, filling his peasant cloak with roses picked in the middle of winter, miraculously imprinting the cloak with her image, and directing Juan to take cloak and roses to the local bishop as proof of her apparition and of her wish that a church be built on the hill on which she had appeared. If you are a skeptic like me, you ask if there is any truth to the tale of Juan Diego and any justification for the strong faith of Mexican Catholics in the miraculous nature of the image. You begin a search for evidence.

Some of the best sources of information about paranormal phenomena are books by Joe Nickell, who has been a stage magician, a private investigator, and a teacher. At least three of his books contain information about the image of Guadalupe. But let's say that you do not have any of these books at hand. For your first search, you will then access the Internet, where, to your surprise perhaps, you will find a plethora of articles in support of the supernatural origin of the image of Guadalupe and relatively few skeptical articles. It seems it is always that way: the ratio of credulous articles to skeptical articles is heavily skewed toward the former. If you are a believer, you might be overjoyed to land on the website "Matrix Drops," which has an article with the following headline: "NASA has called the image of the Virgin of Guadalupe living." Wow, NASA! They really know what they're doing, don't they? Indeed they do, but this article does not. Here are excerpts from it to give you an idea of the nonsense that is out there:

- "It was established, with instruments of the eye-specialist [unnamed], that in the picture, the eyes of Mary's retinas, when exposed to light --similar to the human eye--expand and contract. The researchers have also concluded that the temperature of the cloth, where the image can be observed, is permanently 36.6 degrees [centigrade], such as a healthy human body temperature. The image has also been examined with a stethoscope. The scientists have measured a pulse of 115 beats/min at Mary's belt which corresponds with the number of a fetal heart rate."

- "NASA engineers have also stated the paint with which the image was made does not exist on Earth and has never existed."

- "Aldofo Orozco, research physicist, reports that there is no scientific explanation for the still surviving tilma [the cloth with the image]. Over 10 years similar cloths become ruined by the local moist, salty air."[1]

At this point, if you're a believer, you're packing your bags for Guadalupe. But not so fast. It turns out that the article insists that the woman who appeared in 1531 to Juan Diego was not Jesus's mother but the Mother God of the Aztecs. The author's name is András Kovács; he has written a book entitled *The Biggest Secret: Truth*, which is about the "operation of the spiritual world, the hidden real history of Europe." About the book, we read this: "Spirit families that lived multiple lives on Earth are introduced and their deeds in the perspective of hundreds and thousands of years are recited."[2] I don't know about you, but this information alone makes me want to distrust anything Mr. Kovács writes or has written.

Let us look at the claim that NASA engineers have called the image of the Virgin of Guadalupe "living." The fact-checking organization Snopes calls this claim false. It seems that the false information about the tilma showing "characteristics startlingly like a living human body" goes back to an analysis by a biophysicist Phillip Callahan, in which Callahan supposedly used infrared technology to discover the constant 98.6 degree Fahrenheit temperature of the tilma. Of this claim, Snopes reports that, while "Callahan's original analysis is not readily available, . . . reviews of the decades-old infrared photography of the piece carried out by him did not conclude that the material was metaphysical in origin."[3] The Snopes article continues: "The claim that 'NASA scientists' had affirmed the supernatural nature of the sacred image . . . appears to have been a complete fabrication with no supporting evidence for its extraordinary claims. Research carried out by Callahan for the Center for Applied Research in the Apostolate (CARA, a religious organization) in 1979 by no means amounts to evidence in 2017 that the piece is 'living,' has a heartbeat, or maintains a temperature identical to that of the human body." If you are wondering about Snopes, it calls itself "the definitive fact-checking and Internet reference for urban legends, folklore, myths, rumors, and misinformation." Is it biased? Although Snopes.com has reportedly been cited by the conservative Fox News Channel, the agency receives more complaints of a liberal bias than of a conservative bias.[4]

Another claim of tilma believers is that the cloth is made of a common cactus fiber which, in the absence of a miracle, would purportedly have disintegrated in about a decade. This "proof" of the miraculous nature of the tilma is repeated many times on the Internet, although the claim has little evidence to support it. Catholic authorities on Guadalupe have been reluctant to allow thorough scientific investigations of the tilma; consequently, little is known for certain about the composition of the cloth. It has been reported that two scientists, who had managed to obtain two stands from the edge of the cloth, analyzed the texture of the strands and found that they were hemp, a material that lasts for centuries. Joe Nickell writes of the tilma that "nowhere is there convincing evidence of its supposedly miraculous nature, but everywhere signs of human artistry and fraud."[5] According to Nickell, "infrared photographs show that the hands have been modified, and close-up photography shows that pigment has been applied to the highlight areas of the face sufficiently heavily so as to obscure the texture of the cloth. There is also obvious cracking and flaking of paint all along a vertical seam."[6] If the tilma were, as claimed, of supernatural origin, we would not expect these negative indicators. Nickell refers to an article in the Spanish magazine Proceso that tells of a 1982 secret examination of the famous cloth by an art-restoration expert José Sol Rosales. In Nickell's words, the Spanish article reported that "Rosales examined the cloth with a stereomicroscope and observed that the canvas appeared to be a mixture of linen and hemp or cactus fiber. It had been prepared with a brush coat of white primer (calcium sulfate) [image enthusiasts report that no primer at all was used], and the image was then rendered in distemper (i.e., paint consisting of pigment, water, and a binding medium). [...] Rosales concluded that the image did not originate supernaturally but was instead the work of an artist who used the materials and methods of the sixteenth century (El Vaticano 2002)."[7]

Finally, there seems to be very good evidence that the tilma was not in existence in 1531, when the Virgin Mary is said to have appeared to Juan Diego. Juan de Zumárraga, Archbishop of Mexico, who supposedly sent Juan back to the site of his apparition in search of a miracle, and who is reported to have fallen on his knees at the sight of the roses and the image, apparently wrote nothing about Juan, the apparition, or the miraculous image--nothing at all despite the fact that he was a prolific writer. It is no wonder that skeptic Brian Dunning calls the absence of written comments by Zumárraga about these things a "red flag."[8] According to Dunning (and others), Archbishop Alonso de Montúfar, Zumárraga's successor, commissioned the Aztec artist Marcos Cipac de Aquino to paint a portrait of the Virgin Mary, as a kind of magnet to hasten the conversion of the Aztecs. This portrait, commissioned in 1555 (24 years after the "apparition"), was to become famous as the image of Guadalupe. It took up residence in a church that had been built on the very hill on which the Astecs had worshipped their mother goddess. In time, the story of Juan Diego was invented to add stature to the image and to the church. And what stature it did add! Today, Guadalupe is the most visited church in the world after St. Peter's Basilica in Rome.

1. Andras Kovács, "Matrix Drops."
2. from the website *Avalon Magic Health*.
3. "NASA Has Called the Image of the Virgin of Guadalupe 'Living'?" Snopes. com.
4. "Snopes.com," Wikipedia.
5. Joe Nickell, *Secrets of the Supernatural: Investigating the World's Occult Mysteries*, pp. 115, 116.
6. Joe Nickell, "'Miraculous' Image of Guadalupe," *Skeptical Briefs*, Vol. 12.2 June 2002.
7. Joe Nickell, *Skeptical Briefs*, Vol. 12.2, June 2002.
8. (Brian Dunning, "The Virgin of Guadalupe: Mexico's Virgin of Guadalupe played an important role in the Catholic colonization of the Americas," Skeptoid Podcast #201, April 13, 2010)

Part VI: Questioning Faith

Chapter XVIII
Perspectives on Faith

"What is wanted is not the will to believe, but the will to find out, which is the exact opposite." - Bertrand Russell, *Skeptical Essays*

"The easy confidence with which I know another man's religion is folly teaches me to suspect that my own is also." - Mark Twain, *Biography*

Truth, in the matters of religion, is simply the opinion that has survived." - Oscar Wilde, "The Critic as Artist"

Einstein's God

The intellectual interests of Albert Einstein (1879-1955) were by no means limited to physics and mathematics, but included, for example, ethics, education, pacifism, politics, philanthropy, Zionism, and--as you have probably guessed from the title of this chapter--religion. While it does not follow necessarily that a brilliant physicist has brilliant religious insights, I find Einstein's ideas about religion well worth the time it takes to read them. I hope you will, too.

Albert Einstein did not believe in a personal God. He was, at least at one point in his life, an agnostic and, at another point, a Spinozistic pantheist; that is, he believed, like the philosopher Baruch Spinoza, that God is all that exists (that the universe is part of God). Was Einstein ever an atheist? Certainly not when he was interviewed for a book that appeared in 1930. He said in the interview, "I am not an atheist. I do not know if I can define myself as a Pantheist. The problem involved is too vast for our limited minds. May I not reply with a parable? The human mind, no matter how highly trained, cannot grasp the universe. We are in the position of a little child, entering a huge library whose walls are covered to the ceiling with books in many different tongues. The child knows that someone must have written those books. It does not know who or how. It does not understand the languages in which they are written. The child notes a definite plan in the arrangement of the books, a mysterious order, which it does not comprehend, but only dimly suspects. That, it seems to me, is the attitude of the human mind, even the greatest and most cultured, toward God. We see a universe marvelously arranged, obeying certain laws, but we understand the laws only dimly. Our limited minds cannot grasp the mysterious force that sways the constellations. I am fascinated by Spinoza's Pantheism."[1] Later in life--in 1949, five and a half years before his death--Einstein still denied being an atheist: "I have repeatedly said that in my opinion the idea of a personal God is a childlike one. You may call me an agnostic, but I do not share the crusading spirit of the professional atheist whose fervor is mostly due to a painful act of liberation from the fetters of religious indoctrination received in youth. I prefer an attitude of humility corresponding to the weakness of our intellectual understanding of nature and of our own being."[2] Five years later, only months before his death, Einstein sounded more certain of his disbelief, less like an agnostic than an atheist: "The word God is for me nothing more than the expression and product of human weakness, the Bible a collection of honorable, but still primitive legends."[3]

What about Einstein's pantheism? In a letter to a Japanese scholar, the fifty-year-old Einstein wrote, "Scientific research can reduce superstition by encouraging people to think and view things in terms of cause and effect. Certain it is that a conviction, akin to religious feeling, of the rationality and intelligibility of the world lies behind all scientific work of a higher order. . . . This firm belief, a belief bound up with a deep feeling, in a superior mind that reveals itself in the world of experience, represents my conception of God. In common parlance this may be described as pantheistic (Spinoza)."[4] Around the same time, Einstein wrote, "I believe in Spinoza's God, who reveals himself in the harmony of all that exists, not in a God who concerns himself with the fate and doings of mankind."[5] You will recall perhaps that, in everyday parlance, pantheism is the doctrine that God and nature are the same thing; however, this is not Spinoza's pantheism. Spinoza's God has a mind. We can say with confidence that Einstein was a Spinozistic pantheist, at least for a while.

Consistent with Spinozistic pantheism, Einstein said in 1930, "I cannot imagine a God who rewards and punishes the objects of his creation, whose purposes are modeled after our own--a God, in short, who is but a reflection of human frailty. Neither can I believe that the individual survives the death of his body, although feeble souls harbor such thoughts through fear or ridiculous egotisms."[6] Later in life, Einstein's ideas about an afterlife had not changed. He wrote the following words in 1953 (two years before his death): "I do not believe in immortality of the individual, and I consider ethics to be an exclusively human concern with no superhuman authority behind it."[7] Also, like Spinoza, Einstein was a strict determinist; that is, he did not believe in free will.

Depending on your definition of religion, you could call Einstein a religious person or not. He himself admitted to a certain kind of religiousness: "To know that what is impenetrable to us really exists, manifesting itself as the highest wisdom and the most radiant beauty, which our dull faculties can comprehend only in the most primitive forms--this knowledge, this feeling, is at the center of true religiousness. In this sense, and in this sense only, I belong to the rank of devoutly religious men."[8] In the same article, Einstein distinguishes three human impulses which bring about religious thought: fear, social impulses, and a cosmic religious feeling. Primitive religion is based on fear. The desire for love and support produces a social and moral idea of a supreme being. All religions are a mixture of primitive and moral religion; the higher the level of social life, the greater the influence of the latter. Cosmic religious feeling, which Einstein found only in "religious geniuses," is without dogma, and its God is not anthropomorphic.

If we take Einstein at his word (and I do), he held morality in high esteem: "The most important human endeavor is the striving for morality in our actions."[9] You might be surprised to learn that Einstein also thought highly of Jesus: "No one can read the Gospels without feeling the actual presence of Jesus. His personality pulsates in every word. No myth is filled with such life."[10] But, of course, he rejected Jesus' divinity: "I seriously doubt that Jesus himself said that he was God, for he was too much a Jew to violate that great commandment: 'Hear, O Israel, the Eternal is our God and He is one!'" And he added, "Sometimes I think it would have been better if Jesus had never lived. No name was so abused for the sake of power!"[11] Nor did Einstein consider Jesus the epitome of moral perfection: "It is quite possible that we can do greater things than Jesus, for what is written in the Bible about him is poetically embellished."[12] One cannot read the following words of Einstein without thinking of Jefferson's edited Bible: "If one purges the Judaism of the Prophets and Christianity as Jesus Christ taught it of all subsequent additions, especially those of the priests, one is left with a teaching which is capable of curing all the social ills of humanity."[13]

William Kingdon Clifford: Reason's Role in Faith

William Kingdon Clifford (1845-1879) lived a short life, his death by tuberculosis the possible result of two breakdowns that may have been caused by overwork. He was a brilliant mathematician and philosopher. He was the first to suggest the geometrical underpinnings of gravitation. Albert Einstein, a contemporary, developed his geometric theory of gravitation nine years after Clifford's death. As a philosopher, Clifford was interested in and wrote about the mind and consciousness. Of principal interest to us here is his essay on faith, entitled "The Ethics of Belief," in which he argues that "it is wrong always, everywhere, and for anyone, to believe anything upon insufficient evidence."[14] According to Clifford, blind faith, i.e., belief without the support of adequate evidence, is immoral. Clifford's position on faith was opposed by the famous philosopher William James in his "Will to Believe" lecture, delivered to philosophy students of Yale and Brown Universities.[15] A Wikipedia article refers to Clifford's "The Ethics of Belief" and James's "Will to Believe" as "touchstones for the debate over evidentialism, faith, and overbelief."[16] Evidentialism is the doctrine that evidence is of prime importance in matters of faith.

Clifford begins his essay with a story: A ship owner, about to send a ship full of emigrants to sea, has doubts about the reliability of the ship, which is quite old. He manages to assuage troubling thoughts of an expensive overhaul by considering that the ship has made many successful passages already and by putting his trust in Providence that the vessel will weather any storms this time as well. When the ship sinks with great loss of life, he collects the insurance. According to Clifford, the ship owner "had no right to believe on such evidence as was before him."[17] Then Clifford asks if the owner's guilt would have been diminished if the ship had come through safely. "Not one jot," he replies. It does not matter if he happened to believe something that is true. What matters is whether or not he had a right to believe it, for "the belief held by one man was of great importance to other men."[18] Now Clifford widens the field: "We have no choice but to extend our judgment to all cases of belief whatever."[19] He excuses no one: "No simplicity of mind, no obscurity of station, can escape the universal duty of questioning all that we believe."[20] I like Clifford's subjecting of religious belief to judgment, but "questioning all that we believe"? He modulates this idea later in his essay; you'll see.

Clifford has an idea of why humans are disposed to believe easily: "It is the sense of power attached to the sense of knowledge that makes men desirous of believing, and afraid of doubting."[21] Okay, but I suspect there is more motivation than that going on. How about fear of hell for starters? In any case, Clifford asks, "What would be thought of one who, for the sake of a sweet fruit, should deliberately run the risk of bringing a plague upon his family and neighbors?" Clifford continues: "In like manner, if I let myself believe anything on insufficient evidence, there may be no harm done by the mere belief; it may be true after all, or I may never have occasion to exhibit it in outward acts. But I cannot help doing this great wrong towards Man, that I make myself credulous."[22] And what, one may ask, is the great harm in making oneself credulous?

Clifford is at hand with an explanation: "The danger to society is not merely that it should believe wrong things, though that is great enough; but that it should . . . lose the habit of testing things and inquiring into them; for then it must sink back into savagery."[23]

Many people believe as they do because, their faith having been passed down by their parents, they have never bothered to look further. Clifford judges such persons harshly: "If a man, holding a belief which he was taught in childhood or persuaded of afterwards, keeps down or pushes away any doubts which arise about it in his mind, purposely avoids the reading of books and the company of men that call in question or discuss it, and regards as impious those questions which cannot easily be asked without disturbing it--the life of that man is one long sin against mankind."[24] Ouch, I've been there. You? Surely not everyone who consciously and consistently dispels doubts commits "one long sin against humanity." Surely sin requires an awareness of the immorality of one's action. The indoctrinated are often advised to dispel doubts; it is sinful, they are told by religious leaders whom they trust, to entertain doubts about their religion. Those who buy into this proscription fall into a trap, from which extrication is not easy, but they do not sin, in my opinion.

I do think that Clifford's thinking regarding faith is solid, but I also think he applies his ideas too rigidly. If he was as demanding of himself as he appears to have been of others, I think that I understand why he had two breakdowns and died at the age of 33. On the other hand, I am very comfortable with two statements quoted by Clifford, the first from Milton, the second from Coleridge:[25]

- "A man may be a heretic in the truth; and if he believes things only because his pastor says so, or the assembly so determine, without knowing other reason, though his belief be true, yet the very truth he holds becomes a heresy."

- "He who begins by loving Christianity better than Truth, will proceed by loving his own sect or Church better than Christianity, and in the end loving himself better than all."

Among the insights of Clifford on the importance of evidence and reason in faith are the following two passages:[26]

- "Inquiry into the evidence of a doctrine is not to be made once and for all, and then taken as finally settled. It is never lawful to stifle a doubt; for either it can be honestly answered by means of the inquiry already made, or else it proves that the inquiry was not complete."

- "'But,' says one, 'I am a busy man; I have not time for the long course of study which would be necessary to make me in any degree a competent judge of certain questions, or even able to understand the nature of the arguments.' Then he should have no time to believe." If humans came even close to implementing Clifford's precept, church attendance would plummet. I wonder how many pastors would have to excuse themselves.

Clifford begins the second section of his essay with this question: "Are we then to become universal skeptics, afraid always to put one foot before the other?" Confident this will not happen, he offers this explanation: "The beliefs about right and wrong which guide our actions with men in society, and the beliefs about physical nature which guide our actions in dealing with animate and inanimate bodies, these never suffer from investigation; they can take care of themselves without being propped up by 'acts of faith,' the clamour of paid advocates, or the suppression of contrary evidence."[27] And he notes, in addition, that "there are many cases in which it is our duty to act upon probabilities, although the evidence is not such as to justify present belief."[28]

Next, Clifford asks in what cases human testimony is worthy of belief. His answer is that we must have solid grounds for trusting the veracity, the knowledge, and the judgment of our source. As obvious as these guidelines may be, says Clifford, many people disregard them. They will cite the apparent excellent moral character of their source and disregard the fact that this person's statement is about something that he or she cannot possibly have knowledge of. Mohammed, for example, may have been of high moral character, who spoke the truth as far as he knew it, but where is the evidence that he knew the truth? Also, the longevity of a belief is insufficient reason for accepting it. The belief may have been "founded on fraud" and "propagated by credulity."[29] The fact that Christianity has been around for two thousand years does not argue convincingly for its acceptance. On the other hand, traditional human experiences provide a solid basis for our thoughts and actions. According to Clifford, these experiences give us "conceptions of right" such as justice and beneficence.[30] Clifford argues that these conceptions are instincts, not propositions. Still, he adds, it is our duty to verify any statements that emerge from our observation of the interaction of these instincts.

Finally, Clifford gives this general rule regarding belief in such things as reported historical events and alleged paranormal experiences: "No evidence . . . can justify us in believing the truth of a statement which is contrary to, or outside of, the uniformity of nature." The author continues, "If an event really happened which was not a part of the uniformity of nature, it would have two properties: no evidence could give the right to believe it to any except those whose actual experience it was; and no inference worthy of belief could be founded upon it at all."[31] If I apply that rule to the resurrection of Jesus (to take the central Christian miracle) I must say that, even if Peter saw the risen Jesus, I have no right to believe it. And although Peter may infer from what he witnessed that Jesus is divine, this inference is not worthy of my belief. Can I get an Amen?

In an article in the magazine *Free Inquiry*, Frederik Kaufman writes as follows: "Immanuel Kant based his moral system in the dignity of persons, understood as rational autonomous agents. To flout the standards for proper belief formation is, for Kant, to reject what is most valuable in us and is, therefore, a denial of our dignity; it is to sink to a form of life incompatible with the respect that we owe ourselves in virtue of our essential nature as persons. To the extent that we believe on the basis of self-deception, wishful thinking, insufficient evidence, peer pressure, habituation, upbringing, familiarity, mere assertion, dubious authority, naïvité, or simple unquestioning faith, we fail to respect ourselves as persons. Sincerity of belief and depth of conviction are beside the point."[32] In the debate between James and Clifford, Kaufman sides with Clifford's bold assertion ("it is wrong always, everywhere, and for anyone, to believe anything upon insufficient evidence"). If "suitably qualified," Kaufman says, the assertion is correct. He explains: "Not all failures to believe [to ground one's belief] on sufficient evidence are equally wrong."[33] He contrasts believing that it will not rain today with believing that global warming is no threat to humanity. As for James, Kaufman takes issue with his permission to believe whatever your intellect does not rule out.[34] So do I.

* * * * *

Although William James wrote "The Will to Believe" over a hundred years ago, his idea about the effectiveness of man's passional (James' word) nature, i.e., instincts and emotions, in determining how humans make choices seems to find confirmation in avant-garde twenty-first century psychology, where research tends to show that every choice is made at a subconscious level, and that our conscious reasoning merely serves to confirm what the subconscious has already decided.[35] Even if this is true, we must, in my opinion, continue to hone our reasoning powers in the hope that our conscious conclusions will find their way into our subconscious, where choices are made. If we maintain that the faith of a person whose life is morally empty and whose faith is based on little or no evidence is as valid as the faith of someone who is morally upstanding and who has amassed a broad range of evidence, we have reached a condition where truth, having become relative, is nonexistent. But faith works because it makes people feel good, James seems to say. Consider then an unexamined, feel-good faith that brings parents to scare their children with threats of hell? If this kind of faith is acceptable in religion, why should it not be equally acceptable in politics, where uninformed votes are weighted as heavily as the votes of knowledgeable citizens? Surely the pragmatist, in deciding whether faith works or not, has to look beyond the personal comfort of individual believers. No man is an island.

Jerry A. Coyne: Fact vs. Faith

"Science does not need . . . to organize crusades to kill off heretics and unbelievers." - Morris Cohen, "The Dark Side of Religion," *The Faith of a Liberal*

* * * * *

Is there an inherent conflict between science and religion? Many scientists answer that question affirmatively. Science arrives at conclusions that are testable, thus verifiable or refutable by others. Faith uses insufficient evidence and a "leap" to arrive at its claims, many of which, being totally supernatural, cannot be tested, cannot be proved or disproved. (Actually, one element of religion can be and has been tested: intercessory prayer. When tests have shown no correlation between prayer and a desired outcome, believers counter that God cannot be tested. What would they say if tests confirmed the efficacy of prayer? Of course, they would not only accept the tests, but they would also broadcast the results around the globe.) What do scientists do when solid evidence does not support a particular scientific claim? They reject that claim and seek a correct one based on evidence. What do believers do when solid evidence does not support their religion? Some reject the religion, but most assume that the evidence is wrong. University of Chicago evolutionist Jerry A. Coyne challenges one and all to give him "a single verified fact about reality that came from scripture or revelation alone and then was confirmed only later by science or empirical observation."[36]

What if the natural world were assigned to science and the realm of the supernatural to religion? Science would offer facts, religion would offer faith, and the two areas would exist happily side by side. What is wrong with that? Well, plenty. Try as it might, religion cannot remain totally in the realm of the supernatural. Take abortion, homosexuality, evolution, and euthanasia, all of which religion allots to its own moral judgment. Why? Because religion considers itself the proper arbiter of moral right and wrong in the world. Can it prove it has this right? Of course not; religion cannot prove its own authority. Its standards of morality are based on faith. And faith has, in the past, led the Catholic Church, for example, to refuse an abortion to a woman who would die along with her fetus if the life of the fetus were not terminated. The same Catholic Church, declaring that the principal reason for sex is propagation, rejects artificial birth control as unnatural. Many Christian churches refuse to sanction gay marriage, in part because of an obscure Old Testament proscription of homosexuality; of course, the same churches ride merrily over a plethora of other proscriptions from the same testament. (In the interest of full disclosure, it must be stated that several epistles of the New Testament seem to proscribe homosexuality, although this interpretation is disputed by some.) When religious people arrive at certainty from insufficient evidence, bad things can happen. Coyne quotes the physicist Steven Weinberg, who says, "With or without religion, good people can behave well and bad people can do evil; but for good people to do evil--that takes religion."[37] While this is overstated, it is true that religion can lead good people to do bad things; of course, fanatical political groups can do this as well.

Science works. Scientists have designed product after product that can be seen to work while religion has nothing to show for itself. In the words of Coyne, "Understanding reality, in the sense of being able to use what we know to predict what we don't, is best achieved using the tools of science, and is never achieved using the methods of faith. This is attested by the acknowledged success of science in telling us about everything from the smallest bits of matter to the origin of the universe itself--compared with the abject failure of religion to tell us anything about gods, including whether they exist. While scientific investigations converge on solutions, religious investigations diverge, producing innumerable sects with conflicting and irresolvable claims. Using the predictions of science, we can now land space probes not only on distant planets, but also on distant comets. We can produce 'designer drugs' to target a specific individual's cancer, decide which flu vaccines are most likely to be effective in the coming season, and figure out how finally to wipe out scourges like smallpox and polio from our planet. Religion, in contrast, cannot even tell us if there's an afterlife, much less anything about its nature."[38] Even people who reject science when it contradicts their religion affirm it silently every time they fly on a plane, trust an MRI scan, turn on their TV set, access the Internet, and rely on the GPS in their car.

There is only one science, and it is universal--not American, Chinese, South African, Indonesian, Argentine, or Lebanese. Science is the same everywhere in the world; on the other hand, there are hundreds if not thousands of different religions. When scientists attend international conferences, they find complete agreement on the fundamentals of science among the attendees because the truths of science are based on evidence. How many religious doctrines would find full endorsement at an international conference of religions? None. Those attending such a conference would not even be able to agree on the existence of God because the "truths" of religion are not based on evidence. Here is what Coyne says about his personal experience with scientists from around the world: "When I visit Turkey, Russia, Austria, or India, I can discuss my work with my colleagues without any cultural awkwardness or misunderstandings. Although scientists come in all faiths, including no faith at all, there is no Hindu science, no Muslim science, no Jewish science. There is only science, combining brainpower from the whole world to produce one accepted body of knowledge."[39]

Credulousness (the willingness to believe on insufficient evidence) is not a virtue. According to Coyne, the glorification of faith is a danger to science because it "warps the public understanding of science . . . by claiming that revelation or the guidance of ancient books is just as reliable a guide to truth about our universe as are the tools of science."[40] But it gets worse. In extreme cases, credulousness can lead the unsuspecting to membership in churches like the People's Temple of Jim Jones, the Branch Davidians of David Koresch, and the Church of Scientology of L. Ron Hubbard. Even Christian Science and Jehovah's Witnesses, which are probably considered more mainstream than the aforementioned trio, promote beliefs that all too often have had fatal consequences. Christian Scientists believe that disease is an illusion caused by faulty thinking. This leads some parents to treat their seriously ill children with prayer alone, and the results are devastating. Jehovah's Witnesses refuse blood transfusions. Children who die without a life-saving transfusion are "celebrated by Jehovah's Witnesses as martyrs."[41] Coyne references the May 1994 edition of *Awake!* magazine which includes pictures of twenty-five child martyrs who, according to the magazine, "put God first."[42] Many Americans think that calling someone a "person of faith" is a compliment. This needs to stop, cautions Coyne.

As science has disproved one scriptural claim about the world after another, religion has transformed its "literal truths" into metaphors; however, religion is incapable of disproving the accepted facts of science (if it could, it would be using science). Many modern Christians are willing to relegate the stories of Adam and Eve, of Noah's Ark, and even of the Israelites' migration through the desert--stories long thought to be literally true--to the realm of metaphor. Even some of the events associated with Jesus' birth seem like fair game. But who can say that the Incarnation and the Resurrection are not likewise metaphorical? What is metaphor in the Bible and what is reality? Historical criticism of the Bible points out that myth crept into the stories that people began to tell about Jesus, into stories that were in time written down by the evangelists. Nevertheless, believers continue to believe the "truths" that their churches impart to them. Coyne explains this phenomenon as follows: "You [the believer] start with what you were taught to believe, or what you want to believe, and then accept only those facts that support your prejudices."[43] This manner of thinking is called confirmation bias.

A high percentage of American scientists are atheists. According to Coyne, Pew Research has found that only 33 percent of American scientists polled reported that they believed in God, while 41 percent said they were atheists. This contrasts with the prevalence of belief in God among the general public: 83 percent reported belief in God, while only four percent said they were atheists. According to this poll, scientists are ten times more likely to be atheists than is the American public. Among scientists employed by elite universities, 62 percent say they are atheist or agnostic. The percent goes up to 93 percent for scientists who are members of the American Academy of Sciences.[44]

According to Coyne, "the deadliest blow ever struck by science against faith was Darwin's publication of On the Origin of Species."[45] Coyne calls the attitude of religion toward evolution the clearest example of its resistance to science, and he thinks he knows why this resistance exists: "While not the only scientific theory that contradicts scripture, evolution has implications, involving materialism, human exceptionalism, and morality, that are distressing to many believers." And yet, according to Coyne, evolution "is supported by mountains of scientific data--at least as many data as support the uncontroversial 'germ theory' that infectious diseases are caused by microorganisms."[46] Not surprisingly, rejection of evolution is higher in countries that are more religious. A 2014 Gallup Poll showed that 42 percent of Americans were creationists, who maintain that the earth was created in the last ten thousand years.[47] Here is how Robert Green Ingersoll appraises Charles Darwin's contribution to mankind: "This [19th] century will be called Darwin's century. He was one of the greatest men who ever touched this globe. He has explained more of the phenomena of life than all of the religious teachers. Write the name of Charles Darwin on the one hand and the name of every theologian who ever lived on the other, and from that name has come more light to the world than from all of those. His doctrine of evolution, his doctrine of the survival of the fittest, his doctrine of the origin of species, has removed in every thinking mind the last vestige of orthodox Christianity. He has not only stated, but he has demonstrated, that the inspired writer knew nothing of this world, nothing of the origin of man, nothing of geology, nothing of astronomy, nothing of nature; that the Bible is a book written by ignorance--at the instigation of fear."[48]

Karen Armstrong: The Uncertainty of Faith

Karen Armstrong (b. 1944), author of many books about religion, defines religion not as a system of beliefs but as a way of life. She considers stories about the Buddha, Mohammed, and Jesus, for example, to be myths that, although not historically reliable, "tell us something valuable about the human predicament."[49] Because biblical stories are myths, the Bible "gives us no single orthodox message and demands constant reinterpretation."[50] For Armstrong, the facts of religion are symbols. In her book *The Case for God*, Armstrong maintains that, until around three hundred years ago, "Jews, Christians, and Muslims all knew that revealed truth was symbolic, that scripture could not be interpreted literally, and that sacred texts had multiple meanings."[51] The Church Father Origen referred to the words and stories of the Bible as "images of divine things" [Origen, *On First Principles*],"[52] but modern Christians, especially fundamentalists, have forgotten this. I must say that I find this assertion of Armstrong a trifle perplexing. Although she cites important mystics and theologians in support of a tradition of the symbolic interpretation of the Bible, there seems to be an implied contradiction of this symbolic interpretation in the pronouncements of church councils. When, for example, the Council of Rome in 382 excommunicates those who are unwilling to proclaim that the Holy Spirit is not "of one power and one substance with the Father and the Son," surely it does not consider the Trinity to be a mere symbol. When the Council of Ephesus in 341 places an anathema on all who refuse to confess that Jesus, "having suffered in the flesh and having been crucified in the flesh, tasted death in the flesh," there is no question that the crucifixion of Jesus is understood as more than a symbol. And when the First Lateran Council in 649 condemns all who do not confess that the Word of God descended from heaven, became incarnate by the Holy Spirit and the Virgin Mary, was crucified and buried, rose on the third day and ascended into heaven, and will come again in glory to judge the living and the dead, it could hardly be clearer that the council is not referencing symbols.

Armstrong argues that, for most of the history of Christianity, "faith" meant "trust"; however, with the movement away from myth towards a literal interpretation of Scripture, the meaning of the word "faith" changed to "intellectual assent." Again, I would argue that the words of scores of anathemas require assent by the faithful, not trust. In any case, for Armstrong, the original meaning is the correct one. In her opinion, Christians are not asked to assent intellectually to the dogmas of the divinity of Jesus, the Incarnation, the Redemption, the Resurrection, among others; instead, they should simply trust Jesus. But what, I wonder, does this mean? Armstrong, who is sometimes short on specifics, would surely say that Jesus, a myth, is the symbol of an exemplary way of life, the symbol of a higher way of thinking about God. And as a model of morality, Jesus does have much to teach us. Still, he did, according to the Bible, tell people not to judge, while he himself judged the Pharisees harshly; he did senselessly curse a fig tree and drive a herd of swine over a cliff; and he did make a promise that he did not or could not keep when he said he would return from heaven within the lifetime of some of his contemporaries. Are Christians to act similarly? And if Christians accept the symbolic God of Jesus, they accept the image of a God who slaughtered entire towns in the Old Testament and who in the New Testament puts humans in hell for eternity. Is this an edifying symbol? In general I get it, though: the best way to search for a transcendent God is to "engage with a symbol imaginatively, become ritually and ethically involved with it, and allow it to effect a profound change."[53] The Buddha taught that compassion is indispensable for a release from suffering. For Armstrong, it is indispensable for the opening of one's mind to the transcendent God. She would add that meditation is important, too.

"Transcendence" is the key word for Armstrong in forming an idea of God. Her God is utterly different--so different from anyone or anything known to humans that the only way people can know his attributes (Armstrong does use the pronouns "he" and "his" for God) is by means of analogy. One can say that God is good, for example, or merciful, or just, or perfect, but these adjectives merely hint at God's attributes. The best description of God, according to Armstrong, is apophatic; such a description says what God is not. Thus, God is not good, God is not just, God is not merciful, and God is not perfect. In fact, even if one believes in God, one must say that God does not exist. Humans exist, cars exist, trees exist, but God is altogether different; whatever else God might do, he does not exist. In fact, it has been said, without denying the reality of God, that God is nothing. In Armstrong's words, "it is inaccurate to call God the Supreme Being because God is not a being at all."[54] This does not demean God; it elevates him. When he is so defined, I find it easier to accept him--still, though, I remain uncertain. And so does Armstrong. So important is uncertainty to her that she devotes an entire chapter, entitled "Unknowing," to it. I wholeheartedly agree with her that, when it comes to religion, we humans have to be willing to eschew certainly, to admit that we don't really know. If you want to read a book about religion that makes you think while providing an overview of religious thought through the centuries, I recommend Karen Armstrong's *The Case for God.*

Paul Tillich: Faith as Ultimate Concern

Paul Tillich (1886-1965), highly acclaimed avant-garde Christian theologian, moved in 1933 from his native Germany to the United States, where he held, sequentially, professorships at Union Theological Seminary, Harvard University, and the University of Chicago. When I read Tillich's book *Dynamics of Faith*, I was especially interested in his thoughts about faith, God, and Jesus.

Tillich defines faith as "the state of being ultimately concerned."[55] It is "the total and centered act of the personal self, the act of unconditional, infinite and ultimate concern."[56] Faith, according to Tillich, is "certain in so far as it is an experience of the holy," but "uncertain in so far as the infinite to which it is related is received by a finite being."[57] Tillich goes on to say that faith is not, as it has been traditionally in the Catholic Church, an act of the will that makes up for a lack of evidence, an act made possible only by grace. He claims that Protestants understand faith in two different ways depending on how the phrase "obedience of faith" is interpreted: (1) as "the commitment which is implied in the state of ultimate concern,"[58] and (2) as an arbitrary act of faith. Only with the former is Tillich in agreement. "Our oscillating will," he writes, cannot produce the certainty which belongs to faith."[59] Tillich likewise denies the interpretation of faith as mere feeling or emotion; in his words, "faith claims the whole man."[60]

According to Tillich, "man's ultimate concern must be expressed symbolically."[61] The most important symbol is God. How can God be a symbol? For Tillich as for Karen Armstrong, God is utterly beyond our ability to understand. The only way, therefore, to approach God is through the symbolism of God as he is traditionally seen. This traditional God is a myth, "the basic symbol of faith."[62] His divine attributes (love, justice, etc.) are symbols as well. God's manifestations of himself in the world, be they persons, places, events, or documents, are also symbols. For Tilllich, "Jesus as the Christ" is the central symbol of Christianity, just as Mohammed is the central symbol of Islam. Tillich believes that Jesus, "a transcendent, divine being" who "appears in the fullness of time, lives, dies, and is resurrected" is an historical myth,[63] the central symbol of Christianity. "Nothing less than symbols and myths," asserts Tillich, "can express our ultimate concern."[64]

This does not mean that Tillich did not believe in the historical existence of Jesus, for he did. He writes: "Faith includes certitude about its own foundation--for example, an event in history which has transformed history--for the faithful. But faith does not include historical knowledge about the way in which this event took place."[65] It seems the only thing that would invalidate Tillich's faith would be incontrovertible proof that Jesus never existed. In my opinion, Tillich defines into existence his own religious safety net. Consider the final sentences of the book: "If faith is understood as what it centrally is, ultimate concern, it cannot be undercut by modern science or any kind of philosophy. And it cannot be discredited by its superstitions or authoritarian distortions within and outside churches, sects and movements. *Faith stands upon itself and justifies itself against those who would attack it* [italics mine], because they can attack it only in the name of another faith. It is the triumph of the dynamics of faith that a denial of faith is itself an expression of faith, of an ultimate concern."[66] Chief among the "other faiths" that Tillich has in mind must be evidence-based ideas. I maintain that reason has a demonstrably better track record than faith in arriving at truth.

Parable of the Three Rings

The 18th-century German dramatist Gotthold Ephraim Lessing wrote a play entitled *Nathan der Weise* (*Nathan the Wise*), in which Nathan, a wealthy Jew, in order to avoid having to hand over his fortune to the sultan Saladin, must answer a clever question: Which religion is the true religion: the religion of the Jews, the religion of the Christians, or the religion of the Muslims? (Act III, Scene 7) The wise Nathan, who knows that this is a trick question, answers with a parable. Once there was a precious ring that had the power to make whoever wore it beloved of God and men. The ring had been passed down for generations from father to most-loved son. Finally, however, it came to a father with three sons, all of whom he loved equally and to each of whom he promised the ring. Not knowing what to do, the father took the ring to a skilled craftsman and had two rings made that were identical to the genuine one. That done, the father called each son separately to himself, and after giving each son a ring, the father died. When it became known that the sons had identical rings, the case was brought to court. Since the sons could not agree among themselves which of them the other two loved most (are we surprised that each took himself to be the most loved?), the judge, a wise man, refused to decide the case. It was possible, he opined, that the original ring had been lost and that all three rings were fake. He referred the three brothers to a much wiser judge who one day would have the answer for them. In the meantime, each son should believe in the power of his ring and lead a life becoming a bearer of the true ring. Recognizing the wisdom of Nathan's answer, Saladin embraced Nathan and begged his forgiveness. Although I disagree with the judge's advice that each son believe in the power of his ring (insufficient evidence, I say), the story resonates with me because of its insistence that uncertainty is an essential component of faith.

My Thoughts about Faith

In my ninth year as a Catholic seminarian, I took a vow of celibacy before being ordained a subdeacon. Two days later I declined ordination to the deaconate, and about two years later I was granted a dispensation from my vow. Although I could not say it then, I know now that I would have married eventually even without a dispensation. As I write, I am 82 years old. I was married for 41 years to a more-than-wonderful woman from a small town in Minnesota, who died in 2006. I have three loving and lovable children and seven charming grandchildren. My life has been full and fulfilling, though not without problems, some of which involved faith. During the first years of my marriage, I gradually stopped believing in Christianity. I can no longer enumerate the reasons for my apostasy. I do remember that I wanted more moral freedom than the Catholic Church allowed. After the birth of our third child in three years, my wife and I began using artificial birth control, which the Vatican clearly proscribed. Eventually, I began reading book after book about God and Christianity. I revisited the question that never was answered to my satisfaction in the seminary: How can we know that the Bible is a reliable source of information? It seems that most Christians today simply assume, as I did many years ago, the accuracy or historical reliability of the Bible. All too often, I am afraid, people base their belief in God on what is said in the Bible--end of story. "Yes, Jesus loves me, for the Bible tells me so." To be sure, faith is a funny thing. Some people, for no reason that they can articulate, are absolutely certain of the most improbable things; others base their certainty on the assurances of someone they trust, ignoring the possibility that their source, albeit sincere, may be a deceived deceiver. And then there are those whom I most closely resemble these days, who require a high degree of probability before they leave the boat and try to walk on water.

When I was a child at St. Benedict's Elementary School in Evansville, Indiana, every day began with the nuns shepherding the pupils to church to attend Mass, and once a month we were all escorted over to the church to confess our sins to a priest. I now realize that we children were being indoctrinated, not by culpable individuals who knew that they did not know what they were teaching us, but by indoctrinated indoctrinators. The nuns and the priests had themselves all sat in classrooms as children and listened to "absolutely true" words by persons whose authority they had not known to question. As a kid I was terribly credulous. Until I was out of high school, I could not imagine a priest making a mistake when he spoke about religion. The Catholic Church was the true church. I knew that. My future wife was quite the opposite. Although she had a very religious mother, she somehow realized that the party line was not necessarily right. The nuns who taught her in elementary school used to say that Protestants could not go to heaven. Even as a child, my wife had the good sense to reject this kind of teaching. She had Protestant friends, and she was convinced that they had as much chance of being saved as anyone else. Of all the catechism answers that the nuns had us memorize, I can remember only the answer to the question "Why am I here?": "To love, honor, and serve God and be happy with Him forever in heaven." If any of us children had asked, "How do we know this?" the good sister (once she had recovered from the shock of such brazenness) would probably have said, "Because the Church tells us it is so." A Protestant instructor, asked the same question, would probably have said, "Because it is in the Bible." And what kid would have thought to ask how one knows that the Church is right or that the Bible is right?

My first year at St. Meinrad Seminary was called Fourth Special; it was a kind of hiatus during which I and others who had entered the seminary after high school were allowed to catch up in Latin with those who had entered as high-school freshmen. My principal college courses were philosophy, Latin, Greek, French, and public speaking. There was little choice; with few exceptions, everyone took the same courses. But there were no courses on the Bible. Unless we seminarians made a point of reading the Bible on our own, our sources of biblical knowledge were pretty much limited to the liturgy, sermons, and outside reading. I was altogether unaware of the numerous errors, contradictions, and inconsistencies in the Bible. When I did finally read the entire New Testament on my own during my seminary years in Innsbruck, Austria, I discovered the troubling passages about Jesus' announcement that the end of the world was imminent. How could Jesus be divine if he got it wrong? How could the Bible be divinely inspired if it was factually inaccurate? In the meantime, I have learned that the Bible's eschatological passages are just the tip of a huge iceberg of biblical errors. Many books and articles provide insight, but the total number of books on "the other side of the story" pales in comparison with the vast, seemingly endless, literature of orthodoxy. Why is this? It seems to me that most believers want to read material that reinforces their beliefs. They do not want to hear arguments for the other side. This is true apparently not only in religion but also in politics.

I suspect that many Christians, without a serious examination of evidence, go to church because they need to feel they belong to something that purports to offer a pathway to paradise. They need to believe that they are saved. And Christian intellectuals? Why do some well-informed believers (many priests and ministers as well as a large number of lay intellectuals) continue to believe in Christianity despite an awareness of gross biblical errancy? Some simply place feeling above intellect, intuition-based faith above reason. They feel God speaking to them, so it matters not at all that they have insufficient evidence for what they believe; for them, feeling is evidence. If this is the right approach to religion, then do not Jews, Muslims, Hindus, and Buddhists (to name adherents of only a few of the world's religions) have the same right as Christians to base their faith on feeling? Are all religions equally valid? The faith of many Christians, some of them brilliant people, does not depend on evidence, which they use only to try to bolster their faith. I require also of those who reject Christianity a dependence on evidence. It is simply too easy for emotion to commandeer the ship of reason without the ship's captain, the conscious mind, having any awareness of the takeover. We humans must examine the evidence; surely that is our best hope of arriving at truth.

Have you ever wondered why people continue to believe when they realize that people whom they admire disagree with them? As Linda Zagzebski points out, a conflict arises in believers between self-trust and admiration. Here is the problem as she sees it: "What really bothers us [Zagzebski has in mind believers of all kinds, not just religious believers], I think, is that we recognize admirable people among those who believe differently than we do about certain things and we observe that the beliefs of certain exemplars conflict with each other."[67] In other words, believers are deeply troubled by disagreement among people whom they admire and by disagreement between people they admire and themselves.[68] Do I (let us say I am a lifelong Christian who has given little thought to reasons for believing) have a right to remain a

Christian even though I know several admirable, knowledgeable Muslims? How could I know that I am right and they are wrong? Would I not have an obligation to investigate? Let us say that I do investigate but cannot resolve the disagreement. Can I conscientiously continue to practice my religion as before? And here is one more thought (this one borrowed from Zagzebski): "Respect for others comes from trusting that we are right in the admiration we have for many people who have very different beliefs, and that logically requires us to think of them as like the self I could have been if I had been raised in a different way."[69] Of course, we cannot imitate everyone we admire. What I personally conclude regarding religious faith (or lack of faith) is this: Since innumerable admirable people hold countless conflicting beliefs, agnostic skepticism is the most logical position. This means for me a deep distrust of all religions but without final certitude. I may have strong feelings about religion, but in the end I find myself saying "I do not know." And I do not understand how others can say, after thoughtful study, that they do know.

An intriguing quotation from an 18th-century novel *The Nun* goes like this: "Believe or you will be damned . . . is the strongest argument in theology."[70] Is this true? Do Christians, or do some Christians, shut out the use of reason for fear it will contradict Christian dogma and lead them to hell? Are they even encouraged to do so by clerics and others who elevate faith above reason? The following scene from the above-mentioned novel is narrated by a nun who has been forced into the religious life: "Bewildered in an immense forest during the night, and having only one small torch for my guide, a stranger approaches and thus addresses me: Friend, blow out thy light, if thou wouldst make sure of the right path. This stranger was a priest."[71] The point is that religious faith, unlike the faith of the priest in the forest, ought to be evidence-driven. But in real life, not all decisions to believe are guided by evidence. Some believers do not care a smidgen about evidence. God has given them the grace to believe, they say, and so they believe, period. If God has not given you the same grace (or, it is asserted, if you are not open to God's grace), that is too bad for you. And consider this possibility: even those who accept the notion of evidence-driven faith, may be seeking, or seriously considering, only those reasons that support their desire to believe. And honesty compels me to add one more possibility: I too may be doing much the same thing. I may be seeking only the reasons that support my desire not to believe; if so, for them as for me, this process is, let us hope, playing itself out in the subconscious outside of conscious control. The most we can do is try to approach faith honestly.

At some point in my Catholic upbringing, I was taught to pray "Lord, I believe; help thou my unbelief." The prayer is basically a line from the New Testament, from the Gospel of Mark. The father of a boy who had been possessed by a demon since birth asks Jesus to heal his son. Jesus replies, "If thou canst believe, all things are possible to him who believes." The father cries out, "I do believe; help my unbelief" (Mark 9:22-23). (By the way, wouldn't Jesus, to be logical, have omitted the if-clause from his reply? He would have if he had known all things because the if-clause is meaningless. The conclusion, a divine Jesus would be the first to say, applies without the if-clause as well.) My point is this: While faith is sometimes admirable, it can also sometimes be shameful. If committed partners have lived together for many years, each might have every reason to believe the other if he or she were accused of a crime. But if someone, without examining the evidence carefully, "believes in his heart" that Jesus is his personal lord and savior, that seems to be unwise, or worse; likewise, if someone else, again without a careful examination of the evidence, "believes in her heart" in Allah and in the Koran, is that commendable? "How does that harm anyone?" someone might ask. It is harmful, for example, if people, blindly accepting the tenets of their respective religions, frighten their children with images of a horrible afterlife. It is harmful when believers vote according to their unexamined beliefs. And it is immensely harmful when believers rationalize their hatred of people who believe differently or not at all. My ultimate concern in this matter is whether anyone can justify a religious belief. If Christians, for example, look closely at the Bible and at the history of Christianity, how can they believe and remain true to their rational selves? The same question applies to Muslims when they read the Koran with a truth-seeker's eye and, for that matter, to Mormons (whom not everyone considers to be Christian) when they become familiar with the life of their founder, Joseph Smith. Still, there seem to be many knowledgeable Christians, Muslims, and Mormons who are good people. Is religious faith ever justifiable? Maybe it is for some people, but it would not be for me.

John W. Loftus challenges all Christians to take "the outsider test for faith,"[72] that is, to examine the extraordinary claims of Christianity such as the Incarnation, the Trinity, and the Resurrection with the same skepticism with which they examine the extraordinary claims of other religions. The challenge can be broadened to include all believers. If believers want to take the challenge, they need to find and examine serious arguments in favor of another religion (this kind of information exists in abundance on the Internet). Loftus thinks the believers will easily find reasons to reject these arguments. The next step for those taking the challenge is to imagine they are members of another reli-

gion or of no religion at all (à la John Lennon, perhaps, who asked us
to imagine there's no heaven--remember?). In their imagined role as
outsiders, they should think of reasons for believing in the religion that
they profess. Will they, as outsiders, find the reasons as convincing as
they do when they are on the inside? Loftus thinks not. Me? When I
take the test, I find some Christian evidence intriguing but not compelling, some anti-Christian evidence weak but not disqualifying. But when
I weigh all the evidence, I come down solidly on the side of unbelief.

We need at least to consider the positive perspective on faith presented
by Robert M. Burton, M.D., who, acknowledging that he does not wish
to provide ammunition to fundamentalists, nevertheless draws attention to "mystical moments" undergone by some, the common thread of
which he describes as "an inexplicable feeling of knowing what life is
about without the awareness of any preceding or triggering thought."[73]
Burton likens this felt sense of purpose to the sense of purpose that
most people feel most of the time, which he contrasts with the empty
feeling that we have when this feeling of purpose eludes us. The point
seems to be that all humans enjoy a feeling of knowledge that is not
within conscious control and that religious faith is precisely this kind of
feeling. Of course, such knowledge is fraught with uncertainty. After all,
while a feeling of knowledge tells Christians that Christianity is the true
religion, and a feeling of knowledge tells Muslims that Islam is the true
religion, the feelings of both sides cannot be accurate. Of course, Burton
knows that religious faith is uncertain, but, because he is seeking a kind
of rapprochement between religion and science, he wishes to show that
even the most revered scientific facts are uncertain as well. Not to be
forgotten, however, is the fact that uncertainty attendant on faith and
uncertainty attendant on science differ greatly in degree. Whereas disagreement among various religious leaders on basic religious concepts
(for example, the creation of the world, the divinity of Jesus, even the
existence of God) is widespread, one is hard pressed to find renowned
scientists who question basic scientific theories (for example, gravity,
evolution, and relativity).

1. Albert Einstein, in G. S. Viereck's *Glimpses of the Great*, p. 372-373.
2. Albert Einstein, in a letter of Sept. 28, 1949, to Guy H. Raner Jr., from article
by Michael R. Gilmore in *Skeptic* magazine, Vol. 5, No. 2, 1997.
3. Albert Einstein, in a letter of January 3, 1954, to the philosopher Erik Gutkind.
4. Albert Einstein, "On Scientific Truth," *Ideas and Opinions*, p. 262.
5. Albert Einstein, in a cable to Rabbi Herbert S. Goldstein, April 24, 1929.
6. Albert Einstein, column for *The New York Times*, Nov. 9, 1930.
7. Albert Einstein, in Helen Dukas's *Albert Einstein: The Human Side*, p. 39.
8. Albert Einstein, in an article in *The New York Times* of November 9, 1930,
9. Albert Einstein, "Letter to a Brooklyn minister," Nov. 20, 1950, in Helen

Dukas's *Albert Einstein, The Human Side*, p. 95.

10. Albert Einstein, from "What Life Means to Einstein: An Interview by George Sylvester Viereck," in *The Saturday Evening Post*, Oct. 26, 1929.

11. Albert Einstein, from William Hermanns' *Einstein and the Poet: In Search of the Cosmic Man*, p. 62.

12. Albert Einstein, from William Hermanns' "A Talk with Einstein," Oct. 1943, *Einstein Archive* 55-285.

13. Einstein's *Mein Weltbild*, 1934, published in *Ideas and Opinions*, pp. 184-185.

14. William Kingdon Clifford, "The Ethics of Belief," in *Religion from Tolstoy to Camus*, ed. Walter Kaufmann, p. 206.

15. One finds both Clifford's essay and James's lecture in *Religion from Tolstoy to Camus*, edited by Walter Kaufmann, and in *The Philosophy of Religion: Selected Readings*, edited by Michael Peterson et al.

16. "William Kingdon Clifford," *Wikipedia*

17. Clifford, "The Ethics of Belief," p. 202.

18. Ibid., p. 202.

19. Ibid., p. 204.

20. Ibid., p. 205.

21. Ibid., p. 205.

22. Ibid., p. 206.

23. Ibid., p. 206.

24. Ibid., p. 206.

25. Ibid., p. 207.

26. Ibid., p. 207.

27. Ibid., p. 207.

28. Ibid., p. 208.

29. Ibid., p. 214.

30. Ibid., p. 214.

31. Ibid., p. 219.

32. Frederik Kaufman,"The Right to Believe," *Free Inquiry*, Dec. 2016/Jan. 2017, Vol. 37, No. 1, p. 51. If you wonder why fundamentalists and evangelicals voted overwhelmingly for Donald Trump in the 2016 presidential election, you might want to consider this answer by *New York Times* writer Frank Schaeffer: "White evangelical voters support Trump because they have been conditioned by their religious beliefs to be irrational" (from frankschaeferblog.com, August 11, 2017).

33. Ibid., p. 51.

34. Ibid., p. 51.

35. Jonathan Haidt, *The Righteous Mind.*

36. Jerry A. Coyne, *Faith vs. Fact: Why Science and Religion Are Incompatible*, p. 91. Recently I received a letter from Timothy Smith, chief development officer for the Museum of the Bible, which is under construction in Washington D.C. The letter, of course, asks for a monetary contribution. In his letter, Mr. Smith lauds the Bible for, among other things, having "influenced science." Sadly, the Bible has contributed nothing positive to science. If anything, its contribution has been negative.

37. Steven Weinberg, in Jerry A. Coyne' *Faith vs. Fact: Why Science and*

Religion Are Incompatible, p. 220.

38. Jerry A. Coyne, *Faith vs. Fact: Why Science and Religion Are Incompatible,* p. xx.

39. Ibid., p. 39.

40. Ibid., pp. 225-226.

41. Ibid., p. 232.

42. Ibid., p. 232.

43. Ibid., p. 66.

44. Ibid., p. 12.

45. Ibid., p. 14.

46. Ibid., p. 59.

47. Ibid., p. 60.

48. Robert Green Ingersoll, "Orthodoxy."

49. Karen Armstrong, *The Case for God,* p. 8.

50. Ibid., p. 28.

51. Ibid., p. 324.

52. Ibid., p. 95.

53. Ibid., p. 321.

54. Ibid., p. ix.

55. Paul Tillich, *Dynamics of Faith,* p. 1.

56. Ibid., p. 8.

57. Ibid., p. 16.

58. Ibid., p. 37.

59. Ibid., p. 38.

60. Ibid., p. 39.

61. Ibid., p. 44.

62. Ibid., p. 47.

63. Ibid., p. 54.

64. Ibid., p. 53.

65. Ibid., p. 89.

66. Ibid., pp. 125-126.

67. "Self-trust and the Diversity of Religions," *Readings in Philosophy of Religion: Ancient and Contemporary,* eds. Linda Zagzebski and Timothy D. Miller, pp. 466-467.

68. Ibid., p. 467.

69. Ibid., p. 473.

70. From *The Nun,* a novel ascribed to Denis Diderot, from "Denis Diderot Applies Logic to Christianity," www.jeromekahn123.tripod.com.

71. From Diderot's *The Nun* as quoted in "Theological Controversy: Our Method of Procedure," *The Reasoner: Herald of Progress,* June 3, 1846.

72. John W. Loftus, *Why I Became an Atheist,* pp. 64-78.

73. Robert A. Burton, M.D., *On Being Certain : Believing You Are Right Even When You Are Not,* p. 177.

Any thoughts about the topic of faith versus science? Are both of them sources of truth in their respective realms, even when they contradict each other?

Tom (geologist, middle-school science teacher): *A boy is struck in the chest with a broken bat at a high-school baseball game. A woman runs onto the field, quickly assesses the situation and radios for help. Within twenty minutes a helicopter has retrieved the boy and delivered him to a regional hospital, where a highly trained surgeon is already scrubbed in and ready to receive the patient. Five hours later the surgeon emerges from the operating room, tired but confident in his work. Three months later the youth is again playing ball despite the near-fatal puncture of his left lung. When asked about the traumatic ordeal, the boy's mother replies, "Thank you, Jesus, my boy is alive. By the grace of the Almighty my boy is alive . . . glory to God for this miracle."*

To a person of faith, the mother's response to her son's experience is exactly what it should be, an expression of thanks to the one who is responsible for anything and everything--God. To a person of faith, this is simple expression of their truth and reality.

To a science-based person such as myself, truth and reality take a very different form. Without science, there would be no trained paramedic to assess the situation, there would be no radio on which to call for help, there would be no trained pilot and no helicopter, and there certainly would be no surgeon with the tools, technology, and training to operate on the boy. So where is the divine miracle? And, by the way, does God take naps? Because no benevolent god that I can think of would purposefully impale a boy's chest with a broken bat. Yes, I know . . . "God works in mysterious ways."

Can science help in the search for a possible deity?

Ed (retired owner of a commercial real estate appraisal company, conservationist): *I believe in the scientific method of discovery and in the roles that evolution and selection play in it. It is my understanding that while science has searched for a God or a supernatural being, it has thus far been unable to ascertain even a trace. I believe E. O. Wilson when he says that if we ever found any evidence that there is such a force in the universe, the scientific community would openly embrace it. Many scientists* do accept, however, that the principles that have been utilized thus far, i.e., materialism and reductionism, may have limitations. And some scientists, mostly on the periphery, continue to hold to possibilities of a feature known as "emersion." They say that, under this premise, the whole can be larger than the sum of its parts; even Yuval Harrari recognizes that the brain is not exactly the same as the mind. If the scientific community were to find evidence of this phenomenon, it would indeed change everything, but so far, it has not happened; moreover, it is my understanding that most leading scientists are highly doubtful, as the relevant evidence indicates otherwise.

Chapter XIX

John 3:16

"Stewart had an uncanny knack for being in the perfect spot for the television cameras—and the viewers' eyes." - Monte Burke, "The Resurrection of John 3:16," *Forbes*, 11/12/2009

* * * * *

Have you ever wondered who the person was who used to hold the sign "John 3:16" at sporting events in the 70's and 80's, so that it could be seen by millions of people on TV? His name was Rollen Frederick Stewart, aka "Rock 'n' Rollen" and "Rainbow Man." In 1992, believing the Second Coming was about to happen, he kidnapped two men, barricaded himself in a hotel room, threatened to shoot at airplanes, and placed John 3:16 signs in the hotel-room windows.

My intention here is simply to inform, not to imply that the messenger demeans the message. After all, many others have continued what Stewart began; as far as I know, they are fine people. Tim Tebow, professional quarterback, wrote John 3:16 on his eye black for the 2009 BCS championship game. I cheered for Tebow when he played for the Denver Broncos. I hope he makes it big in professional sports if that is what he really wants to do.

The text of John 3:16 must stand or fall on its own merits. Here it is: "For God so loved the world that he gave his only-begotten Son, that those who believe in him shall not perish, but may have life everlasting." If you are a Christian, ask yourself what you would think of these words if you were not a Christian. God has a son, you say? How weird. I know that people often anthropomorphize animals, but God? People have sons, but why would one think that the omniscient, omnipotent creator of the world has a son? How about a daughter? And does god have grandchildren? You say he sent this son to the world so that people would not perish if they believed in him. What specifically did God's son have to accomplish while he was in the world? He had to die for our sins? Really? God sent his son to the world to die for our sins so that we will not perish if we believe in this son? What do you mean by "perish"? Go to hell, you say? Suffer for all eternity? Holy crap! Why would a kind God (you say you are certain that God is kind, in fact all-kind, omnibenevolent?) create beings who might end up in unimaginable horror? You must be joking. But, of course, Christians are not joking. John 3:16 is the heart and soul--or should I, an agnostic vegetarian, say the tofu and potatoes?--of their faith.

Chapter XX
A Gift from My Nephew

"It ain't what you don't know that gets you in trouble; it's what you know for sure that just ain't so" - attributed (incorrectly, I hear) to Mark Twain

* * * * *

Recently, one of my nephews, concerned about my immortal soul, sent me a book by Mark Cahill, a Christian fundamentalist and author of five books, two of which reportedly have combined sales of well over one million copies. Cahill tells his readers that he takes every opportunity --on sidewalks, in hotels, on airplanes, in restaurants--to ask people if they know where they will be if they die that night. If their response leaves him an open door, Cahill, who knows that he knows the answers to life's important questions, launches into what people need to do to avoid going to hell. The title of the book I received is *One Heartbeat Away: Your Journey into Eternity*. Christian preachers used to try to scare the hell out of people with threats of eternal damnation. Cahill still does.[1] Among the things that he knows are the existence of God and the inerrancy of the Bible. The Bible tells him there is no such thing as a small sin; therefore, in the eyes of God, anger, even in a child, is the same as murder. Thus all are in need of Jesus if they are to avoid hell. Let us examine Cahill's evidence for his infallible pronouncements.

As a proof for God's existence, Cahill hauls out the old idea that the design of the universe points to a divine architect. This is Thomas Aquinas's argument from design (the "watchmaker" proof), which most philosophers have found wanting. Cahill tries to bring in Charles Darwin, Stephen Hawking, and Albert Einstein in support of his argument for the existence of God, while conveniently failing to mention that Darwin was an agnostic, that Einstein, who at times referred to himself as an agnostic, was a Spinozistic pantheist, and that Hawking is an atheist. Is Cahill trying to deceive through disingenuousness, or does he simply not know these basic facts about the men whose authority he invokes?

Next, Cahill attempts to discredit evolution, specifically macroevolution (evolution between species), which he maintains "has never been observed; therefore, it is not scientific."[2] Of course, as a non-scientist (he and I share that deficiency), Cahill cannot argue persuasively on this topic from his own authority, so he summons experts, as he should. Who, though, is the first "expert" called? Believe it or not, it is Ken Ham, the man who built the Creation Museum and the Ark Encounter in Kentucky, the man who argues that the earth is only about 6000 years old. To the expertise of Ham, Cahill adds that of Martin Moe, who holds a master's degree in zoology and marine biology. Cahill uses a quotation from George Gaylord Simpson, an eminent evolutionist, with the intention of showing that life cannot have come into being from non-life without a creator. He neglects to say that Simpson was an agnostic and that he thought that macroevolution could be fully explained in terms of microevolution (evolution within a species). And by using only a partial quotation from Francis Crick, one of the discoverers of the structure of DNA, Cahill implies that Crick thought the appearance of life from non-life impossible, whereas the continuation of the quotation reveals Crick's acknowledgement of the possibility of just such a transition. Crick was an avowed humanist who hated Christianity. Either Cahill acted disingenuously in his misuse of the authority of Simpson and Crick, or he "quote mined" (a practice he criticizes later in his book).

This brings us to what I consider the most important chapter in Cahill's book, Chapter 3, entitled "The Red Silver Dollar." It is about the Bible. "The unity, harmony, and accuracy of the Bible," writes Cahill, "cannot be compared with that of any other book. The Bible is, by its very existence, evidence of a Divine Hand writing through devoted men."[3] I consider this statement nonsensical. Among the claims Cahill makes for the Bible are the following: (1) the Bible is "free of any known contradictions"[4]; (2) the historical accuracy of the Bible is supported by the fact that "there were seventeen secular historians who wrote about the death of Jesus by crucifixion"[5]; (3) more than 25,000 archaeological finds "reveal the Bible as being true"[6]; (4) among the "most convincing pieces of evidence supporting the Bible is the scientific nature of that book"[7]; (5) "except for the End Time return of Jesus, every single prophecy [Cahill says there are more than 2000 in the Old Testament alone]--including those about political, religious, intellectual, and geographic events leading up to the return of Jesus Christ to earth--has been fulfilled down to the smallest detail."[8] All five of these points are utterly incorrect. To understand why, please see the relevant sections of this book (especially Chapters III through VI) or, better yet, one or more of several relevant books listed in the bibliography, perhaps especially *The Rejection of Pascal's Wager: A Skeptic's Guide to the Bible and the Historical Jesus*, by Paul Tobin.

Not surprisingly, Cahill has chapters on hell, the Ten Commandments, and God's plan for salvation. If you follow Cahill's advice, you will not go to hell. Otherwise, well, you know. At least Cahill does say that it is not a happy day for God when someone dies and goes to hell. And he wonders if it will be a happy day for God when you die.[9] What a guy!

1. I am reminded of the famous sermon by 18th-century preacher and theologian Jonathan Edwards "Sinners in the Hands of an Angry God," in which he says, "The God that holds you over the pit of Hell, much as one holds a spider, or some loathsome insect over the fire, abhors you, and is dreadfully provoked."

2. Mark Cahill, *One Heartbeat Away: Your Journey into Eternity,* p. 30.

3. Ibid., p. 62.

4. Ibid., p. 64. For a refutation of this assertion, *please see Chapters II, III, and IV of The Virtue of Uncertainty.*

5. Ibid., p. 64. Please see Chapter III of *The Virtue of Uncertainty* for a much more accurate count of the number of first- and second-century secular historians who wrote about Jesus' death by crucifixion.

6. Ibid., p. 65. Please see Chapter IV of *The Virtue of Uncertainty* for the status of archaeology vis-a-vis the Bible.

7. Ibid., p. 65. The Bible contains a number of mathematical and scientific errors and has added nothing in the way of new scientific information.

8. Ibid., p. 69. Please see Chapter V of *The Virtue of Uncertainty* for an account of the inaccuracy of biblical prophecies.

9. Ibid., p. 97.

Chapter XXI
Embracing Uncertainty

"Let us console ourselves with the hypothesis--a not altogether impossible one--that the starry universe and whatever gods there be do not worry about us at all, and will not resent our enjoying whatever humane and enlightened comfort and whatever vision of truth and beauty our world offers us." - Morris Cohen, *The Faith of a Liberal*

"Most scholars who write about the ancient world feel obliged to warn their readers that our knowledge can be at best partial and that certainty is seldom attained. A book about a first-century Jew who lived in a rather unimportant part of the Roman empire must be prefaced by such a warning." - E. P. Sanders, "Preface," *The Historical Figure of Jesus*

"True religion, I believe, begins in doubt and continues in spiritual exploration. Debased religion begins in fear and ends in certainty." - Neal Gabler, "Why the Trump Era Won't Pass Without Serious Damage to America," billmoyer.com

* * * * *

I wrote the following poem about twenty years ago and have tweaked it several times over the years. It is not autobiographical, but it does express a personal point of view--one that has become increasingly important to me, one that may resonate with you.

Three Preachers

Betaking myself to Hyde Park one fine day,
Three preachers I happened to hear.
With time on my hands and a curious mind,
To each of the three I drew near.

The first with harangue of unending invective
Held dozens of folks in his spell.
Inexorably, without pity or shame,
He condemned all the sinners to hell.

With little regard for his manner or words,
I strolled to the next preacher's box.
This self-acclaimed shepherd, soft-spoken and glib,
Circled his prey like a fox.

He prefaced importunate grasps for our quid

With beloved words from the Psalms.
Illicit intentions concealed from the masses,
This man would get none of my alms.

Disgusted, I hastened to hear the third preacher,
Whose hearers were no more than six.
He stammered and stuttered and jerked when he spoke,
A bundle of twitters and tics.

His idiosyncrasies made him more human,
And I started enjoying the scene.
He asked the hard questions, suggested some answers,
But with an incredulous mien,

Which hinted that questions are answered by questions,
With pain of uncertainty rife.
This is the preacher who captured my ear.
His viewpoint unfettered my life.

It would be a boon to the entire earth if all people of faith added to their credos the simple words "but I may be wrong." Religiously inspired zealotry would disappear. Surely the 9/11 hijackers would not have flown planes into the World Trade Center and into the Pentagon without the certainty that this was Allah's will? These men were violent fundamentalists. They allowed religious certitude to sweep aside the demands of mankind's natural moral code. It is my hope that the influence of all fundamentalist denominations will begin to wane as more and more evidence dissuasive of religious certitude makes its way to the light of day and gains entry into the minds of the public.

Perhaps you, like me, have decided that religion is indeed, as Karl Marx famously said, a kind of opiate, and that you can live a better life by casting its allures aside. If you choose this course through life, you will not know, nor will you claim to know, the answers to some of life's important questions: Why am I here? Does God exist? If so, what is God like? Is there more than one god, say a god of good and a god of evil? What happens to me when I die? If there is a god who rewards and punishes in an afterlife, how can I live my life to improve my chances of a happy outcome? My personal assumption (just a guess really) is that God exists (only one), that she (to grab a pronoun at random) looks favorably on acts of kindness towards one's fellow creatures. My assumption may be wrong, but I cannot see how a life of kindness can be wrong. If you are like me, you feel better when you are kind. More importantly, it makes the world a better place. Kindness precludes hatred and extreme possessiveness. It means loving and sharing. And kindness is not proud. Among the many things that I do not know is this: Am I morally one speck better or worse than anyone else? Maybe this question, too, will be answered in an afterlife. If there is an afterlife.

When we seminarians returned to the Canisianum from Christmas break in January of 1962, those of us who were scheduled to be ordained to the priesthood in the early spring found small altars in our rooms. We knew why, of course: they were props to help us learn to say Mass. My altar bothered me. It did more than that: it hit me over the head with the imminence of ordination. It seemed that it was really going to happen, this thing that I dreaded. I practiced very little. My question about the trustworthiness, of the Bible had still not been answered. Later I would be able to articulate that I had spent nine years preparing to do something I did not want to do, that the celibate life of a priest was not for me. I had entered St. Meinrad Seminary in southern Indiana after my high-school girlfriend told me she intended to become a missionary nun. Heartbroken, I wondered if (or, more precisely, feared that) this was a sign that I had a vocation to the priesthood. If God was calling and I did not answer, would I not be risking damnation? It was the fear of hell that brought me to the seminary. It was this fear that kept me there.

Around the time the altar appeared in my room, I began to be troubled by Bible passages like Matt. 16: 27-28: "For the Son of Man is to come with his angels in the glory of his Father, and then he will render to everyone according to his conduct. Amen, I say to you, there are some of those standing here who will not taste death, till they have seen the Son of Man coming in his kingdom." But this did not happen. One of the most basic tenets of Christianity is that Jesus was divine. Yet it seems obvious that Jesus made a mistake. I could not put aside this doubt. I could not leap over it and feel good. How was I to preach what I myself found difficult to believe? What an utterly miserable, indeed immoral, life that would be.

A few years after I left the seminary, I left the Church. In time, I found my way to agnosticism, a philosophy that, despite not providing certainty, continues to comfort me in my eighties. If you are a person who believes in Christianity with total conviction, I have a wish and a challenge for you. I wish that you would abandon your absolute certitude. I challenge you to read the Bible thoroughly and thoughtfully, and to acquaint yourself well with the history of Christianity and with the history of your particular denomination. Examine scrupulously the available evidence, for doing so will raise doubts in your mind. Don't repress the doubts. Embrace them. Perhaps you will be able to say with me: I am not certain that

I am right. You may decide, in the end, to continue to believe, if faith brings you peace and joy, but please admit that you may be wrong. If large numbers of believers adopt a similar attitude, surely our world will become a more tolerant place--religiously, socially, politically.

Toward the end of his book *The First Coming*, University of Chicago avant-garde Christian theologian Thomas Sheehan places himself squarely among uncertain humanity, right there with Jesus and all the rest of us: "Jesus words ['the kingdom of God is at hand'] . . . are an interpretation that requires yet further interpretation, and so on ad infinitum. But in all these efforts of understanding the message of his kingdom of God, the point is to see the *inevitability of interpretation*, that is, to see that what makes us human is our inexorable finitude, which condemns us to being acts of indirection and mediation, where all is 'hints and guesses / Hints followed by guesses' [T. S. Elliot]. [...] We are the inevitability of taking and mis-taking ourselves and the world as this or that; we are the inevitability of heresy. That is to say: All of us, including Jesus, are inevitably and forever a question to which there is no answer."[1] To that even I can say Amen. I hope you can, too.

1. Thomas Sheehan, *The First Coming: How the Kingdom of God Became Christianity*, pp. 225, 226. Among Sheehan's radical ideas is this: "Salvation was no longer to be understood as the forgiving of a debt or as the reward for being good. [...] His [Jesus'] proclamation [of the Kingdom of God] marked the death of religion and religion's God and heralded the beginning of the postreligious experience: the abdication of "God" in favor of his hidden presence among human beings" (pp. 61-62). Sheehan is a professor at Loyola University in Chicago.

Is doubt an appropriate religious attitude?

PT: *Doubt is valid in religion even as it is valid in any serious pursuit for truth. Scientific data aren't reported with 100% certainty. Questioning a belief allows one to challenge oneself as well as others. The results could be a deeper understanding of faith... or not. It shouldn't be condemned as a failure in one's faith. Absolute certainty in matters of faith can lead to a fundamentalism, the results of which are seen in societies around the globe. This kind of absolutism cannot be proved, but it is still used to justify xenophobia, wars, economic disparities (castes), and genocide.*

George: *Doubt is the ally of reason. That which defies reason--as do most articles of religious faith--should be rejected as impeding human progress.*

As you know from having read this book, I am an agnostic. I know nothing at all about God: not which adjectives, if any, describe God; not whether God is a he, a she, or an it . . . or none of these; not how God wants us humans to act; not even whether God exists. Thus I do not love God. Please keep this in mind when you read the following poem, which I wrote in the persona of a believer. It is a love song primarily to a human being, secondarily to a possible creator of the world.

Tell Me Why

I keep hearing the song that we heard on TV
Last night as we lay in our bed:
That lovely old song with the name "Tell Me Why"*
Turns meaningful love on its head.*

Imagine, my Love, that I sang you this song
Intending my love to construe.
I'd say that the reason I love you, Sweetheart,
Is that God the creator made you.

Would you be delighted to hear words like these?
I really don't think there's a chance.
For God the creator made not only you,
But spiders and crickets and ants.

The words make more sense with one three-letter change
Though at first they may strike you as odd.
Just give them a moment, let them sink in:
God made you, that's why I love God.

* The final line of the song is "Because God made you, that's why I love you."

Partial Bibliography

Allegro, John M. *The Dead Sea Scrolls and the Christian Myth*, 2nd rev. ed. Buffalo: Prometheus Books, 1992.

Allen, Steve. *Steve Allen on the Bible, Religion, and Morality*. Buffalo: Prometheus Books, 1990.

Allen, Steve. *More Steve Allen on the Bible, Religion, and Morality*. Buffalo: Prometheus Books, 1993.

Aquinas, Thomas. *The Summa Theologica*, transl. Fathers of the English Dominican Province. Benziger Bros. edition, 1947. www.dhspriory.org.

Armstrong, Karen. *The Bible: A Biography*. New York: Atlantic Monthly Press, 2007.

Armstrong, Karen. *The Case for God*. New York: Anchor, 2009.

Armstrong, Karen. *Fields of Blood: Religion and the History of Violence*. New York: Alfred A. Knopf, 2014.

Armstrong, Karen. *A History of God*. New York: Random House, 1993.

Asadi, Muhammed. "Paul and the Invention of Christianity," *Atheist Ground*. www.bigissueground.com.

Aslan, Reza. *Zealot: The Life and Times of Jesus of Nazareth.* New York: Random House, 2013.

Avalos, Hector. *The End of Biblical Studies*. Amherst: Prometheus Books, 2007.

Baier, Colin J. and Bradley R. E. Wright. "'If You Love Me, Keep My Commandments': A Meta-Analysis of the Effect of Religion on Crime," abstract. www.sagejournals.com.

Barker, Dan. *Losing Faith in Faith: From Preacher to Atheist*. Madison: Freedom From Religion Foundation, 1983.

Beit-Hallahmi, Benjamin and Michael Argyle. *The Psychology of Religious Behavior, Belief, and Experience*. London: Routledge, 1997.

Blackmore, Susan. "Why I Have Given Up," in *Skeptical Odysseys: Personal Accounts by the World's Leading Paranormal Inquirers*. Paul Kurtz, ed. Amherst: Prometheus Books, 2001, pp. 85-94.

Brown, Tom. "Did Jesus Die on Good Friday?" www.tbm.org.

Burton, Robert A., M.D. *On Being Certain: Believing You Are Right Even When You're Not*. New York: St. Martin's Griffin, 2008.

Cahill, Mark. *One Heartbeat Away: Your Journey into Eternity*. Rockwall, TX: BDM Publishing, 2005.

Calvin, John. *The Institutes of the Christian Religion*, transl. Henry Baeveridge. www.ntslibrary.com.

Cartlidge, David R. and David L. Dungan, eds. *Documents for the Study of the Gospels*. Great Britain: Collins Liturgical Publications, 1980.

Cheetham, Nicholas. *Keepers of the Keys: A History of the Popes from St. Peter to John Paul II*. New York: Scribner, 1983.

Chemnov, Ron. *Alexander Hamilton*. New York: Penguin Books, 2005.

Clifford, William Kingdon. "The Ethics of Belief," in *Religion from Tolstoy to Camus*. Walter Kaufmann, ed. New York: Harper & Row, 1961.

Code of Canon Law. www.vatican.va/archive/ENG1104.

Coyne, Jerry A. *Faith vs. Fact: Why Science and Religion Are Not Compatible*. New York: Viking Penguin, 2015.

Cronin, K. J. "The Name of God as Revealed in Exodus 3:14: An explanation of its meaning." www.exodus-314.com.

Crossan, John Dominic. *Who Is Jesus?* New York: Harper Paperbacks: 1996.

Denzinger, Heinrich. *Enchiridion Symbolorum, Definitionum et Declarationum de Rebus Fidei et Morum,* ed. 21-23. Freiburg im Breisgau: Herder, 1937.

Doyle, Rev. Kenneth. "What teachings are declared infallible?" www. catholiccourier.com.

Dukas, Helen and Banesh Hoffmann. *Albert Einstein: The Human Side.* Princeton, N.J.: Princeton University Press, 1979.

Dunn, Edmond J. *What is Theology?* Mystic, CT: Twenty-Third Publications, 1998.

Edwards, Jonathan. "Sinners in the Hands of an Angry God," *Anthology of American Literature,* 2nd ed., vol. 1. New York: Macmillan, 1980, pp. 236-247.

Ehrman, Bart D. *Jesus: Apocalyptic Prophet of the New Millennium.* New York: Oxford University Press, 1999.

Ehrman, Bart. "Josephus's Clearest Claim about the Burial of Crucified Victims." www.ehrmanblog.org.

Ehrman, Bart D. *The New Testament: A Historical Introduction to the Early Christian Writings.* 2nd ed. New York: Oxford University Press, 2000.

Ehrman, Bart. "Paul's Importance in Early Christianity?" www.ehrmanblog.org.

Einstein, Albert. *Ideas and Opinions,* transl. Sonja Bargmann. New York: Crown Publishers, 1954.

Evans, C. Stephen. "Moral Arguments for the Existence of God," *Stanford Encyclopedia of Philosophy.* www.plato.stanford.edu.

Fox, Robin Lane. *The Unauthorized Version: Truth and Fiction in The Bible.* New York: Vintage Books, 1991.

Funk, Robert W. and the Jesus Seminar. *The Acts of Jesus: The*

Search for the Authentic Deeds of Jesus. San Francisco: Harper, 1998.

Funk, Robert W., Roy W. Hoover, and the Jesus Seminar. *The Five Gospels: The Search for the Authentic Words of Jesus*. New York: Macmillan, 1993.

Gathercole, S. J. "The Critical and Dogmatic Agenda of Albert Schweitzer's *The Quest for the Historical Jesus*." www.tyndalehouse. com.

The Gospel of Thomas, transl. W. R. Schroedel. www.goodnewsinc.net.

Grant, James. *John Adams: Party of One*. New York: Farrar, Straus and Giroux, 2005.

Green, Steven K. *Inventing a Christian America: The Myth of a Religious Founding*. Oxford: Oxford University Press, 2015.

Harari, Yuval Noah. *Sapiens: A Brief History of Humankind* New York: HarperCollins, 2015.

Harris, Sam. *The End of Faith: Religion, Terror, and the Future of Reason*. New York: W. W. Norton, 2004.

Harris, Sam. *Free Will*. New York: Free Press, 2012.

Hart, David Bentley. *Atheist Delusions: The Christian Revolution and Its Fashionable Enemies*. New Haven: Yale University Press, 2009.

Haught, John F. *Science and Faith: A New Introduction*. New York: Paulist Press, 2012.

Hopper, Paul. "Fresh Evidence: The Forged Jesus Passage in Josephus." www.vridar.org.

Jacoby, Susan. *Strange Gods: A Secular History of Conversion*. New York: Pantheon Books, 2016.

James, William. "The Will To Believe," in *Religion from Tolstoy to Camus*. Walter Kaufmann, ed. New York: Harper & Row, 1961.

"Josephus and Jesus: The Testimonium Flavianum Question." www.earlychristianwritings.com.

Josephus, Flavius. *The Antiquities of the Jews*. www.documentacatholicaomnia.eu..

Kane, Greg. *Pagan Origins of the Christ Myth*. www.pocm.info.

Kaufmann, Walter. *Critique of Religion and Philosophy*. Princeton: Princeton University Press,1958.

Kaufmann, Walter. *The Faith of a Heretic*. Garden City: Doubleday, 1963.

Kant Immanuel. "Religion within the Boundaries of Mere Reason," in *Religion within the Boundaries of Mere Reason and Other Writings*. Allen Wood and George di Giovanni, eds. Cambridge: Cambridge University Press, 1998.

Kaufmann, Walter. *Religion from Tolstoy to Camus*. New York: Harper & Row, 1961.

Kirby, Peter. "The Historicity of the Empty Tomb Evaluated." www.infidels.org.

Lewis, C. S.. *Mere Christianity*. Macmillan: New York, 1960.

Loftus, John W., ed. *The Christian Delusion*. Amherst: Prometheus Books, 2010.

Loftus, John W. *Why I Became an Atheist: A Former Preacher Rejects Christianity*. Amherst: Prometheus Books, 2012.

Luther, Martin. *The Bondage of the Will*, transl. Philip S. Watson. www.lutheransonline.com.

Maccoby, Hyam. *The Mythmaker: Paul and the Invention of Christianity*. San Francisco: Harper & Row, 1987.

Mack, Burton L. *Who Wrote the New Testament? The Making of the Christian Myth*. San Francisco: Harper, 1989.

Marius, Richard. *Martin Luther: The Christian Between God and Death*. Cambridge: The Belknap Press, 1999.

Marshall, George, N. *Buddha: His Quest for Serenity*. Schenkman: Rochester, Vermont, 1990.

McBrien, Richard P. *Catholicism: Study Edition*. Minneapolis: Winston Press, 1981.

McBrien, Richard P. *Lives of the Popes: The Pontiffs from St. Peter to Benedict XVI*. San Francisco: Harper, 2000.

McClory, Robert. "The Gospel According to Thomas Sheehan," *Chicago Reader*, Apr. 20, 1989. www.chicagoreader.com.

McKinsey, C. Dennis. *The Encyclopedia of Biblical Errancy*. Amherst: Prometheus Books, 1995.

Miethe, Terry L. and Anthony G. N. Flew. *Does God Exist? A Believer and an Atheist Debate*. San Francisco: Harper, 1991.

Miller, Robert J. "Did Jesus Fulfill Prophecy?" Westar Institute. www.westarinstitute.org..

Morgan, Donald. "Bible Absurdities." www.infidels.org.

Miller, John C. *Alexander Hamilton and the Growth of the New Nation*. New Brunswick: Transaction Publishers, 2004.

Nickell, Joe. *Looking for a Miracle: Weeping Icons, Relics, Stigmata, Visions & Healing Cures*. Prometheus Books: Buffalo, NY, 1993.

Nickell, Joe. *Relics of the Christ*. University of Kentucky Press, Lexington: Lexington, 2007.

Nickell, Joe. *Secrets of the Supernatural: Investigating the World's Occult Mysteries*. Buffalo: Prometheus Books, 1988.

Norwich, John Julius. *Absolute Monarchs: A History of the Papacy*. New York: Random House, 2012.

Pagels, Elaine and Karen L. King. *Reading Judas: The Gospel of Judas and the Shaping of Christianity*. England: Penguin Books, 2008.

Paine, Thomas. *The Age of Reason: Being an Investigation of True and Fabulous Theology*. Buffalo: Prometheus Books, 1984.

Pascal, Blaise. *Pensées,* transl. W. F. Trotter. www.leaderu.com.

"Paul's Mythology: The Unspoken Bible." www.usbible.com.

Peterson, Michael et al, eds. *The Philosophy of Religion: Selected Readings*. New York: Oxford University Press, 1996.

Pius X, "Syllabus Condemning the Errors of the Modernists," *Lamentabili Sane*. www.papalencyclicals.net.

Randi, James. *The Faith Healers*. Buffalo: Prometheus Books, 1989.

Russell, Bertrand. *A History of Western Philosophy*. New York: Simon and Schuster, 1945.

Russell, Bertrand. *Why I Am Not a Christian*. New York: Simon and Schuster,1957.

Reimarus, Samuel, *Fragments from Reimarus Consisting of Brief Critical Remarks on the Object of Jesus and His Disciples as Seen in the New Testament*, transl. Rev. Charles Voysey. www.books.google.com.

Sagan, Carl. *The Demon-Haunted World: Science as a Candle in the Dark*. New York: Ballantine Books, 1996.

Sanders, E. P. *The Historical Figure of Jesus*. London: Allen Lane, 1993.

Schweitzer, Albert. *The Quest of the Historical Jesus: A critical Study of Its Progress from Reimarus to Wrede,* transl. W. Montgomery. London: Adam and Charles Black, 1910.

Sheaffer, Robert. *The Making of the Messiah: Christianity and Resentment*. Buffalo: Prometheus Books, 1991.

Sheehan, Thomas. *The First Coming: How the Kingdom of God Became Christianity*. New York: Random House, 1986.

Spinoza, Benedict de [Baruch]. *The Ethics*, transl. R. H. M. Elwes. www.gutenberg.org.

Stenger, Victor J. *The New Atheism: Taking a Stand for Science and Reason*. Amherst: Prometheus Books, 2009.

Sturgis, Matthew. *It Ain't Necessarily So: Investigating the Truth of the Biblical Past*. London: Headline, 2001.

Till, Farrell. "Prophecies: Imaginary and Unfulfilled," *The Secular Web: A Drop of Reason in a Pool of Confusion*. www.infidels.org.

Tillich, Paul. *Dynamics of Faith*. New York: Harper & Row, 1957.

Tobin, Paul. *The Rejection of Pascal's Wager: A Skeptic's Guide to the Bible and the Historical Jesus*. England: Authors OnLine ltd, 2009.

Tolstoy, Leo. *The Gospel in Brief*, transl. Aylmer Maude. www.fredsakademiet.dk.

Tolstoy, Leo. *My Religion*, transl. Huntington Smith. London: Walter Scott, 1889. www.books.google.com.

Voltaire. *Philosophical Dictionary*. New York: Carlton House. www.gutenberg.org.

Waterworth, J., ed. and transl. *The Council of Trent: The Canons and Decrees of the Sacred and Oecumenical Council of Trent*. www.history.hanover.edu.

Wells, Steve, annotator. *The Skeptic's Annotated Bible: The King James Version from a Skeptic's Point of View*. SAB Books, 2013.

White, L. Michael. *From Jesus to Christianity*. San Francisco: Harper, 2004.

White, L. Michael. *Scripting Jesus: The Gospels in Rewrite*. New York: HarperCollins, 2010.

Zagzebski, Linda and Timothy D. Miller. *Readings in Philosophy of Religion: Ancient to Contemporary.* Chichester: Wiley-Blackwell, 2009.

Zuckerman, Phil. "Atheism, Secularity, and Well-Being: How the Findings of Social Science Counter Negative Stereotypes and Assumptions." www.pitweb.pitzer.edu.

Zuckerman, Phil. "Is Faith Good for Us?" www.onlineopinion.com.

Xygalatas, Dimitris. "True North: Is religion vs. atheism really an indicator of morality?" The Courier-Journal, October 29, 2017.

Index

Other books by Eugene R. Moutoux

Essential German: A No-frills Approach to Reading and Writing German

Unbekannt und Unbeachtet: German Fairy Tales You May Have Missed

Drawing Sentences: A Guide to Diagramming

Diagramming Step by Step: One Hundred and Fifty-five Steps to
Diagramming Excellence

Analyzing the Grammar of Literature: Diagrams of 130 Long Sentences
from British and American Writers

Latin Derivatives: A Toolbox for College and Career Success

2016 Latin Derivatives for Latin Students

* * * * *

Website: www.german-latin-english.com.

www.ingramcontent.com/pod-product-compliance
Lightning Source LLC
Chambersburg PA
CBHW052038090426
42739CB00010B/1963